First World War
and Army of Occupation
War Diary
France, Belgium and Germany

4 CAVALRY DIVISION
Mhow Cavalry Brigade
Headquarters,
'A' Battery Royal Horse Artillery,
2 Lancers (Gardner's Horse),
6th Dragoons (Inniskilling),
38 Central Indian Horse, Brigade Signal Troop,
11 Cavalry Machine Gun Squadron and Royal Army
Veterinary Corps
Mobile Veterinary Section
31 December 1916 - 28 February 1918

WO95/1160

The Naval & Military Press Ltd
www.nmarchive.com
Published in association with The National Archives

Published by

The Naval & Military Press Ltd

Unit 10 Ridgewood Industrial Park,

Uckfield, East Sussex,

TN22 5QE England

Tel: +44 (0) 1825 749494

www.naval-military-press.com

www.nmarchive.com

This diary has been reprinted in facsimile from the original. Any imperfections are inevitably reproduced and the quality may fall short of modern type and cartographic standards.

© Crown Copyright
Images reproduced by permission of The National Archives, London, England, 2015.

Contents

Document type	Place/Title	Date From	Date To
Heading	1917 4th Cavalry Division Mhow Cavalry Brigade Bde Headquarters. Jan-1917-1918 March		
Heading	War Diary of Headquarters. Mhow Cavalry Brigade. From 1st January 1917 To 31st January 1917		
War Diary	Escarbotin	01/01/1917	25/02/1917
Heading	War Diary of Head Quarters Mhow Cavalry Brigade. From 1st March 1917 To 31st March 1917		
War Diary	Escarbotin	09/03/1917	19/03/1917
War Diary	Drucat	20/03/1917	20/03/1917
War Diary	St. Leger	21/03/1917	21/03/1917
War Diary	Aveluy	22/03/1917	31/03/1917
Heading	War Diary of Headquarters Mhow Cavalry Brigade From 1-4-17 To 30-4-17.		
War Diary	Aveluy	01/04/1917	03/04/1917
War Diary	Miraumont	09/04/1917	13/04/1917
War Diary	Sarton	17/04/1917	28/04/1917
Operation(al) Order(s)	Mhow Cavalry Brigade Operation Order No.2.	28/03/1917	28/03/1917
Operation(al) Order(s)	Mhow Cavalry Brigade Operation Order No. 2	28/03/1917	28/03/1917
Operation(al) Order(s)	Mhow Cav. Bde. Operation Order No. 3.	09/04/1917	09/04/1917
Operation(al) Order(s)	Mhow Bde Operation Order No.4.	01/04/1917	01/04/1917
Operation(al) Order(s)	M H O W. Cavalry Brigade Operation Order No. 4.	09/04/1917	09/04/1917
Heading	War Diary of Headquarters Mhow Cavalry Brigade From 1st May 1917 To 30th June 1917.		
War Diary	Sarton	01/05/1917	17/05/1917
War Diary	St Christ	18/05/1917	24/05/1917
War Diary	Roisel L.7.B.	24/05/1917	31/05/1917
Operation(al) Order(s)	Mhow Cavalry Brigade. Operation Order No.5.	13/05/1917	13/05/1917
Miscellaneous			
Operation(al) Order(s)	Mhow Cav Bde Operation Order No. 6		
Operation(al) Order(s)	Mhow Cavalry Bde Operation Order No. 7	16/05/1917	16/05/1917
Operation(al) Order(s)	Mhow Cavalry Brigade. Operation Order No. 8.	21/05/1917	21/05/1917
Miscellaneous	Relief 22nd/23rd May.		
Miscellaneous	Reliefs 23rd/24th May 1917		
Operation(al) Order(s)	Mhow And Sialkot Dismounted Regt. Operation Order No. 1.	22/05/1917	22/05/1917
Heading	War Diary of Headquarters Mhow Cavalry Brigade From 1st June 1917 To 30th June 1917.		
War Diary	Sheet 62C. N.E. L.7d.7.7.	01/06/1917	04/06/1917
War Diary	Camp Hamelet	05/06/1917	17/06/1917
War Diary	Camp Ennemain & B. Sector.	18/06/1917	30/06/1917
Operation(al) Order(s)	Mhow Cavalry Brigade Order No.9	14/06/1917	14/06/1917
Miscellaneous	Relief Table issued With Whom Cavalry Brigade Order No.9 of 14th June 1817.	14/06/1917	14/06/1917
Operation(al) Order(s)	Mhow Cavalry Brigade Order No. 10	14/06/1917	14/06/1917
Operation(al) Order(s)	Mhow Cavalry Brigade Order No. 12.	26/06/1917	26/06/1917
Miscellaneous	Relief Table Issued with 4th Dismounted Brigade Operation Order On. 9.		
Heading	War Diary of Head Quarters Mhow Cavalry Bde From 1st July 1917 To 31st July 1917.		
War Diary	Ruelles Wood & Camp Ennemain	01/07/1917	10/07/1917

Type	Description	Start	End
War Diary	Camp Ennemain	11/07/1917	31/07/1917
Miscellaneous	No. B.M.149. Reference 4th Cavalry Division Map 1/2500.		
Miscellaneous	Appendix "A"		
Operation(al) Order(s)	4th Dismounted Brigade Order No. 12.	02/07/1917	02/07/1917
Operation(al) Order(s)	4th Dismounted Brigade Order No.13.	05/07/1917	05/07/1917
Miscellaneous	Relief Table Issued With 4th Dismounted Brigade Order No.13.		
Heading	War Diary of Mhow Bde Head Quarters From 1st Aug 1917 To 31 Aug 31 Aug 1917		
War Diary	Ennemain	01/08/1917	31/08/1917
Heading	War Diary of Head Quarters. Mhow Cavalry Bde From 1st Sept. 1917 To 30th Sept. 1917		
War Diary	Ennemain	01/09/1917	30/09/1917
Operation(al) Order(s)	Mhow Cavalry Brigade Order No. 14.	18/09/1917	18/09/1917
Miscellaneous	Appendix "A" to Mhow Cavalry Brigade Order No. 14		
Operation(al) Order(s)	Mhow Cavalry Brigade Order No. 15.	20/09/1917	20/09/1917
Operation(al) Order(s)	Mhow Cavalry Brigade Order No. 16	20/09/1917	20/09/1917
Operation(al) Order(s)	Mhow Cavalry Brigade Order No. 17.	28/09/1917	28/09/1917
Miscellaneous	Table "A"		
Heading	War Diary of Head Quarters Mhow Cavalry Brigade From 1-10-17 To 31-10-17		
War Diary	Ennemain	03/10/1917	29/10/1917
Heading	War Diary of 4 Div Headquarters Mhow Cav Bde From 1-11-17 To 30-11-17		
War Diary	Ennemain	01/11/1917	21/11/1917
War Diary	Fins	22/11/1917	23/11/1917
War Diary	Ennemain	24/11/1917	30/11/1917
Operation(al) Order(s)	Mhow Cavalry Brigade Order No. 17.	19/11/1917	19/11/1917
Miscellaneous	March Table. Issued With Mhow Cavalry Brigade Order No. 17.		
Operation(al) Order(s)	Mhow Cav Bde Order No. 18.	20/11/1917	20/11/1917
Operation(al) Order(s)	Mhow Cavalry Brigade Order No. 20	25/11/1917	25/11/1917
Heading	War Diary of Headquarters, Mhow Cavalry Brigade. From, 1-12-17. To 31-12-17.		
War Diary	St. Emilie	01/12/1917	01/12/1917
War Diary	W 30 f 5.3 (Sheet 5 7 C)		
War Diary	Peiziere W 30 f 5.3 (Sheet 57c)	01/12/1917	01/12/1917
War Diary	Peiziere	01/12/1917	01/12/1917
War Diary	Epehy	01/12/1917	02/12/1917
War Diary	St Emilie	02/12/1917	03/12/1917
War Diary	Ennemain	07/12/1917	31/12/1917
Miscellaneous	Summary of Operations, Mhow Cavalry Brigade, November 30th To December 2nd 1917.		
Miscellaneous	Operations Carried Out by Mhow Cavalry Brigade On December 1st 1917.		
Map	Maps		
Heading	War Diary of 4 Div Headquarters. Mhow Cavalry Brigade. From 1-1-18 To 31-1-18.		
War Diary	Ennemain	01/01/1918	31/01/1918
Heading	War Diary of 4 Cav Div H. Qrs. Mhow Cavalry Bde From. 1st February 1918 To 28th February 1918		
War Diary	Centre Sector Cav. Corps Front	01/02/1918	11/02/1918
War Diary	Courcelles Area	12/02/1918	28/02/1918
War Diary	Poix.	01/03/1918	21/03/1918

Type	Description	Start	End
Heading	1917 4th Cavalry Division Mhow Cavalry Brigade "A" Battery R. H. A. Jan-Nov 1917		
Heading	War Diary of "A" Battery, Royal Horse Artillery From 1st January 1917 To 31st January 1917		
War Diary	Molliens Aux-Bois	01/01/1917	03/01/1917
War Diary	Longpre	04/01/1917	04/01/1917
War Diary	Toeufles	05/01/1917	05/01/1917
War Diary	Sallenelle	08/01/1917	26/01/1917
Heading	A Battery, Royal Horse Artillery. 1st To 28th February 1917.		
War Diary	Sallenelle	01/02/1917	26/02/1917
War Diary	Havernas Albert.	27/02/1917	28/02/1917
Heading	A Battery, R.H.A. From 1st To 31st March 1917.		
War Diary	(Prison Camp) Albert	01/03/1917	04/03/1917
War Diary	Bonneville	05/03/1917	09/03/1917
War Diary	St Ouen	10/03/1917	17/03/1917
War Diary	Aveluy	18/03/1917	22/03/1917
War Diary	Ervillers	23/03/1917	31/03/1917
Heading	War Diary of "A" Battery R.H.A. From 1-4-17 To 30-4-17.		
War Diary	Ervillers	01/04/1917	14/04/1917
War Diary	Miraumont	15/04/1917	15/04/1917
War Diary	Mailly-Mailet	16/04/1917	16/04/1917
War Diary	Sarton	17/04/1917	25/04/1917
Heading	A Battery Royal Horse Artillery. From 1st May To 30th June 1917.		
War Diary	Sarton	01/05/1917	09/05/1917
War Diary	Meaulte	12/05/1917	12/05/1917
War Diary	Courcelles	13/05/1917	15/05/1917
War Diary	St Christ	17/05/1917	19/05/1917
War Diary	Boucly	20/05/1917	30/05/1917
Heading	A Battery, Royal Horse Artillery. From 1st To 31st July 1917.		
War Diary	Boucly	01/07/1917	29/07/1917
Heading	A Battery, Royal Horse Artillery. From 1st To 31st August 1917.		
War Diary	Carpeza Copse	01/08/1917	10/08/1917
War Diary	Vadencourt	11/08/1917	15/10/1917
War Diary	Athies	16/10/1917	01/11/1917
War Diary	Vaux Wood	14/11/1917	17/11/1917
War Diary	Beaucamp.	19/11/1917	22/11/1917
War Diary	Marcoing	26/11/1917	26/11/1917
War Diary	Beaucamp.	28/11/1917	28/11/1917
War Diary	Athies.	29/11/1917	29/11/1917
War Diary	Villers-Faucon	30/11/1917	30/11/1917
Operation(al) Order(s)	Mhow Brigade Operation Order No.2. Appendix 2	24/09/1916	24/09/1916
Heading	4th Cav. Dv. Mhow Cav. Bde Diary Dec 17. 0f "A" R. H. A. Is Missing		
Miscellaneous	To Withdraw to this road.		
Heading	1917-18 4th Cavalry Division Mhow Cavalry Brigade 2nd Lancers Jan 1917-Mar 1918		
Heading	War Diary of 2nd Lancers (Gardner's Horse). From 1st January 1917 To 31st January 1917		
War Diary		09/01/1917	28/01/1917
Heading	War Diary of 2nd Lancers I. A. From 1-2-17 To 28-2-17		

War Diary	Lancheres		03/02/1917	27/02/1917
Heading	War Diary. 2nd Lancers. (G.H.) From 1-3-1917 To 31-3-17. Volume XIII.			
War Diary	Lancheres		09/03/1917	17/03/1917
War Diary	Pt Laviers		19/03/1917	19/03/1917
War Diary	St Ouen		20/03/1917	20/03/1917
War Diary	Aveluy		21/03/1917	22/03/1917
War Diary	Miraumont		29/03/1917	29/03/1917
Heading	War Diary of 2nd Lancers From 1-4-17 To 30-4-17.			
War Diary	Miraumont		01/04/1917	13/04/1917
Heading	War Diary of 2nd Lancers. From 1st May 1917. To 30th June 1917.			
War Diary	Templeux		23/05/1917	28/05/1917
War Diary	Gd Priel Wood		29/05/1917	31/05/1917
War Diary	U Rville		01/05/1917	15/05/1917
War Diary	Heilly		16/05/1917	16/05/1917
War Diary	Bray		17/05/1917	17/05/1917
War Diary	St Christ		19/05/1917	27/05/1917
Heading	War Diary of 2nd Lancers From 1st June 1917. To 30th June 1917.			
War Diary	Gd Priel Wood		01/06/1917	04/06/1917
War Diary	Hamelet		04/06/1917	17/06/1917
War Diary	Athies		22/06/1917	30/06/1917
Heading	War Diary of 2nd Lancers. (G.H.) From 1st July 1917 To 31 July 1917 (Volume XIII)			
War Diary	Ennemain		01/07/1917	30/07/1917
Heading	War Diary of 2nd Lancers. (G.H.) From 1-8-1917 To 31-8-17 (Volume XIII).			
War Diary			04/08/1917	31/08/1917
Heading	War Diary 2nd Lancers (G.H.) From 1-9-1917 To 30-9-1917. (Volume XIII).			
War Diary	Athies		05/09/1917	30/09/1917
Heading	War Diary of 2nd Lancers From 1-10-17 To 31-10-17			
War Diary	Athies		01/10/1917	31/10/1917
Heading	War Diary of 2nd (Bengal) Lancers. From 1-11-17 To 30-11-17			
War Diary	Athies		10/11/1917	30/11/1917
War Diary	St Emile		30/11/1917	30/11/1917
Heading	War Diary of 2nd Lancers From, 1-12-17. To 31-12-17.			
War Diary	St Emilie		01/12/1917	31/12/1917
Heading	War Diary 2nd Lancers (G.H.) From 1/3/1918 To 30/3/1918 (Lancers) (Volume XIII).			
War Diary	Athies		01/01/1918	01/02/1918
War Diary	N. E. Avilleret		01/02/1918	01/02/1918
War Diary	Athies		02/02/1918	02/02/1918
War Diary	N. E. Avilleret		02/02/1918	02/02/1918
War Diary	Guillaucourt		03/02/1918	03/02/1918
War Diary	Guignemicourt		04/02/1918	04/02/1918
War Diary	N. E. Avilleret		05/02/1918	05/02/1918
War Diary	Fresnoy-au-Val		09/02/1918	01/03/1918
War Diary	Saleux		20/03/1918	20/03/1918
War Diary	Marseille		23/03/1918	30/03/1918
Heading	1917-18 4th Cavalry Division Mhow Cavalry Brigade 6th Inniskilling Dragoons Jan 1917-Feb 1918 From 1 Cav Div Mhow Cav Bde To 7 Cav Bde 3 Cav Div			

Heading	War Diary of 6th Inniskilling Dragoons. From 1st January 1917 To 31st January 1917		
War Diary	Escarbotin.	01/01/1917	29/01/1917
Heading	War Diary of The Inniskilling Dragoons. For February 1917 Volume. Series.		
War Diary	Escarbotin.	01/02/1917	22/02/1917
Heading	War Diary March 1917 From 1st To 31 March 1917		
War Diary	Escarbotin	01/03/1917	19/03/1917
War Diary	Drucat	19/03/1917	20/03/1917
War Diary	St Leger	21/03/1917	21/03/1917
War Diary	Aveluy	22/03/1917	31/03/1917
Heading	War Diary of 6th Inniskilling Dragoons From 1-4-17. To 30-4-17.		
War Diary	Aveluy	01/04/1917	02/04/1917
War Diary	Miraumont	03/04/1917	12/04/1917
War Diary	Authie	13/04/1917	24/04/1917
War Diary	Thievres	25/04/1917	30/04/1917
Operation(al) Order(s)	Mhow. Cav. Bde. Operation Order No.3.	09/04/1917	09/04/1917
Heading	War Diary of Inniskilling Dragoons For May 1917 & June 1917.		
War Diary	Thievres.	01/05/1917	15/05/1917
War Diary	Mericourt	16/05/1917	16/05/1917
War Diary	Bray	17/05/1917	17/05/1917
War Diary	Camp. O. 35. C.	18/05/1917	20/05/1917
War Diary	St. Christ.	21/05/1917	23/05/1917
War Diary	Hargicourt.	24/05/1917	24/05/1917
War Diary	St Christ.	24/05/1917	24/05/1917
War Diary	Hargicourt.	25/05/1917	25/05/1917
War Diary	St Christ.	25/05/1917	25/05/1917
War Diary	Hargicourt.	26/05/1917	26/05/1917
War Diary	St. Christ.	26/05/1917	26/05/1917
War Diary	Hargicourt.	27/05/1917	27/05/1917
War Diary	St Christ.	27/05/1917	27/05/1917
War Diary	Hargicourt.	28/05/1917	28/05/1917
War Diary	St Christ.	28/05/1917	28/05/1917
War Diary	Hargicourt.	29/05/1917	29/05/1917
War Diary	St. Christ.	29/05/1917	29/05/1917
War Diary	Hargicourt.	30/05/1917	30/05/1917
War Diary	St. Christ.	30/05/1917	30/05/1917
War Diary	Hargicourt.	31/05/1917	31/05/1917
War Diary	St. Christ.	31/05/1917	31/05/1917
Heading	War Diary of 6th Inniskilling Dragoons From 1st June 1917. To 30th June 1917.		
War Diary	St. Christ.	01/06/1917	01/06/1917
War Diary	Hargicourt.	03/06/1917	03/06/1917
War Diary	St. Christ.	04/06/1917	04/06/1917
War Diary	Hamelet.	05/06/1917	17/06/1917
War Diary	Hargicourt.	17/06/1917	17/06/1917
War Diary	Ennemain.	18/06/1917	18/06/1917
War Diary	Hargicourt.	18/06/1917	18/06/1917
War Diary	Ennemain.	19/06/1917	19/06/1917
War Diary	Hargicourt.	19/06/1917	20/06/1917
War Diary	Ennemain.	28/06/1917	28/06/1917
War Diary	Hargicourt.	22/06/1917	28/06/1917
War Diary	Ennemain	28/06/1917	28/06/1917
War Diary	Hargicourt	29/06/1917	29/06/1917

War Diary	Ennemain	29/06/1917	30/06/1917
War Diary	Hargicourt	30/06/1917	30/06/1917
Heading	War Diary of The Inniskilling Dragoons From 1st July 1917 To 31st July 1917.		
War Diary	Hargicourt	01/07/1917	09/07/1917
War Diary	Ennemain	10/07/1917	31/07/1917
Miscellaneous	No. B.M. 149. Reference 4th Cavalry Div. Map 1/2500.	28/06/1917	28/06/1917
Miscellaneous	Right Platoon Leader		
Miscellaneous	4th Dismounted Brigade. Special Order.	02/07/1917	02/07/1917
Miscellaneous	Orders for Raid Night of 1/2 July 17		
Heading	War Diary of Inniskilling Dragoons. From 1st. August 1917 To 31st. Aug.		
War Diary	Ennemain	01/08/1917	31/08/1917
Heading	War Diary of Inniskilling Dragoons. For September 1917		
War Diary	Ennemain	01/09/1917	30/09/1917
Heading	War Diary of Inniskilling Dragoons 1st October To 31st October 1917.		
War Diary	Ennemain.	01/10/1917	31/10/1917
Heading	War Diary of Inniskilling Dragoons. November 1st To November 30th 1917 Volume No.		
War Diary	Ennemain.	01/11/1917	21/11/1917
War Diary	Fins Area	22/11/1917	22/11/1917
War Diary	Fins	23/11/1917	23/11/1917
War Diary	Ennemain.	24/11/1917	24/11/1917
War Diary	N. W. Villers Faucom	25/11/1917	25/11/1917
War Diary	Villers Faucon	25/11/1917	25/11/1917
War Diary	Ennemain	26/11/1917	30/11/1917
War Diary	P. 30. D.	30/11/1917	30/11/1917
Heading	War Diary of Inniskilling Dragoons For December 1917. Vol. No.		
War Diary	Villers Guislain Ridge	01/12/1917	03/12/1917
War Diary	Ennemain	04/12/1917	31/12/1917
Miscellaneous			
Miscellaneous	Summary of Operation, Mhow Cavalry Brigade, November 30th To December 2nd 1917.	04/12/1917	04/12/1917
Miscellaneous	Report on The Operation Of "C" Squadron, Inniskilling Dragoons, On Decr. 1st 1917.		
Miscellaneous	Rations Carried out by the Inniskilling Dragoons on December 1st. 1917.		
War Diary	Ennemain	01/01/1918	31/01/1918
Heading	War Diary of The Inniskilling Dragoons. From; 1st February 1918 To: 28th. February 1918. Volume. No.		
War Diary	Ennemain	01/01/1918	02/01/1918
War Diary	Marcelcave	03/01/1918	03/01/1918
War Diary	Molliens Vidame	04/01/1918	04/01/1918
War Diary	Selincourt	05/01/1918	28/01/1918
War Diary	Cote Wood	27/01/1918	27/01/1918
War Diary	The Egg (Hargicourt Sector Cav. Corps Front).	28/01/1918	02/02/1918
War Diary	Support Line (Cote Wood)	03/02/1918	08/02/1918
War Diary	The Egg (Hargicourt)	09/02/1918	11/02/1918
War Diary	Cote Wood	12/02/1918	12/02/1918
Miscellaneous			

Heading	1917-18 4th Cavalry Division Mhow Cavalry Brigade 38th (K. G. O.) Central India Horse Jan 1917-Mar 1918 From Ind Cav Div Box 1176 To Egypt 4cav Div 10 Cav Bde		
Heading	War Diary of 38th (K. G. O.) Central India Horse. From 1st January 1917 To 31st January 1917		
War Diary	Nibas	02/01/1917	27/01/1917
Heading	War Diary of 38th (K. G. O.) C. I. Horse For February 1917		
War Diary	Nibas	03/02/1917	26/02/1917
Heading	War Diary of 38th (K. G. O.) C. I. Horse For March 1917		
War Diary	Nibas	01/03/1917	19/03/1917
War Diary	Caours	20/03/1917	20/03/1917
War Diary	Berteaucourt	21/03/1917	21/03/1917
War Diary	Aveluy	24/03/1917	25/03/1917
Heading	War Diary of 38th. (K. G. O.) C. I. Horse From 1st To 30th April 1917.		
War Diary	Aveluy	03/04/1917	03/04/1917
War Diary	Camp	10/04/1917	13/04/1917
War Diary	Sarton	26/04/1917	30/04/1917
Heading	War Diary of 38th (K. G. O.) C. I. Horse For May June 1917.		
War Diary	Sarton	02/05/1917	15/05/1917
War Diary	Mericourt	16/05/1917	16/05/1917
War Diary	Cappy	17/05/1917	17/05/1917
War Diary	St. Christ	19/05/1917	31/05/1917
Heading	War Diary of 38th (K. G. O.) C.I Horse For June 1917		
War Diary	St. Christ	04/06/1917	04/06/1917
War Diary	Hamelet	05/06/1917	17/06/1917
War Diary	Ennemain	20/06/1917	29/06/1917
Heading	War Diary of C I H Coy. For June 1917		
War Diary		15/06/1917	30/06/1917
Heading	War Diary of 38th (K. G. O.) C. I. Horse For July 1917		
War Diary	Ennemain	02/07/1917	31/07/1917
War Diary	B 3 Left Subsector E of Hargicourt	02/07/1917	02/07/1917
Heading	War Diary of 38th (K. G. O.) C. I. Horse For August 1917		
War Diary	Ennemain	06/08/1917	31/08/1917
Heading	War Diary of 38th. (K. G. O.) Central India Horse For September 1917.		
War Diary	Ennemain	02/09/1917	22/09/1917
War Diary		01/09/1917	14/09/1917
War Diary	Na. Asscension Farm	22/09/1917	26/09/1917
War Diary	Trenches Na Ascension Farm	26/09/1917	29/09/1917
War Diary	Trenches	29/09/1917	30/09/1917
Heading	War Diary of The 38th. King Georges Own Central India Horse For The Month Of October 1917.		
War Diary	Ennemain	01/10/1917	26/10/1917
Heading	War Diary of 38th (K. G. O.) C I Horse For November 17		
War Diary	Ennemain	02/11/1917	21/11/1917
War Diary	Fins	23/11/1917	23/11/1917
War Diary	Ennemain	24/11/1917	30/11/1917
Heading	War Diary of 38th. Central India Horse For The Month of December 1917		

War Diary	St. Emelie	30/11/1917	01/12/1917
War Diary	Epehy	02/12/1917	02/12/1917
War Diary	St. Emelie	03/12/1917	03/12/1917
War Diary	Ennemain	08/12/1917	31/12/1917
Heading	War Diary 38th (K. G. O.) C. I. Horse For January 1918		
War Diary	Ennemain	01/01/1918	29/01/1918
Heading	War Diary Div Mhow Bde 38th (K. G. O.) C. I. Horse For February 1918		
Miscellaneous	Messages And Signals.		
War Diary	Field	28/01/1918	07/02/1918
War Diary	Ennemain	01/02/1918	02/02/1918
War Diary	Bayonvillers	03/02/1918	04/02/1918
War Diary	Fricamps	15/02/1918	28/02/1918
War Diary		08/02/1918	15/02/1918
War Diary	Ericamps	01/03/1918	21/03/1918
War Diary	Marseilles	24/03/1918	30/03/1918
Heading	1917 4th Cavalry Division Mhow Cavalry Brigade Signal Troop Jan 1917-Mar 1918		
Heading	War Diary of Signal Troop, Mhow Cavalry Brigade. From 1st January 1917 To 31st January 1917		
War Diary	In the Field	01/01/1917	24/01/1917
Heading	War Diary. of Signal Troop Mhow Cav Bde From 1-2-17 To 28-2-17		
War Diary	Field	01/02/1917	28/02/1917
Heading	War Diary of Signal Troop Mhow Cavalry Brigade From 1st March 1917 To 31st March 1917		
War Diary	Field	01/03/1917	31/03/1917
Heading	War Diary of Signal Troop Mhow Cavalry Brigade From 1-4-17 To 30-4-17.		
War Diary	In the Field	01/04/1917	30/04/1917
Heading	War Diary of Signal Troop Mhow Cavalry Brigade From 1st May 1917. To 30th June 1917.		
War Diary	In the Field	01/05/1917	31/05/1917
Heading	War Diary of Signal Troop Mhow Cav Bde From 1st June 1917. To 30th June 1917.		
War Diary	St Christ-Brios	01/06/1917	03/06/1917
War Diary	Hamelet	04/06/1917	16/06/1917
War Diary	Authies	17/06/1917	27/07/1917
War Diary	Ennemain	29/07/1917	30/07/1917
Heading	War Diary of Signal Troop Mhow Cavalry Brigade From 1st July 1917 To 31st July 1917		
War Diary	In the Field	01/07/1917	31/07/1917
Heading	War Diary of Signal Troop, Mhow Cavalry Bde From 1-8-1917 To 31-8-1917		
War Diary	In the Field	01/08/1917	31/08/1917
Heading	War Diary of the Mhow Brigade Signal Troop From 1st Sept" 17 To 30th Sept" 1917		
War Diary	In the Field	01/09/1917	30/09/1917
Heading	War Diary of Signal Troop Mhow Cav Bde From 1-10-17 To 31-10-17		
War Diary	In the Field	01/10/1917	31/10/1917
Heading	War Diary of Signal Troop Mhow Cavalry Brigade From 1-11-17 To 30-11-17		
War Diary	In the Field	01/11/1917	30/11/1917

Heading	War Diary. of Signal Troop Mhow Cav Bde Fro, 1-12-17. To 31-12-17.		
War Diary	In the Field	01/12/1917	31/12/1917
Heading	War Diary. 4 Div Mhow. Bde Signal Troop For January 1918.		
War Diary	In the Field	01/01/1918	31/01/1918
Heading	War Diary of Mhow Bde Signal Troop From. 1st February 1918. To 28th February 1918.		
War Diary	In the Field	01/02/1918	28/02/1918
War Diary	St. Sauflieu	01/03/1918	11/03/1918
War Diary	Marseilles	17/03/1918	21/03/1918
War Diary	Alexandria	28/03/1918	29/03/1918
War Diary	Tel El Kebir	30/03/1918	31/03/1918
Heading	1917-18 4th Cavalry Division Mhow Cavalry Brigade 11th Machine Gun Squadron Jan 1917-Mar 1918		
Heading	War Diary of Machine Gun Squadron Mhow Cavalry Brigade From 1st January 1917 To 31st January 1917.		
War Diary	Offeux	31/12/1916	31/01/1917
Heading	War Diary of No. 11. Squadron M.G. Corps (cav) (Mhow Cavalry Brigade) From 1-2-17 To 28-2-17		
War Diary	Offeux.	01/02/1917	28/02/1917
Heading	War Diary of No 11 Machine Gun Sqdn Machine Gun Corps (Cav) Confidential From 1st To 31st March 1917		
War Diary	Offeux	01/03/1917	07/03/1917
War Diary	Franleu	08/03/1917	18/03/1917
War Diary	Le Plessiel	19/03/1917	19/03/1917
War Diary	Berteaucourt	20/03/1917	20/03/1917
War Diary	Aveluy	21/03/1917	31/03/1917
Heading	War Diary No 11 Sqdn M.G. Corps (Cav) April 1917		
War Diary	Aveluy	01/04/1917	01/04/1917
War Diary	Miraumont	02/04/1917	11/04/1917
War Diary	Authie	13/04/1917	13/04/1917
War Diary	Thievres	15/04/1917	15/04/1917
War Diary	Amplier	25/04/1917	30/04/1917
Heading	War Diary For May 1917 June 1917 No 11. Sqnd. M.G. Corps. (Cav). Field May 31st. 1917		
War Diary	Amplin	01/05/1917	13/05/1917
War Diary	Heilly	14/05/1917	15/05/1917
War Diary	Bray	15/05/1917	16/05/1917
War Diary	Due S. Of. Brie 62 E 1 : 40,000	16/05/1917	16/05/1917
War Diary	U.3.b. 62c 1/40,000 Due S. Of Brie.	17/05/1917	22/05/1917
War Diary	L. 10. a. 6:6. 62c. NE. 1:20,000 H.Qs. No. 11 Sqdm M.G. Caps. Codes M.Q.	23/05/1917	23/05/1917
War Diary	L. 10. a. 6:6. 62c. N.E. 1:20,000 H.Q. No.11 Sqdn. M.G. Caps. Codes M.Q	24/05/1917	24/05/1917
War Diary	L. 10. a.6:6: 62c. N. E. 1/20.000 H.Q. NO. 11 Sqsn. M.8. Caps. Codes:- M. Q.	25/05/1917	26/05/1917
War Diary	L. 10. a. 6:6: 62c No.E.1/20000 H.Q. No.11. Sqa M.G.Caps Coded Muse M.X.	28/05/1917	28/05/1917
Miscellaneous	L. 10. a. 6:6: 62c No.E.1/20.000 H.Q. No.11. Sqdn M.G. Corps Coded Muse	28/05/1917	28/05/1917
War Diary	L. 10. a. 6:6: 60c No.E. 1/20.000 H.Q. No.11.Sqa M.G.Cops Muse	29/05/1917	30/05/1917
Heading	War Diary June 1917 No 11 Sqdn M.G. Corps. (Cavalry)		
War Diary	Map Ref 62c N. E. L 10. A. 6.6.	01/06/1917	02/06/1917

War Diary	Hamelet	03/06/1917	14/06/1917
War Diary	Cote Wood L.10. A. 3.2.	15/06/1917	15/06/1917
War Diary	Cote Wood	15/06/1917	30/06/1917
Map	Appendix I to War Diary June 1917 No 11 Sqdn M.G Corps (Cav) 30.06.17		
Heading	War Diary July 1917 No 11 Sqdn. M.G. Corps (Cav)		
War Diary	H.Q. Cote Wood L.10.C.32. 62C N.E.	01/07/1917	08/07/1917
War Diary	Ennemain	09/07/1917	11/07/1917
Heading	No 11 Sqdn. Machine Gun Corps (Cav) War Diary August 1917		
War Diary	Ennemain	01/08/1917	10/08/1917
War Diary	Epehey Sector	10/08/1917	22/08/1917
War Diary	Hargicourt Sector	22/08/1917	31/08/1917
Heading	War Diary No 11 Sqdn M.G. Corps (cavalry) September 1917		
War Diary	Hargicourt Sector	01/09/1917	29/09/1917
Heading	War Diary of No 11 Squadron Machine Gun Corps (Cavalry) October 1917		
War Diary	Ennemain	01/10/1917	01/10/1917
War Diary	Athies	03/10/1917	30/10/1917
Heading	War Diary No 11 Sqdn M.G. Corps (Cav) November 1917		
War Diary	Athies	01/11/1917	18/11/1917
War Diary	Dessart wood	19/11/1917	23/11/1917
War Diary	Athies	25/11/1917	30/11/1917
Heading	No 11 Squadron Machine Gun Corps (Cav) War Diary December 1917		
War Diary	Brtt Emilie	01/12/1917	01/12/1917
War Diary	E. 18 d 6.5	02/12/1917	03/12/1917
War Diary	Athies	04/12/1917	31/12/1917
Heading	War Diary of 4 Div Mhow Bde No 11 Squadron M.G.C. (Cav) For January 1918		
War Diary	Athies	01/01/1918	31/01/1918
Heading	War Diary of 11th Machine Gun Squadron For February, 1918		
Heading	Athies	01/01/1918	31/01/1918
War Diary	Villeret Sector	01/02/1918	01/02/1918
War Diary	Athies	02/02/1918	02/02/1918
War Diary	Wiencourt	03/02/1918	03/02/1918
War Diary	Bovelles	04/02/1918	04/02/1918
War Diary	Villeret Sector	14/02/1918	15/02/1918
War Diary	Aubin	26/02/1918	26/02/1918
War Diary	Dommartin	27/02/1918	27/02/1918
War Diary	Harbonnier	28/02/1918	28/02/1918
Heading	War Diary of No 11 Squadron M G C. (Cav) Attached To 32 Division For March 1918		
War Diary	Brusle	01/03/1918	13/03/1918
War Diary	Brae	14/03/1918	14/03/1918
War Diary	Vaire-Sur-Corbie	15/03/1918	15/03/1918
War Diary	Vers	16/03/1918	16/03/1918
War Diary	Franciers	17/03/1918	18/03/1918
War Diary	L'Etoile	18/03/1918	25/03/1918
War Diary	Bellacourt	26/03/1918	27/03/1918
War Diary	Humbercamp	28/03/1918	28/03/1918
War Diary	Quesnoy Farm	28/03/1918	28/03/1918
War Diary	Quesnoy. Fm.	29/03/1918	31/03/1918

Heading	1917-18 4th Cavalry Division Mhow Cavalry Brigade Mobile Vety Section Jan 1917-Feb 1918		
Heading	War Diary of Mobile Veterinary Section, Mhow Cavalry Brigade. From 1st January 1917. To 31st January 1917.		
War Diary	Belloy Sur Mer	15/01/1917	31/01/1917
War Diary	Belloy Sur Mer	01/01/1917	14/01/1917
Heading	War Diary of Mobile Veterinary Section Mhow Cavalry Brigade From 1-2-17 To 28-2-17		
War Diary	Belloy	01/02/1917	14/02/1917
War Diary	Friville	15/02/1917	28/02/1917
Heading	War Diary of Mobile Veterinary Section Mhow Cavalry Brigade From 1st March 1917 To 31st March 1917		
War Diary	Friville	01/03/1917	19/03/1917
War Diary	Drucat	20/03/1917	20/03/1917
War Diary	St Leger	21/03/1917	21/03/1917
War Diary	Aveluy	22/03/1917	31/03/1917
Heading	War Diary of Mobile Veterinary Section Mhow Cavalry Brigade From 1-4-17. To 30-4-17		
War Diary	Aveluy	01/04/1917	03/04/1917
War Diary	Miramont	04/04/1917	13/04/1917
War Diary	Sarton	14/04/1917	30/04/1917
Heading	War Diary of Mobile Veterinary Section Mhow Cavalry Brigade From 1st May 1917. To 30th June 1917.		
War Diary	Sarton	01/05/1917	14/05/1917
War Diary	Mericourt	15/05/1917	15/05/1917
War Diary	Cappy	16/05/1917	16/05/1917
War Diary	St Christ	17/05/1917	31/05/1917
Heading	War Diary of Mobile Vety Section Mhow Cavalry Bde From 1st June 1917. To 30th June 1917.		
War Diary	St Christ	01/06/1917	17/06/1917
War Diary	Ennemain	18/06/1917	30/06/1917
Heading	War Diary of Mobile Veterinary Section Mhow Cavalry Brigade From 1st July 1917 To 31st July 1917		
War Diary	Ennemain	01/07/1917	31/07/1917
Heading	War Diary of Mobile Veterinary Section Mhow Cavalry Bde. From 1 Aug 1917 To 31 Aug 1917		
War Diary	Ennemaine	01/08/1917	31/08/1917
Heading	War Diary of Mobile Veterinary Section Mhow Cavalry Bde From 1-9-17 To 30.9.17		
War Diary	Ennemaine	01/09/1917	30/09/1917
Heading	War Diary of Mobile Veterinary Section Mhow Cavalry Brigade From 1-10-17 To 31-10-17		
War Diary	Ennemain	01/10/1917	31/10/1917
Heading	War Diary of Mobile Veterinary Section Mhow Cav Bde Form 1-11-17 to 30-11-17		
War Diary	Ennemain	01/11/1917	30/11/1917
Heading	War Diary of Mobile Veterinary Section Mhow Cavalry Brigade Fro, 1-12-17. To 31-12-17.		
War Diary	St. Emile	01/12/1917	02/12/1917
War Diary	Ennemain	03/12/1917	31/12/1917
Heading	War Diary Mobile Veterinary Section Mhow Bde For January 1918		
War Diary	Ennemain	01/01/1918	31/01/1918
Heading	War Diary of 4 Div Mhow Mobile Veterinary Section From, 1st February 1918. To 28th February 1918.		

War Diary	Ennemain	01/02/1918	02/02/1918
War Diary	Marcelcave	03/02/1918	03/02/1918
War Diary	Pont De Metz	04/02/1918	04/02/1918
War Diary	Courcelles	05/02/1918	28/02/1918

1917
4TH CAVALRY DIVISION
MHOW CAVALRY BRIGADE

BDE HEADQUARTERS.

JAN - 1917 — 1918 MARCH

SERIAL NO. 114

Confidential
War Diary
of

HEADQUARTERS, MHOW CAVALRY BRIGADE.

FROM 1st JANUARY 1917 **TO** 31st JANUARY 1917

Army Form C. 2118.

WAR DIARY
or
INTELLIGENCE SUMMARY Head Quarters
Indian Cavalry Brigade

(Erase heading not required.)

Instructions regarding War Diaries and Intelligence Summaries are contained in F. S. Regs, Part II. and the Staff Manual respectively. Title Pages will be prepared in manuscript.

Place	Date	Hour	Summary of Events and Information	Remarks and references to Appendices
JANUARY 1917				
ESCARBOTIN	1st to 6th		Squadron & Regimental Training & Musketry. 3 weeks course completed.	
	6th	5pm	Capt. HARVEY K.D. Guards took up appts of Staff Capt. (temporary)	
	8th		Advance Party Pioneer Bn. left for MONDICOURT for recce tour of duty.	
	11th		Pioneer Bn. left for MONDICOURT.	
	12th		Lt. Col. Croke 35th C.H. proceeded to MONDICOURT to take over command from Capt. MONCRIEFF	
	15th		Major BENNETT 2nd Lancers relieved Lt. Colonel COOKE.	
	26th		Captain ROBERTSON 2nd Lancers 40. I.O. Ranks. 16 British O.Rs. left for MONDICOURT by lorry as a relief to Pioneer Bn.	
	27th		Capt. SHERWOOD SMITH attd. 2nd Lancers 40 I.O. Ranks & 16 British O.Rs. rejoined from MONDICOURT on relief.	

Gould Capt.
Brigade Major
Indian Cav. Bde.

Army Form C. 2118.

WAR DIARY
INTELLIGENCE SUMMARY
(Erase heading not required.)

MHOW CAVALRY BRIGADE

Place	Date	Hour	Summary of Events and Information	Remarks and references to Appendices
ESCARBOTIN	Feb. 1917 3rd		3 Officers, 1 Medical Officer, 1 Sub. Asst. Surgeon, 16 British O.Rs, 40 Indian O.Rs left by lorry as a relief to Pioneer Bn. at MONDICOURT	M.
	4th		3 Officers, 1 Medical Officer, 1 Sub. Asst. Surgeon, 18 British O.Rs, 38 Indian O.Rs returned by lorry from MONDICOURT	M.
	13th	10 a.m.	7 Officers 22 British ORs 3/0s 24 Indian ORs left by lorry as a relief to Pioneer Bn at MONDICOURT	RR.
	14th		5 Officers 8 British OR 3/0s 25 IORs returned by lorry from MONDICOURT	RR
	16th		Capt Gould Brigade Major, left for GHQ to go thro Junior Staff Course	RR.
	25th		A battery RHA left billeting area under orders of LUCKNOW BDE & proceeded to a billeting area near TALMAS	RR.

S.E. Harvey Capt.
for Bde Major.
Mhow Cavalry Brigade

Serial No. 114.

CONFIDENTIAL
WAR DIARY.
of
Head Quarters
MHOW Cavalry Brigade.
from 1st March 1917 to 31st March 1917

Army Form C. 2118.

WAR DIARY
or
INTELLIGENCE SUMMARY.
(Erase heading not required.)

Head Quarters
Mhow Cav. Bde.

Instructions regarding War Diaries and Intelligence Summaries are contained in F. S. Regs. Part II. and the Staff Manual respectively. Title pages will be prepared in manuscript.

Place	Date	Hour	Summary of Events and Information	Remarks and references to Appendices
ESCARBOTIN	1917 9.3.	9 a.m.	2 B. Os. 36 O.Rs. from 2nd Lancers left by lorry as relief to 2nd Lancers Pioneer Coy. at MONDICOURT.	R.R.
	10.3.	11.30 a.m.	11th M. G. Sqn. moved billets from OFFEUX to FRANLEU.	R.R.
	11.3.	9 a.m.	5 B.Os. 32 O.Rs. from Inniskillings left by lorry as relief to Inniskilling Pioneer Coy.	R.R.
	13.3.	9 a.m.	Relief from 2.L. and 38th C.C.H. left by lorry for MONDICOURT.	S.C.H.
	14.3		A similar party rejoined from MONDICOURT in relief.	S.C.H.
	17.3	3 a.m.	Mhow Pioneer Bn. Lion Tpt. detrained at WOINCOURT and rejoined their units.	S.C.H.
	18.3	1 p.m.	Tpt. of Pioneer Bn. arrived.	S.C.H.
	19.3	1 a.m.	U. Bty. R.H.A. and Lucknow Cav. Fd. And. joined the Brigade.	S.C.H.
	"	2 p.m.	Bde. moved billets about DRUCAT.	S.C.H.
DRUCAT	20.3	10 a.m.	Bde. moved billets about ST LEGER LES DOMART.	S.C.H.
ST LEGER.	21.3	10.30 a.m.	Bde. moved to a bivouac near AVELUY arriving 7 p.m.	S.C.H.
AVELUY.	22.3	10 p.m.	"B" echelon rejoined after having been left at RUBEMPRE owing to bad roads.	S.C.H.
	24.3		Reconnaissance of approach to V Corps line carried out.	4y/24
	25.3		Bde. found working party for work on roads consisting of 7 officers & 175 men. Working party found us to for 24 tt.	

WAR DIARY
or
INTELLIGENCE SUMMARY

(Erase heading not required.)

Army Form C. 2118.

Head Quarters
Inshaw Corps B de

Place	Date	Hour	Summary of Events and Information	Remarks and references to Appendices
AVELUY	1917 26.3		Working party found as for 25th. B.Wing in arrived from Junior Staff School 5 pm.	Nil.
	27/3		Bde. found 12 bayg'mrs & 24 men for moving Lucknow Bde. Dump. 25 men for working at R.H.	
		7 pm	Party of 2 Officers & 155 O.Rs. left for ACHIET LE GRAND for work at new Rail Head. 1 Officer & 16 O.Rs. for pitching new camp left for MIRAUMONT by rail.	Nil. Nil.
	28.3		50 tents with N.C.O. and 4 men sent up MIRAUMONT for new camp.	Nil.
	29.3	10.30 am	Lucknow camp complete with A.M.S. solution left for new camp near IRLES.	Nil.
		3 pm	Divisional mounted men rejoined the Bde. arrived under orders of Division.	Nil.
	30.3		Move of remainder of Bde. postponed until 1.4.17	
	31.3		" " " " " 3.4.17	

Grunth Capt.
Bde. Major
Indian Cav. Bde.

Serial No. 114.

--------C O N F I D E N T I A L.--------

WAR   DIARY   OF

Headquarters
Mhow Cavalry Brigade

From 1 - 4 - 17.   to   30 - 4 - 17.

Army Form C. 2118.

WAR DIARY
of
INTELLIGENCE SUMMARY. Xth Cavalry Brigade

Headquarters

(Erase heading not required.)

Instructions regarding War Diaries and Intelligence Summaries are contained in F. S. Regs., Part II. and the Staff Manual respectively. Title pages will be prepared in manuscript.

Place	Date	Hour	Summary of Events and Information	Remarks and references to Appendices
AVELUY	M.29.		at AVELUY	
	3rd	9am	Units moved independently over camp between MIRAUMONT~IRLES looking portion of 50 men for rest. working daily at road repairs.	
MIRAUMONT.	9.4.17	9.15pm	Order recd from Div. to move at 11.30am 10.4.17 to Square B.28.	
	10.4.17	11.30am	Bde. marched & arrived in portion of stations 5am. Recd. order to return to camp at MIRAUMONT 7.10 am. Arrived in camp 10 am. 4P.M. orders recd to move 2.45am. 11th.	
	11.4.17	2.45am	Bde. marched & arrived B.28. 6am. 9.40am. moved up to Rly. line E. of MORY. 10.20 a.m. moved between L.B.28. Remained here until 3.40pm. when orders were received to return to camp MIRAUMONT. Arrived in camp 6.30pm.	
	12.4.17	10.45am	Bde. put at 2 hours notice. 8.30pm. Warning Order of movement to back area in the following day received.	
	13.4.17	10.30am	Bde. marched to SARTON AUTHIE area and arrived 4.30pm.	
SARTON.	17.4.17	3.30pm	"A" Bty. R.H.A. rejoined Xth Bde. from the Line.	
	24.4		117 Remounts received for the Brigade.	
	25.4		Whirl-Whirling Coy. on left AUTHIE for THIEVRES and FAMECHON. Australia	

Army Form C. 2118.

WAR DIARY
or
INTELLIGENCE SUMMARY.
(Erase heading not required.)

Instructions regarding War Diaries and Intelligence Summaries are contained in F. S. Regs., Part II. and the Staff Manual respectively. Title pages will be prepared in manuscript.

Place	Date	Hour	Summary of Events and Information	Remarks and references to Appendices
SARTON	25.4		Cav. Bde. Ambce. moving into SARTON and M.G. Sqn. to ORVILLEand AMPLIER.	Nil.
	26.4		Cmdg Offr. inspected 1 Sqn. per aft. to M.G. Sqn. and Household A Bty. and Section Ammunition Column	Nil.
	28.4		1 Section M.G. Sqn. moved from ORVILLE to AUTHIEULLE. 4 Horses evacuated from the Bde. from 21st inst. of which 27 from A Bty RHA.	Nil.

Gmdl Cpt.
Brig Major
Inhos Cavalry Brigade.

Copy No. 17

S E C R E T.

MHOW CAVALRY BRIGADE Operation Order No. 2.

Reference Sheets 57.D. and 57.C. 1:40000.   28-3-17.

1. Mhow Cavalry Brigade will move into camp on North side of road between MIRAUMONT and IRLES, One Regiment moving on 29th instant, remainder of Brigade on 30th.

2. ROUTE. West bank of River ANCRE - Cross at HAMEL to East Bank - GRANDCOURT - MIRAUMONT.

3. 2nd Lancers complete with "A" and "B" Echelons will move tomorrow 29th instant. Hour of starting will be communicated to this office this evening.

4. Inniskilling Dragoons, 38th C.I.Horse, Bde. Hd. Qrs and M.G.Sqdn. will march independently on the 30th inst, starting at 9-0.a.m., 10-0.a.m., 10-45.a.m. and 11-0.a.m. respectively.

5. Regiments should detail a strong party to follow in rear of "B" Echelon as the roads are in very bad condition.

6. Billets must be left scrupulously clean and units will leave behind 1 Officer and 16 other ranks (M.G.Squadron 1 officer and 8 other ranks) to go through camp and billets after the units departure.

7. Rations will be delivered by rail at MIRAUMONT.

8. Brigade Report Centre will close at AVELUY at 10-30.a.m. and open in camp on arrival.

ACKNOWLEDGE.

Captain.
Brigade Major.

Issued at 4-0.p.m.

Copy No. 2. Inniskilling Dragoons.
     3. 2nd Lancers.
     4. 38th C.I.Horse.
     5. M.G.Squadron.
     6. Signal Troop.
     7. B.T.O.
     8. B.S.O.
     9. Mob. Vet. Section.
    10. 4th Cavalry Division.

SECRET.   Copy No.

MHOW CAVALRY BRIGADE Operation Order No. 2.

Reference Sheets 57.D. and 57.C. 1/40,000.   28-3-17.

1. Mhow Cavalry Brigade will move into Camp on North side of road between MIRAUMONT and Irles, One Regiment moving on 29th instant remainder of Brigade on 30th.
   ROUTE
2. West bank of River ANCRE – Cross at HAMEL to east bank – ~~GRANDCOURT~~ GRANDCOURT – MIRAUMONT.

3. 2nd Lancers complete with "A" and "B" Echelons will move tomorrow 29th inst. Hour of starting will be communicated to this office this evening.

4. Inniskilling Dragoons, 38th C.I.Horse, Bde. H. Qrs and M.G.Sqdn. will march independently on the 30th inst, starting at 9-0,a.m. 10.a.m., 10.45.a.m. and 11.a.m. respectively.

5. Regiments should detail a strong party to follow in rear of "B" Echelon as the roads are in a very bad condition.

6. Billets must be left scrupulously clean and units will leave behind one Officer and 16 other ranks (M.G.Sqdn 1 Officer and 8 other ranks) to go through camp and billets after the units departure.

6. Rations will be delivered by rail at MIRAUMONT.

8. Brigade report centre will close at AVELOY at 10-30.a.m. and open in Camp on arrival.

                                    (sgd) G.Gould.   Captain
                                           Brigade Major........

Issued at 4-0 p.m.

Copy No.2. Inniskilling Dragoons
       3. 2nd Lancers
       4. 38th C.I.Horse.
       5. M.G.Squadron.
       6- Signal Troop.
       7. B.T.O.
       8. B.S.O.
       9. Mob Vet Section.
      10. 4th Cavalry Division.

SECRET.
MHOW CAV. BDE. OPERATION ORDER No.3.
Reference Sheets 1:40,000. 57C & 51B.

Copy No. 18.
9-4-17.

1. The Fifth Army is attacking at Zero (on a date to be notified later) in accordance with the plan already circulated.

2. The Brigade will move to a position of readiness in Square B.28. South of MORY.
   Starting Point. Eastern extremity of C.I.H.Lines.
   TIME. Will be notified later.
   ROUTE. IRLES - Cross roads in G.22.c.9.0. - 5 roads junction - BIHUCOURT - SAPIGNIES - Thence by Cavalry Track to Square B.28.

   Order of March. Bde. H.Q., 38th C.I.Horse., Pack Mounted Section., M.G. Squadron., 2nd Lancers., Inniskilling Dragoons.

3. O.C. 38th C.I.Horse will detail one troop under a British Officer to clear the road by which the Brigade is moving.

4. Fighting Troops of Lucknow Bde. will follow Mhow Bde, starting one hour after head of Mhow Bde passes Starting Point.

5. A1 Echelon, under Lieut PECK, 2nd Lancers, will follow Lucknow A1 Echelon which will follow in rear of Lucknow Bde Fighting Troops.
   Officers led horses in order of units will march at the head of A1 under Lieut HILDER, Inniskilling Dragoons.
   A2 Echelon under Lieut DUDGEON Inniskilling Dragoons will follow Lucknow Bde A2 Echelon. M.V.Sec will march in rear of Cyclists with Echelon A2.
   "B" Echelon under B.T.O. will move under orders of O.C.,A.S.C.

6. All cyclists, less those with "B" Echelon, will march under the senior Cyclist N.C.O. of the Inniskilling Dragoons, in rear of Echelon A2.
   At least 2 cyclists per unit will be left with "B" Echelon during operations.

7. All units will water at the SAPIGNES water point, and water bottles and water carts must be filled at this place, as there is little water beyond

8. On arrival at Position of readiness all units will off saddle.

9. At Position of Readiness, Brigade Report Centre will be near the MORY - FAVREUIL road and Gallopers will report here immediately on arrival.

ACKNOWLEDGE.

Captain.
Brigade Major.
Mhow Cavalry Brigade.

Issued at 1-0.p.m.

Copy No.	To.
1.	Office.
2.	6th Dragoons.
3.	2nd Lancers.
4.	38th C.I.Horse.
5.	M.G.Squadron.
6.	Signal Troop.
7.	M.V.Sec.
8.	B.T.O.
9.	B.S.O.
10.	Ambala C.F.A.
11.	O.C. A1.
12.	O.C. A2.
13.	O.C. Led Horses.
14.	Lucknow Bde.
15.	4th Cav Div.
16.	Camp Comdt.
17,18 & 19.	Diary.

SECRET.
MHOW CAV. BDE. OPERATION ORDER No.3.
Reference Sheets 1:40,000. 57C & 51B.

Copy No. 17.
9-4-17.

1. The Fifth Army is attacking at Zero (on a date to be notified later) in accordance with the plan already circulated.

2. The Brigade will move to a position of readiness in Square B.28. South of MORY.
   Starting Point. Eastern extremity of C.I.H.Lines.
   TIME. Will be notified later.
   ROUTE. IRLES - Cross roads in G.22.c.9.0. - 5 roads junction -BIHUCOURT - SAPIGNIES - Thence by Cavalry Track to Square B.28.

   Order of March. Bde. H.Q., 38th C.I.Horse., Pack Mounted Section., M.G. Squadron., 2nd Lancers., Inniskilling Dragoons.

3. O.C. 38th C.I.Horse will detail one troop under a British Officer to clear the road by which the Brigade is moving.

4. Fighting Troops of Lucknow Bde. will follow Mhow Bde, starting one hour after head of Mhow Bde passes Starting Point.

5. A1 Echelon, under Lieut PECK, 2nd Lancers, will follow Lucknow A1 Echelon which will follow in rear of Lucknow Bde Fighting Troops.
   Officers led horses in order of units will march at the head of A1 under Lieut HILDER, Inniskilling Dragoons.
   A2 Echelon under Lieut DUDGEON Inniskilling Dragoons will follow Lucknow Bde A2 Echelon. M.V.Sec will march in rear of Cyclists with Echelon A2.
   "B" Echelon under B.T.O. will move under orders of O.C.,A.S.C.

6. All cyclists, less those with "B" Echelon, will march under the senior Cyclist N.C.O. of the Inniskilling Dragoons, in rear of Echelon A2.
   At least 2 cyclists per unit will be left with "B" Echelon during operations.

7. All units will water at the SAPIGNES water point, and water bottles and water carts must be filled at this place, as there is little water beyond

8. On arrival at Position of readiness all units will off saddle.

9. At Position of Readiness, Brigade Report Centre will be near the MORY - FAVREUIL road and Gallopers will report here immediately on arrival.

ACKNOWLEDGE.

Captain.
Brigade Major.
Mhow Cavalry Brigade.

Issued at 1-0.p.m.
```
Copy No.      To.
   1.    Office.
   2.    6th Dragoons.
   3.    2nd Lancers.
   4.    38th C.I.Horse.
   5.    M.G.Squadron.
   6.    Signal Troop.
   7.    M.V.Sec.
   8.    B.T.O.
   9.    B.S.O.
  10.    Ambala C.F.A.
  11.    O.C. A1.
  12.    O.C. A2.
  13.    O.C. Led Horses.
  14.    Lucknow Bde.
  15.    4th Cav. Div.
  16.    Camp Comdt.
17,18 & 19. Diary.
```

Mhow Bde Operation Order No 4.

Memo.
Reference Mhow Cav Bde Operation Order No 3. of date.

The Brigade will march at 1.30.a.m., 10th inst.

Headquarters passing Starting Point at this hour.

Units will not leave their Camping Ground before it is time for them to take their place in the Column.

9.30 pm.   [signed] Captain
                       Brigade Major.
9-4-17. Mhow Cav Bde
To Ordinary Distribution.

S E C R E T.

M H O W. Cavalry Brigade Operation order No. 4.

Memo.

    Reference Mhow Cavalry Brigade Operation Order No 3. of date.

    The Brigade will march at 1-30 a.m., 10th inst.

    Headquarters passing starting point at this hour.

    Units will not leave their Camping ground before it is ~~their~~ time for them to take their place in the Column.

                                      (sgd) G.Gould Captain
                                       Brigade Major Mhow Cavalry Bde.

9.30 p.m.

9-4-17.

To.   Ordinary Distribution.

Serial No. 111

CONFIDENTIAL.

WAR DIARY.

of

Headquarters
Mhow Cavalry Brigade

from 1st May 1917.   to ~~31st May 1917.~~ 30th June 1917.

Army Form C. 2118.

WAR DIARY
INTELLIGENCE SUMMARY.
(Erase heading not required.)

Headquarters, 15th new Bde

Place	Date	Hour	Summary of Events and Information	Remarks and references to Appendices
SARTON.	MAY 1917. 1st.		General routine work.	
	to 11th.		do do	
	12th.		Orders to transfer to Fourth Army received.	
	13th.		General Routine work.	
	14th.		do do	
	15th. 10am		Bde marched to HEILLY and MERICOURT. Halted 1½ hours at CONTAY to water and feed. Arrived 3pm. Headquarters in MERICOURT.	July
	16th. 10.15am.		Bde marched to BRAY and CAPPY. Arrived 1pm. HQ in CAPPY.	
	17th. 9am		Bde marched to ST CHRIST BRIOST and went into Camp on arrival at 1pm.	July
ST CHRIST.	18th.		General routine work.	
	19th. 11am		"A" Bty. R.H.A. & 1 M.G. of the Brigade from OURVILLES. L.t. O. Bisset 15 G M.G. Section taking over of B Section from 176 th. M.G Bde Afferer Partier went to his treatment M.G. Sqdn. arrived July 6 July number	July
	23rd.		"Dismounted Bde" marched up in three parties, horses being sent-back after arrival. Relief commenced at 8.30 pm Bde H.Q. Anx. ROISEL. 10 Rounded up.	
	24th. 1.30am		Relief completed without incident. Quiet night. Projectile ful Haig	

WAR DIARY
or
INTELLIGENCE SUMMARY.

Army Form C. 2118.

Place	Date	Hour	Summary of Events and Information	Remarks and references to Appendices
	MAY 1917.			
ROISEL	24.5		Arrived Command of Lt. Peter at 7.30 a.m. & Bde. H.Q. An. moved to L.76.	66.
L.7.B.	25.5		Situation normal. Lt. Peter w.m. Some shelling of TEMPLE by X.I.O.R. sounded.	66.
	26th.		Quiet m. 6 men of 38th Cavalry wounded during afternoon by premature. One man Inniskillings killed and four wounded by m.m. enemy fire. Two men Inniskillings wounded during night. 17th. Lancers 1 O.R. wounded.	66.
	27th.		Patrols from all units in B1 & B2. Subsection out during the night. 3 parties of the enemy being encountered. Hostile Artillery moderately active. Papers were taken from a dead German, nothing of importance. Gas Alert on Lud Lancers 1.10 R. sounded 30th Cr. Ls. to 5 stables being fired. No casualties known. Gas Alert on.	66.
	28th.		Sne patrols out during night. Bwang L 3t. shelled by a hung gun from 6.45am to 7.25 am about 50 shells being fired. No casualties known. Gas Alert on.	66.
	29th.		Small day light raid carried out by two men M.G. Corps, two Germans reported killed. Identification brought in. Later. New Subsector taken over from 36th. Poona Horse. Relief Completed 2.30 a.m. Quiet night. Gas Alert. Taken S/o. 1 Officer 2 O.R. wounded.	66.
	30th.		29th Lancers relieved Inniskillings in L.3.a. Inniskillings moved in to B1 Subsector, arriving 12.10 am.	66.
	31st		Quiet night. Inniskillings took over two posts from 17th. Lancers. Inniskillings took over two posts and a support post from 17th Lancers. One man M.G. Sqn. killed.	66.

Alfred Capt.
Intelligence Cav. Bde.

SECRET. Copy No. 14

MHOW CAVALRY BRIGADE. OPERATION ORDER No.5.

Reference Map 1:100000, LENS & AMIENS.   13-5-17.

1. The Division is being transferred to the Fourth Army and will move thereto on 15th, 16th and 17th instants.

2. (a) Mhow Cav.Bde will move via M—
   Cross Roads 300 yards N.E. of last E of BEAUQUESNE – RAINCHEVAL – CONTAY – FRANVILLERS – HEILLY – RIBMONT – MERICOURT STA.
   (b) Starting point Cross Roads at Northern entrance to MARIEUX.
   (c) Time 10 a.m.
   (d) Order of March. Brigade Head Quarters. Inniskilling Dragoons. 38th C.I.Horse. 2nd Lancers. M.G.Sqdn. Ambala Cav Fd Amb. "A" Echelon in order of units under command of Lieut LUPTON 6th Dragoons. Cyclists. "B" Echelon in order of units under command of Major Prichard 38th C.I.H.

3. Cyclists will move in a formed body under the command of the Senior Cyclist N.C.O. Inniskilling Dragoons.

4. Fighting troops will maintain an average rate of march of 5 miles per hour, exclusive of halts.

5. An interval of 500 yards will be maintained between units.

6. Billeting parties will rendezvous at Bde Starting point at 8-30 a.m. and march under the Senior Officer present.
   They will report on arrival at MERICOURT – L'ABBE to Staff Captain at Town Majors Office.

7. 1 troop of the rear Regiment will follow immediately behind "B" Echelon under orders of B.T.O.

8. Attention is directed to orders regarding Gallopers, certificates on leaving and entering billets, reports as to position of report centres, Officers left behind to settle claims, etc, etc, Brigade Standing Orders Ne.5 and 7, Reports (s)

9. *The Brigade will water at CONTAY.*

Captain
Brigade Major
Mhow Cavalry Brigade.

Issued 13/5/17
To.
   Normal distribution.

1 —
2 —
3 —
4 —
5 —
6 General & ADC on leave.
7 —
8 —
9 —
12
13 th order to move.
14 —

18 General returned

Secret   Copy No. 14

15th Can Cav Bde Operation Order No. 6

1. The 15th will continue the march tomorrow 16th inst.

2. (a) Route. Cross roads 5000 yds South of MERICOURT–L'ABBE, main road to HAPPY and CAPPY.

   (b) Starting Point. Cross roads 500 yds West of (a) on MERICOURT (MERICOURT–SAILLY LE SEC road).

   (c) Time 10.15 a.m.

3. Order of March. RCD, 1st CMR, QR, 5th C.M. Horse, 2nd Lancers Ambala Car Mtr Amb, 6th Inniskilling Dragoons; M.G. Sqdn; "A" Echelon in order of units; Cyclists; "B" Echelon in order of units; RHA Section

3. O.C 5th C.I. Horse will detail one Troop to act as Advance Guard.

4. Artillery parties will parade at the Starting Point at 8 a.m. and proceed under the command of the Senior Officer Artillery.

5. Billets are allotted as under:—
   15th H.Q.
   5th C.I Horse } CAPPY

                                          P.T.O.

A? Section
? FA / LANEUVILLE.

Train, Killing Division
M.G. Sqdn } BRAY.

Billeting Parties will apply to Town
Majors for details of Billets which have
been arranged.

6—10. as in paras 3, 4, 5, 7 & 8 of
O.O. N° 5. of 13th inst.

Issued by D.R.
at 5:15 pm
Normal Distribution. [signature] Captain
Brigade Major.
?har. Co. R.E.

Secret   Copy No. 9

Mhow Cavalry Bde Operation Order No 7.
16-5-17.

1. The Brigade will continue the march tomorrow 17th inst. to an area about ST CHRIST BRIOST.

2. (a) Route via ESTREES and BRIE.
   (b) Starting Point, where ESTREES road leaves CAPPY Village.
   (c) Time 9 a.m.
   (d) Order of March:- Bde H.Qrs. 2nd Lancers; Australia CFA; M.G. Sqdn; Inniskilling Dragoons, 38th C.I.Horse; Cyclists.

3. O.C. 2nd Lancers will detail one Troop to act as advance guard.

4. (a) Units will be followed by their "A" Echelon.
   (b) Divl Hd Qrs. with their "A" and "B" Echelons will follow the Cyclists.
   (c) "B" Echelon of the Bde will follow Divl Hd Qrs "B" Echelon in order of units. Head of "B" Echelon 2nd Lancers will not enter BRAY-CAPPY road until "B" Echelon Divl Hd Qrs has passed.
   "B" Echelon 38th C.I.Horse will join in in rear of the "B" Echelon Column at CAPPY.
   "B" Echelon of the Bde will be clear of VILLERS - CARBONNEL by 1-30 pm.

5. Camp parties will meet Staff Captain at the Starting Point at 8-30 am.

P.T.O.

6—10 a.m. in paras. 3, 4, 5, 7 and 8
O.O. No 5 of 18th inst.

(Sgd) .... Captain,
Brigade Major.

Issued to Squads 3-30 p.m.
for Verbal Distribution

SECRET.   Mhow Cavalry Brigade. Operation Order No.6.   Copy No. 34

Reference Sheets 1/20,000. 62.c.N.E. & 62.b.N.W.   22-5-17.

1. The Dismounted Regiments and M.G.Squadrons of MHOW and SIALKOT Bdes will take over from the 176th Infantry Brigade, in the sector L.22.a.7.6.- L.4.b.4.7. on the nights of 22nd/23rd and 23rd/24th May 1917. Relief to be completed by morning of 24th.

2. The Sector is divided into two Sub-sectors, Right and Left, dividing line approximately L.10 and L.11.Central.

3. The Right Sub-sector. will be commanded by Lieut Colonel NEWNHAM, 6th Cavalry and will compose the 17th Lancers and 6th Cavalry. Headquarters at L.10.c.5.4.

   The Left Sub-sector.will be commanded by Lieut Colonel PATERSON, D.S.O. Inniskilling Dragoons, and will compose the Inniskilling Dragoons and 38th C.I.Horse. Headquarters at L.10.a.6.6.

   The Reserve. will be commanded by Lieut Colonel TURNER, 2nd Lancers, and will compose the 2nd Lancers and 19th Lancers. Headquarters in HERVILLY.

   The Reserve will eventually be required to take over a third Sub-sector on the Right.

4. Reliefs will be carried out in accordance with attached tables.

   Officers Commanding Sub-sectors and Reserve will issue their own orders for the march up, and arrange for the return of horses.

   It might be found of assistance to take some men up in G.S.Wagons, 14 men can ride in a G.S.Wagon.

5. (a) The strength of the Advance Parties has been worked out so that 1 N.C.O. and 2 men can be attached to each platoon, and one officer to each company.
   When the relief is carried out two troops will take over from each Infantry platoon.

   (b) There should be some snipers amongst the selected privates sent. They will work with the Infantry snipers until the relief is completed.

   (c) On the night of 23rd/24th May the patrols will be found by the Infantry. One N.C.O. or man of the Advance Party will accompany each patrol. The patrol reports will be handed over to the Relieving troops on the morning of the 24th May.

   (d) The trench routine as carried out by the 176th Infantry Bde. will be continued by the MHOW and SIALKOT Bdes during their tour in the trenches, and Advance Parties will make themselves thoroughly conversant with this routine.

6. 176th Infantry Bde have kindly consented to leave the 2nds-in-Command and one officer per company of the 2/5 N.Staffords and 2/6th South Staffords (the Bns. holding the advanced and intermediate lines) for 24 hours after the relief has been completed.

7. Medical arrangements will be as in A.D.M.S. Nos 2058 and 2071 of 20th inst. O.C. Ambala C.F.A. will arrange with units of MHOW Bde and 19th Lancers for the necessary establishment and equipment for the Left Sub-sector and the two regiments in Reserve.

8. Communications will be taken over from 176th Infy. Bde. by 8.p.m. 23rd inst.
   The attention of all is drawn to Code names and calls issued under G.I./2/8 of 20th inst. Messages will not be sent by buzzer forward of Bde. Hd. Qrs.

P.T.O.

9. Brigade Hd. Qrs. will close at ST CHRIST at 2.p.m. 23rd inst and will open at ROISEL (House East end of village) at same hour.

Brigade Signal Office will be at L.7.b.8.2.

Issued to Signals at 5-30.p.m.

                                                     Captain.

Normal distribution also :-
12 copies to Sialkot Bde.   Brigade Major.
6 extra to Mhow Bde.   Mhow and Sialkot Dismounted Regiments.
1 to 176th Infty. Bde.

****

SECRET.   ADMINISTRATIVE INSTRUCTIONS.

1. Advance Parties will take over the Battn. Grenade, S.A.A. and R.E. Dumps in their Sub-sectors, obtain details of the contents of each and sign receipts.
Trench stores will be taken over in the same manner.

2. 300 petrol tins (150 in each sub-sector) will be handed over to incoming units. If there are petrol tins with the Reserve Battns, these will also be taken over.

As many more as possible should be taken up full by units taking over, as all water has to come by water cart from ROISEL.

3. (a) Rations will be delivered by Reserve Park to Sub-sector and Reserve Headquarters and from there will be distributed under Regimental arrangements.
Time and place at which guides should meet ration carts will be notified later.

(b) First issue of rations will be on night of 24th/25th. Units will be rationed to and for the 24th inst before leaving present camps.

4. (a) Transport lines of Mhow and Sialkot Dismounted Regts. will be situated near ROISEL, exact locality will be notified later.

(b) Tents should be taken up to accommodate transport personnel.

(c) The B.T.Os of Mhow and Sialkot Bde. will live at their respective horse lines and will supervise the horses of their Bde. M.G. Squadrons.

(d) They will obtain "Town Orders" from Town Major ROISEL and comply with them.

                                                   Captain.
                                                 Staff Captain.
              Mhow and Sialkot Dismounted Regiments.

Issued as above.

A.H.

RELIEFS 22nd/23rd May.

UNIT.	STRENGTH.	ROUTE.	TO ARRIVE AT.	TIME.	REMARKS.
Nos 10 & 11. M.G.Squadrons.	Complete at scale for trenches.	ENNEMAIN - ATHIES.- MONS-EN-CHAUSSEE - BOUVINCOURT.	ROISEL.	7-30.p.m. 22nd.	To be clear of ATHIES by 4-45. p.m. Horses to be sent back from ROISEL. Roads not to be used by mounted men and by transport as little as possible. Route to be reconnoitred under orders of O.C.No.11. M.G. Sqdn.
Hd. Qrs. Left Sub-sector.	Complete.	MONS-EN-CHAUSSEE - BOUVINCOURT - ROISEL.	Main cross roads centre of TEMPLEUX.	8-30.p.m. 22nd.	Horses will be sent back from this point where guides will meet units.
Inniskilling Dgns.	2 Sqdn. Officers. 8 N.C.Os. 16 selected privates.	--- do ---	--do--	--do--	Roads not to be used by mounted men and by transport as little as possible. Route to be reconnoitred under orders of O.C. Left Sub-sector.
38th C.I.Horse.	2nd-in-Command. 2 Sqdn. Officers. 8 N.C.Os. 16 selected Sowars.	--- do ---	--do--	--do--	
Hd. Qrs. Right Sub-sector.	Complete.	MONS-EN-CHAUSSEE - BOUVINCOURT - HERVILLY.	L.14.Central.	8-30.p.m.	--do-- Route to be reconnoitred under orders of O.C.Right Sub-sector.
17th Lancers.	2nd-in-Command. 2 Sqdn. Officers. 8 N.C.Os. 16 selected privates.	--- do ---	--do--	--do--	
6th Cavalry.	2 Sqdn. Officers. 8 N.C.Os. 16 selected Sowars.	--- do ---	--do--	--do--	

Relief 22nd/23rd - Continued.

Unit.	Strength	Route.	To arrive at.	Time.	Remarks.
Hd. Qrs. Reserve Squadron	One Officer one or two men.	MONS-EN-CHAUSSÉE — BOUVINCOURT.	HERVILLY	Afternoon 22nd	To select a position for Hd. Qrs. Reserve in vicinity of Square L.7.d.
2nd L. Lancers.	— do —	— do —	— do —	— do —	To select a position for 2nd Lancers in vicinity of Square L.7.d.
19th Lancers	— do —	— do —	— do —	— do —	To select a position for 19th Lancers in vicinity of Square L.14.d.

Retirn 23rd/24th May 1917

Unit	Strength	Route	To arrive at	Time	Remarks
Bde Hd Qrs	At French Strength	Any	POISEL	4.30 p.m.	Representative will be at 17th Bty Bde H.Q. from 2 p.m.
2nd Lancers 19th Lancers	Complete at scale for trenches, less advance parties.	ENNEMAIN — ATHIES — MONS-EN-CHAUSSEE — BOUVINCOURT.	HERVILLY	Afternoon of 23rd	To move on to Camping ground in L.7.d & L.7.d after dark. Unit to avoid the roads. Transport to avoid the roads as much as possible. Party to be reconnoitred under orders of O.C. Reserve. Horses to be sent back after arrival at HERVILLY. 19th Lancers to join in in rear of 2nd Lancers at ENNEMAIN.
Inniskilling Dgns. 38th C.I. Horse.	— do —	V.4 — V.35 — P.26. e.9.4. — P.21. — BOUVINCOURT — NOBESCOURT Fme — POISEL.	Main Cprs. Roads Centre of TEMPLEUX.	8.30 p.m.	Horses will be sent back from this point where guides will meet units. Unit to avoid the roads. Transport to avoid the roads as much as possible. Route to be reconnoitred under orders of O.C. Left Sub Sector.
17th Lancers 6th Cavalry	— do —	MONS-EN-CHAUSSEE — ESTREES-EN-CHAUSSEE — VRAIGNES — HANCOURT — HERVILLY.	L-14 Central.	8.30 p.m.	— do — Route to be reconnoitred under orders of O.C. Right Sub Sector.

SECRET.   Copy No.
          Mhow and Sialkot Dismounted Regt. Operation Order No.1.
In continuation of Mhow Cavalry Brigade Operation Order No.8. of 21st
inst.   22-5-17.
                      are
1. The following orders/issued in correction and amplification of Mhow
Cavalry Brigade Operation Order No.8. of 21st instant. :-

2. CORRECTIONS. Para 3. for "HERVILLY" read "L.7.d."
   para 6. for "2/5 N.Staffords" read "2/5 South Staffords".

   Table of reliefs 22nd/23rd May :- under heading "Strength" for Hd.Qrs.
   Left Sub-sector delete "complete" and substitute "2nd-in-Command and
   4 O.Rs."
   Similarly for Hd.Qrs. Right Sub-sector substitute "C.O. and 4 O.Rs."

   Table of Reliefs 23rd/24th May :- under headings "to arrive at" and
   "time", for Inniskilling Dragoons and 38th C.I.Horse, delete "main
   cross roads centre of TEMPLEUX. 8-30.p.m." and substitute "500 yards
   East of 176th Infantry Bde. Hd. Qrs in ROISEL" "7-45.p.m.",
   Similarly for 17th Lancers and 6th Cavalry, delete "L.14.central.8-30.
   p.m." and substitute "HERVILLY S.W.end" "8.p.m.".

3. The following will be the nomenclature adopted :-
   The Sector will be known as "B" Sector.
   It will be divided into "B"1. and "B"2. Sub-sectors, commanded respect-
   ively by Lieut Colonel NETTHAM and Lieut Colonel PETERSON, D.S.O.

   The RESERVE. Commanded by Lieut Colonel TURNER.

   Each Sub-sector and the reserve will consist of 2 regiments which will
   be known by their present names and Cavalry terms will be used, e.g.
   Squadron equalling 60 - 70 men, a Troop equalling 15 - 17 men.

   Thus 2 squadrons will equal one Company and will take over from one
   Company, and 2 troops will equal one platoon and will take over from
   one platoon.

4. The Sector is held as follows :-

   "B"1 Sub-sector. 2 Coys in Advanced line.
                    2 Coys in Intermediate Line.

   They will be relieved as follows :-
                    (Right Coy relieved by 8 troops 17th Lancers.
   Advanced Line.   (Left Coy   "   " "   "   6th Cavalry.

                    (Right Coy relieved by 8 troops 17th Lancers.
   Intermediate Line.(Left Coy   "   " "   "   6th Cavalry.

   "B"2 Sub-sector. 3 Companies in Advanced Line.
                    1 Coy in Intermediate Line.

   They will be relieved as follows :-
                    (Right Coy. relieved by 8 troops Inniskilling Dragoons.
   Advanced Line.   (Right two platoons Centre Coy, by 4 troops " -"-
                    (Left   "   "   "   "   " by 4 troops 38th C.I.H.
                    (Left Coy. relieved by 8 troops 38th C.I.Horse.
   Intermediate Line.(Right two platoons relieved by 4 troops Innisk Dgns.
                    (Left two   "   "   " by 4 troops 38th C.I.H.

5. On the night of 23rd/24th May, after dismounting and before marching
   up. Troops will be formed for the march up by regiments in order :-
   Right Regt. in front with their troops for Advanced line leading, Right
   in Front. Followed by troops of the same regt for intermediate line,
   also with their Right in Front.
   The Left Regiment of the Sub-sector will follow with its troops similarly in order, the Right in Front.
   This order must be strictly complied with as otherwise confusion will
   be caused.
   The 2/5 South Staffords in "B"1 Sub-sector and the 2/6 South Staffords
   in "B"2 Sub-sector are providing guides, and unless troops are formed
   up in the order indicated they may not arrive at their correct desti-
   nation.

6. Box Respirators will be placed in the "Alert Position" on arrival at the forming up places, viz S.W. end of HERVILLY and 500 yds East of 176th Infty. Bde Hd. Qrs. and will be worn in this position during the relief.

7. (a) The Reserve, under Lieut Colonel TURNER will be at HERVILLY by 6.p.m. 23rd instant.

   (b) Lieut Colonel TURNER will detail an officer from 2nd Lancers to take over all documents (including the Defence Scheme) Maps, etc., from 2/5 North Staffords at HERVILLY at 3.p.m. on 23rd inst. Similarly an officer from 19th Lancers to take over documents (including the defence scheme), maps, etc., from 2/6 North Staffords at ROISEL, at 3.p.m. on 23rd instant.

8. The previous instructions re tents to be taken up by 2nd Lancers and 19th Lancers are cancelled.
   The following numbers only may now be taken :-
   Reserve Headquarters.   2 Tents.
   2nd Lancers.........   2 tents.
   19th Lancers.........   2 tents.

9. Reference concluding portion of para 5 above :-
   Guides from "B"1 Sub-sector will meet 17th Lancers and 6th Cavalry at cross roads K.23.d.4.2. (outskirts of HERVILLY) at 8.p.m. 23rd inst.
   One man from 2/5 South Staffords to every 2 troops, also one man from the advance party to each 2 troops.
   Guides from "B"2 Sub-sector will meet Inniskilling Dragoons and 38th C.I.Horse at the crater K.12.d.2.5. at 8-30.p.m., 23rd inst. In this Sub-sector two troops only may move forward at a time; 200 yds interval will be maintained between every two troops; first two troops to arrive at the Crater at 8-30.p.m.

10. Transport of both Sub-sectors and the Reserve will not move forward of the forming up places before 9-10.p.m.
    A Guide from the transport of the Battalions being relieved will meet transport for "B"1 and "B"2 Sub-sectors before this hour.

11. The following officers will be in command of the led horses on the return march :-
    17th Lancers.   ) Major CRAIGIE, 6th Cavalry.
    6th Cavalry.   )

    Inniskilling Dgns.) Major LEWIS, 38th C.I.Horse.
    38th C.I.Horse.   )

    2nd Lancers.   ) Major KNOWLES.D.S.O. 2nd Lancers.
    19th Lancers.)

12. Brigadier General Neil HAIG. C.M.G. will assume command of "B" Sector at 7-30.a.m. on 24th inst. From this hour Brigade Head Quarters will be situated at L.7.b.

                                                    G. Gould.
                                                    Brigade Major.

Issued to Signals   Mhow & Sialkot Dismounted Regiments.
    at 6.p.m.
Normal distribution. also :-
12 copies to Sialkot Bde.
6 extra to Mhow Bde.
1 to 176th Infantry Bde.

A.H.

CONFIDENTIAL.

WAR DIARY

of

Headquarters
Mhow Cavalry Brigade

from 1st June 1917.   to 30th June 1917.

WAR DIARY
INTELLIGENCE SUMMARY
(Erase heading not required)

Army Form C. 2118.

Headquarters Mhow Cav Bde

Place	Date	Hour	Summary of Events and Information	Remarks and references to Appendices
Sht 62cN.E. L.7d.7.7.d.	JUNE 2nd.		Situation normal. 1 man Machine Gun Sqn. killed 1 man Mhow Regt. wounded. Patrol front of Unnamed Farm shelled during the morning. Casualties 1 Indian Officer (CHH.) 2 British O.R. (17th Lancers) 9 Indian O.R. (8 CHH. 1, 2h.) all wounded. 11th M.G. Sqn. relieved by 12th M.G. Sqn. relief completed by 12:10 a.m. on 3rd.	Aply Aply
	3rd.		Quiet day, no casualties. Relief of MHOW Bde. by LUCKNOW Bde. commenced 9pm.	Aply
	4th.	12.30am	Completed by 12.30 a.m. Brg. Genl. Maxwell Took over command of the sector from Brg. Genl. Haig. 12 n.n. Bde. moved into camp at HAMLET.	Aply
CAMP HAMLET		2.30pm	Dismounted Reinforcement Company under command of Major Sir T. Tancred Bart. marched to HERVILLY in relief of Lucknow.	Aply Aply
	5th & 13th.		Troop, Squadron & Regt. Training.	
	14th.	8pm	Advance Parties of 3 Officers & 30 N.C.O.s & men with 18 Signallers for Regt. moved up to "B" Sector for general tour of duty in the trenches. No.11 M.G. Sqn. took over from No. 10 M.G. Sqn. in the line, relief completed by 3 a.m. 15th.	Aply
	15th.	7.30pm	Mhow Cav. Regt. Reinforcement 30 Officers left at Trench Strength for B Sector. Relief completed without incident at 3.30 a.m. 16th.	Aply Aply
	16th.	5am	Dismounted Reinforcement Company regained at Camp HAMLET from HERVILLY	Aply Aply

Army Form C. 2118.

WAR DIARY
INTELLIGENCE SUMMARY.
(Erase heading not required.)

Instructions regarding War Diaries and Intelligence Summaries are contained in F. S. Regs., Part II. and the Staff Manual respectively. Title pages will be prepared in manuscript.

Place	Date	Hour	Summary of Events and Information	Remarks and references to Appendices
CAMP HAMELET	17th	9am	Brigade less 1st moved in trenches marched to Camp ENNEMAIN, arriving 11.45am. 1.B.O.R. died of wounds (Musketting Ser.) 2.B.O.R. wounded (Musketting Ser.) L.1.O.R. wounded	
CAMP ENNEMAIN (B. Sector)			(3, 2nd Lancers, 138th C.I. Horse)	
	18th		Routine work.	
	19th		2.1.O.R. (38th C.I. Horse) wounded.	
	20th		Routine work.	
	21st		1.1.O.R. (38th C.I. Horse) wounded.	
	22nd		1.B.O.R. (1st M.G. Sqn.) wounded.	
	23rd		2 platoons Musketting Ser. relieved in Bm Subsector by two platoons K.D.G.s. I.B.A.R. wounded. (11th M.G. Sqn.)	
	24th		Routine work.	
	25th		1.1.O.R. (2 Lancers) wounded.	
	26th		1.1.O.R. killed, 1.1.O.R. wounded, both 38th C.I. Horse.	
	27th		Routine work.	
	28th	11.30pm	A minor raid was carried out by 38th C.I. Horse. New TRENCH was entered and at least five Germans were killed, several others believed to have been wounded. Owing to	

Army Form C. 2118.

WAR DIARY
or
INTELLIGENCE SUMMARY.
(Erase heading not required.)

Instructions regarding War Diaries and Intelligence Summaries are contained in F. S. Regs., Part II and the Staff Manual respectively. Title pages will be prepared in manuscript.

Place	Date	Hour	Summary of Events and Information	Remarks and references to Appendices
CAMPENNEMAIN and B. Sect.	27th	11.30pm	The flight of the garrison of the portion of the trench entered, it was not possible to secure any prisoners. Casualties in above raid. Lieut. R.H.M. DURAND and Lieut. WILSON wounded. 11. I.O.R.s wounded.	
		11.30pm	A strong patrol from the 2nd Lancers proceeded towards the junction of the Railway and Sunken Road at L.12.a.35.70. An entrance was cut through the wire 50 ft west of this point. A thorough search was made for 150 yds. up the Sunken road and along the Rly. Cutting but no Germans were seen and the supposed post was found unoccupied.	do.
	28th		Routine work.	
	29th		Lieut. R.H.M. DURAND 38th. C.I. Horse died of his wounds. Bri.Genl. NEIL HAIG. C.M.G. arrived and assumed command of 4th Dismtd. Bde. from Br. Genl. M.F. GAGE. D.S.O. 2nd Lancers retired no platoon from back seen.	do.
	30th		2nd Lancers relieved one platoon by a platoon from the back area. Casualties. 1 munshi Ubig Brajmin 1.0.R. killed. 3 O.R.s wounded.	do.

Kennedy Capt.
Brig Major
Indian Cavalry Bde.

S E C R E T.   Copy No. 13
            MHOW CAVALRY BRIGADE ORDER No.9.   14-6-17.

Reference Map 1/20,000. Sheets 62c.N.E. & 62b.N.W.

1. Reliefs of Units in "B" Sector will be carried out on the nights of 14th/15th and 15th/16th insts, in accordance with attached table. Strength of Units will be as for last tour of duty in the trenches.

2. The arrangement of all details as to relief of garrisons of Posts, Supports and "Brown Line" will be arranged by Subsector Commanders concerned.

3. Advance Parties will move up to the line as follows, and will take over all Trench Stores giving receipts :-

Inniskilling Dragoons....3 Officers 30 O.Rs.) To report at B.3. Sub-
38th C.I.Horse............3 B.Os. 30 I.O.Rs.) sector H.Q. 9.30.p.m.
                                                14th/15th inst. Not to
                                                take horses beyond
                                                TEMPLEUX.

2nd Lancers....3 B.Os, 24 I.O.Rs.   To report at B.5. Subsector H.Q.
                                    9.30.p.m. 14th/15th inst. Not to
                                    take horses beyond L.14.central.

18 Signallers per unit will also accompany Advance Parties.

4. Guides for all Posts, etc., will be detailed by Subsector Comdrs. on night 15th/16th inst, to meet Relieving Units and conduct them to their positions as under :-

Inniskilling Dragoons. L.2.c.2.2. at 9.45.p.m. Night 15th/16th.
38th C.I.Horse.. .....   --do--   --do--   --do--
2nd Lancers. L.14.central. 9.30.p.m. Night 15th/16th.

Units will proceed dismounted from present camp.
Inniskilling Dragoons and 38th C.I.Horse, Inniskilling Dragoons leading, will parade on HAMELET - ROISEL road, head 600 yds East of the E East end of the village at 8.30.p.m. on the 15th inst, and will proceed at 200 yds interval between platoons to L.2.c.2.2. where they will be met by guides from the units to be relieved.

2nd Lancers will parade in their present camp at 7.30.p.m. 15th inst. and will proceed via HERVILLY and HESBECOURT to L.14.central where they will be met at 9.30.p.m. by guides from the unit to be relieved.

Advance parties on 14th inst, may ride to TEMPLEUX for Inniskillings and 38th C.I.Horse, and to L.14.central for 2nd Lancers, but men must be sent to bring the horses back.

5. Transport as required for Relieving Units and their Advance Parties will proceed direct to the Subsectors H.Q. concerned following the routes allotted to units. Not to enter TEMPLEUX and HERVILLY before 10.p.m. and 9.p.m. respectively on either night.

O.C. B.3. Subsector is arranging for Traffic Control at his Headquarters.

6. Officers and other ranks of Mhow Bde employed on Divisional Intelligence duties will be relieved at "Depot AMERIKA" TEMPLEUX by Sialkot Brigade, under arrangements already made by 4th Dismounted Brigade, and will on relief rejoin their units in back area. Lieut Page 38th C.I.Horse will perform the duties of Intelligence Officer in B.3. Subsector.

7. The Mhow Dismounted Reinforcements Company, after relief by 6th Cavalry on night of 15th/16th June will rejoin their units in Camp HAMELET, under orders to be issued by Major Sir T.TANCRED, Bart.

                                                                        8.

8. Brigadier General L.L.MAXWELL, C.M.G. Commanding 4th Dismounted Brigade, and Staff will be relieved by Brigadier General M.F.GAGE, D.S.O. and Staff at 10.a.m. on 17th instant.
Lieut Col. H.F.WICKHAM, K.D.Gs, Commanding B.3. Subsector and Staff will be relieved by Lieut Colonel A.F.BROWNE, 38th C.I.Horse and Staff on night of 16th/17th June. The actual command of the Subsector will not pass to the incoming Subsector Commander until 24 hours after completion of relief of Units.

9. Box Respirators will be worn in the "Alert" position during the Relief.

10. Such Regimental Transport as is being retained for use with 4th Dismounted Brigade will, after having delivered loads at appointed places on night 15th/16th return to 4th Dismounted Brigade Transport Lines. ROISEL and report to B.T.O. Mhow Bde. under whose orders it will remain.

11. B.T.O. Mhow Bde will arrange to take over the portion of the 4th Dismounted Bde Transport lines, when it is evacuated by Lucknow Bde.

12. A Quartermaster for 4th Dismounted Bde is being detailed by Inniskilling Dragoons. He will be at Transport lines by 8.a.m. 16th, live there and carry out duties as laid down in S.C.830.

13. Code word for completion of relief on night 15th/16th June XXXXXXXX "ACCUMULATION" to be reported to 4th Dismounted Bde and Mhow Cavalry Brigade.

ACKNOWLEDGE.

                                            Captain.
                                            Brigade Major.

14-6-17.

Issued at 10.30.a.m.

Copies to :-

No.1. 4th Cavalry Division.
   2. 4th Dismounted Bde.
   3. Lieut Col. Browne.
   4. Inniskilling Dragoons.
   5. 2nd Lancers.
   6. 38th C.I.Horse.
   7. No.11. M.G.Squadron.
   8. B.T.O. Mhow.
   9. B.S.O. Mhow.
  10. Lieut Smith, Signalling Officer, B.3.
  11. Captain Davison (Divisional Intelligence Duties).
  12. Quartermaster ROISEL.
  13 - 16 Files.

SECRET.

RELIEF TABLE issued with 1HOW CAVALRY BRIGADE ORDER No.9. of 14th June 1917.

DATE.	SUBSECTOR.	RELIEVING UNIT.	RELIEVED UNIT.	REMARKS.
14th/15th June.	B.1. and B.2.	11th M.G.Squadron.	10th M.G.Squadron.	Arranged between Officers Commanding concerned.
15th/16th June	B.2. Left.	2nd Lancers.	6th Cavalry.	6th Cavalry Relieve Mhow Dismounted Reinforcement Company at HERVILLY.
	B.3. Right.	Inniskilling Dragoons.	K.D.Guards.	
	B.3. Left.	38th C.I.Horse.	29th Lancers.	

1How Dismounted Reinforcement Company, after relief by 6th Cavalry, rejoin their units in camp at HAMELET.

Secret   Copy No. 13

MHOW CAVALRY BRIGADE OPERATION ORDER NO.10.   14/8/17.

Reference Map:- 1/40,000 Sheet 62.c.

1. (a). MHOW Cavalry Brigade less the personnel in the Line will move to Camp ENNEMAIN on the 17th inst.
   (b). ORDER OF MARCH. Brigade Hd Qrs, Inniskilling Dragoons, 2nd Lancers, M.G.Squadron, 38th C.I.Horse, Mob Vet Section, 500 yards distance between Regiments.
   (c). ROUTE. By Horse transport tracks, avoiding roads, to ATHIES, and ENNEMAIN.
   O.C. Inniskilling Dragoons will arrange to have the route reconnoitred beforehand, and will report on the route selected to Bde Hd Qrs.
   (d). STARTING POINT. Inniskilling Dragoons Camp.
   (e). TIME.   9 a.m.

2. Bde Hd Qrs will take over the Bde Hd Qrs Camp at ATHIES.
   Inniskilling Dragoons will take over the camp of the 17th Lancers at ENNEMAIN.
   2nd Lancers will take over the camp of the 6th Cavalry at ENNEMAIN.
   38th C.I.H will take over the camp of the 19th Lancers at ENNEMAIN.
   No 11 M.G.Sqdn will take over the camp of the No 10 M.G.Sqdn at ENNEMAIN.

3. All huts, tents, and bivouacs, beyond men's own blankets and ground sheets will be handed over and taken over by the outgoing & incoming units respectively.

4. Units will send forward parties under one officer each, on the morning of the 16th inst to take over their camps in the ENNEMAIN area.

5. Ambulances will stand fast and be administered by the Brigades in whose areas they are after the move.

6. Chaff cutters will be handed over between units in order to save transport.

7. O.C., A.S.C. will distribute rug wagons on the 16th inst. These will return to their unit on the evening of the 17th inst.

8. "A" & "B" Echelons will accompany units.

9. Brigade Hd Qrs will close at HAMELET at 9 a.m. on the 17th inst, and open at ATHIES at the same hour.

Acknowledge.

Issued at 4 p.m.
Copies to :-
No.1 4th Cav Div.
    2 Sialkot Bde 'Rear'
    3 Inniskilling Ds.
    4 2nd Lancers.
    5 38th C.I.H.
    6 No.11 M.G.Sqdn.
    7 ~~Major Pritchard (acting Bde.)~~ Ambala Cav. Fd. Amb.
    8 B.S.O.
    9 M.V.S.
   10 Signals
   11 Camp Commandant
   12 - 14 Office Diary & Files.

                                            Captain
                                Bde Major, Mhow Cavalry Brigade.

SECRET.   MHOW CAVALRY BRIGADE ORDER No.12.   Copy No. 10

Reference Map 1/40000. Sheet 62.c.   26-6-17.

1. Reliefs will be carried out in 'B' Sector on night 29th/30th June in accordance with accompanying table.
    Lieut Colonel C.C.Newnham, 6th Cavalry and Staff will relieve Lieut Col. W.G.K.Green, 36th Jacob's Horse and Staff in command B.1.
    Lt. Col. H.H.F.Turner 2nd Lancers and Staff will relieve Lt. Col. P.B.Sangster, D.S.O. 29th Lancers and Staff in command B.2.
    All details of relief will be arranged between Sub-sector Commanders concerned.
    Command of Sub-sectors will pass on completion of relief.
    Lieut Col. Turner should spend 24 hours in B.2. Sub-sector before the relief takes place.

2. Major C.R.Terrot, D.S.O., Inniskilling Dragoons and Staff and Capt. Humfrey, 11th M.G.Squadron will respectively relieve O.C. B.3. Sub-sector and Staff and Major J.N.Simonds, Commanding Machine Guns in the Line, on the 29th inst, at 10.a.m.

    Any wheeled transport required for taking in kits of relieving Staff will move up to B.3. Sub-sector H.Q. on the night of 28th/29th June and bring out any kit of relieved Staff requiring to be moved by wheeled transport.

    Personal kit may be taken up on Pack on the morning of the 29th which Pack will carry out the personal kit of the relieved staff.

    Arrangements to be made between O.C. B.3. Sub-sector and Major C.R.Terror, D.S.O.

3. Box Respirators will be worn in the "Alert position" during the Reliefs.

4. Brigadier General Neil Haig, C.M.G. and Staff will relieve Brig. General M.F.Gage, D.S.O. and Staff at 10.a.m. on 29th inst.

5. Completion of relief will be reported by code word "SUNSPOT".

    ACKNOWLEDGE.

                                            S.(Haw)
                                                 Captain.
                                            for, Brigade Major.
                                            Mhow Cavalry Brigade.

Copy No.1. 4th Cavalry Division.
       2. O.C. B.2. Sub-sector.
       3. " B.3.   "
       4. Lieut Colonel H.H.F.Turner.
       5. Major C.R.Terrot, D.S.O.
       6. Inniskilling Dragoons.
       7. 38th C.I.Horse.
       8. Captain Humfrey.
       9. O.C. 4th Dismounted Brigade.

RELIEF TABLE ISSUED WITH 4th DISMOUNTED BRIGADE OPERATION ORDER NO. 9.

Date.	Sub-Sector.	Relieving Unit.	Relieved Unit.	Move after relief.	Remarks.
June 29/30.	B.1.(Right)	19th Lancers.	Jodhpur Lancers.	HAMELET.	To Divnl Reserve.
	B.1.(Left)	6th Cavalry.	36th J.Horse.	L.S.b.	To Sector Reserve. Moving across country. Route to be reconnoitred.
	B.2.(Right)	17th Lancers.	29th Lancers.	2 Platoons to HAMELET. 2 Platoons to HERVILLY.	To Divnl Reserve. The 2 Platoons HERVILLY will be relieved by 2 Platoons K.D.Gds. on night 1/2nd, and will rejoin regiment at HAMELET.
	L.S.b.	36th J.Horse	2 Platoons K.D.Gds.	HERVILLY.	To Divnl Reserve.
July 1/2nd	B.3.(Right)	2 Platoons Inniskillings	2 Platoons K.D.Gds.	HERVILLY.	To Divnl Reserve. To relieve 2 Platoons 29th Lancers.
July 2/3rd.		10th M.G.Sqdn.	12th M.G.S.	HAMELET.	

CONFIDENTIAL. Serial No. 114.

WAR   DIARY

of

Head Quarters Mhow Cavalry Bde

from 1st July, 1917   to 31st July, 1917

Army Form C. 2118.

WAR DIARY
INTELLIGENCE SUMMARY.
(Erase heading not required).

Instructions regarding War Diaries and Intelligence Summaries are contained in F. S. Regs., Part II. and the Staff Manual respectively. Title pages will be prepared in manuscript.

Place	Date	Hour	Summary of Events and Information	Remarks and references to Appendices
RUELLES WOOD (Camp) ENNEMAIN.	1st.		Situation unusual.	
	2nd.	1 A.M.	A successful raid was carried out in COLOGNE FARMS by the Inniskilling two (2 Platoons) and 1 Officer, 100 R's. 4th Field Squadron. All objectives attained were effected and at least 60 of the enemy were killed by the Raiding Party. The Artillery must have accounted for many more, also the Engineers who made many dugouts and exploded 350 lbs. of H.E. Lieut. DUDGEON Raid leader. Lieut. DUNNE (killed) and Lieut. KEMMIS platoon leaders. Lieut. LLOYD R.A. and Lieut. F. hurt, under Lieut. LLOYD. Communication wires (infantry) R.A. & M.G. groups were most successful. The raid lasted half an hour. Casualties in Raid Lieut A.S. DUNNE Inniskilling two killed. " " 1 B.O.Rs. " 29. O. Rs. " wounded. 38th C.I. Horse " wounded.	df.
			In addition 3 Indian O.R. Inniskillings 1 O.R. 38th C.I. Horse killed 1 " " wounded	ab.
	3rd.		38th C.I. Horse killed and brought in in Germans. Hostile Artillery T.M's active. Casualties Inniskilling dragoons 2 B.O.Rs. killed. 4 B.O.Rs. wounded. 2nd Lancers 1 I.O.R wounded 38th C.I. Horse 1 I.O.R. killed 5 I.O.Rs. wounded.	ch.

WAR DIARY
or
INTELLIGENCE SUMMARY.
(Erase heading not required.)

Army Form C. 2118.

Place	Date	Hour	Summary of Events and Information	Remarks and references to Appendices
RUELLES WOOD (Camp) ENNEMAIN	4th.		Hostile Artillery activity about normal on left of Katun. Casualties 2.I.O.Rs. 2nd Lancers killed.	
	5th.		Situation normal. Casualties 2.I.O.Rs. 3 I.O.R. Lancers wounded.	
	6th.		Our hostile hostile shelling at intervals mostly on left-sector. Casualties 2nd Lancers 1. I.O.R. 2nd Lancers wounded. 2.I.O.Rs.	
	7th.		30 H.C.H.M wounded. 1.I.O.R. 3 I.C.H.M wounded. Situation normal. 5 O.Rs. Inniskilling Dragoons killed. 10.R. Inniskilling wounded. 13 N.C.O.s men Inniskillings awarded military medal (Decorated). Enemy bombarded Right sector attempted a minor operation between hill 95 & line.	
		1pm	at(?) Fred Smith bay. Relieving Bn. (102nd) arrived in the trenches for Advance Parties of the Relieving Bn. (102nd) arrived in the trenches for 24 hours attachment.	
	8th.		Situation normal. Casualties Inniskillings 2 O.Rs. killed, 3 Ptes. C.1. Horse Lieut. PINNEY and 2 Indian Officers wounded. 1. I.O.R. killed. 4. O.Rs. wounded	
	9th.	2.30 a.m.	Relief of Inniskillings Dragoons & 3rd C.H. me by 23rd Northumberland Fusiliers & 6 guns by 11 M.G. Sqn. by 103rd Inf. Cy. completed.	
	10th.	3 am	Relief of Battalions by 22nd Northumberland Fusiliers and 6 guns 2nd 11 M.G. Sqn. by 102nd M.G. Cy. completed.	
		9 am	£ OC 102nd L.I. Brd. 2FR now command of B. Bde. from Bn. Ind. A. Hd.	

Army Form C. 2118.

WAR DIARY
or
INTELLIGENCE SUMMARY.
(Erase heading not required.)

Instructions regarding War Diaries and Intelligence Summaries are contained in F. S. Regs., Part II. and the Staff Manual respectively. Title pages will be prepared in manuscript.

Place	Date	Hour	Summary of Events and Information	Remarks and references to Appendices
CAMP. ENNE MAIN.	13th		Ordinary routine work	Wx/Tel
	14th	9.15 am	OC Inspected Squad generals. escort 38th LH C/ Horse in marching order	S.C.H.
			C. Sqdn. Francis Wills B.M. left to join cavalry depot as recent squadron.	Wx/—
	16th	9.15 am	Lieut Shilling Bris. arr'd. M.G. Sqn "	Wx/Tel
	17th–26th		Ordinary routine work	Wx/Tel
	27th		Intensive training for troop & squadron commanders.	S.C.H.
	28th to 31st		Intensive training for troops & squadrons.	

S. (Harvey) Capt.
for Bde. Major
Inverness Cavalry Brigade.

SECRET.   No. B.M.149.   Copy No.

Reference 4th Cavalry Division Map 1/2500.

NOT TO BE TAKEN BEYOND SUBSECTOR HEADQUARTERS.

Operation for a date to be fixed later.

The following instructions are issued in supercession of those contained in MHOW Bde. Order NO.11 of 24th inst., which should now be destroyed.

1. It is proposed to :-
   (a) Raid COLOGNE FARM and inflict as much loss as possible on the enemy.

   (b) Destroy any works and dugouts found.

   (c) Carry off Machine Guns.

2. The troops to be employed are :-

   (a) 3 Officers and 23 Other ranks Inniskilling Dragoons.

   (b) 1 R.E. Officer and – Sappers, 4th Field Squadron.

   (c) As much Artillery as can be placed at our disposal, including Heavy, Medium and Light Trench Mortars.

   (d) 20 Machine guns, dispositions and targets given in Appendix A.

   (e) Bearer parties for casualties, included in (a) above.

3. The area to be raided and operated in by our troops will be restricted to :-

   S.E. Limit. A line drawn from L.6.c.2.0. to a point L.6.c.65.40. in COLOGNE SUPPORT TRENCH.

   East Limit. ~~A line drawn from~~ L.6.c.65.40. to L.6.c.5.8. in same trench.

   North Limit. A line drawn from L.6.c.0.8. to L.6.c.5.8.

   All above bounds are inclusive to the raiding party.

   Artillery and M.G. Barrages have been calculated to enclose these limits, leaving a safe margin to the troops operating.

4. Assaulting Troops, distribution and objectives as given in para 5, will at Zero – 24 minutes on the night fixed for the raid be disposed as follows :-
   Right Platoon. in splinter proof shelters about L.6.c.1.1.
   Left Platoon. in the fire trench, about L.5.d.7.8.

   The Garrison of the Quarry, with the exception of 1 Hotchkiss Rifle and 6 men in the Russian Sap L.6.c.½.3. will have vacated the front line by Zero – 24 minutes and gone into their dugouts and splinterproof trench.

   The trench garrison will re-occupy the front line at Zero hour.

   The trench Garrison of the trench in which the left Platoon assemble will not vacate their position.

   The Right Platoon will leave their Shelter at Zero – 1 minute, form up ocer the parapet, and start advancing to their objectives at Zero +1 minute.
   The Artillery Rolling barrage will start to move forward at Zero + 2 minutes.

The Artillery Enfilade Barrage will start to move forward at Zero + 3 minutes.

The Left Platoon will leave their trench at Zero - 1 minute and will be formed up in front of the parapet by Zero hour, when they will advance to their objectives.

Artullery Barrage timings the same as for Right Platoon.

Heavy trench Mortars open fire at Zero - 1 minute.

Medium Trench Mortars will fire on the wire from Zero - 4 minutes to Zero hour after which they will lengthen range.

Stokes Mortars open fire at Zero hour - 4 minutes and lengthen range at Zero + 3 minutes.

5. The Assulting troops will be divided into two parties to be known as the right or Dunne's Platoon, and the Left or KEMMIS' Platoon. The distribution and objectives of these two platoons are as under:

RIGHT PLATOON.

1st Wave.   Platoon Leader......Lieut Dunne.
                                    1 Runner
                                    1 Trumpeter.

        Right Blocking Party...1 Cpl. and 5 men, establish a
                                bombing block in COLOGNE SUPPORT
                                TRENCH at L.6.c.6.4.
                                1 Bomber and 2 carriers in party.

        Centre Blocking party...1 Cpl. and 2 men, establish a bombing
                                block in COLOGNE SUPPORT TRENCH
                                at L.6.c.5.5. (where road crosses
                                trench)
                                1 Bomber and two carriers.

        Eeft Blocking party....1 Cpl and 3 men, establish a bombing
                                block in COLOGNE SUPPORT TRENCH
                                at L.6.c.65.65.
                                1 Bomber and two carriers.

        Forward party.........1 Cpl and 4 men, go to farm building
                                just East of COLOGNE SUPPORT TRENCH
                                1 Bomber and two carriers.

    Total Strength of 1st Wave Right Platoon :-
            1 Officer
            4 Corporals
            1 Trumpeter
            15 men.

2nd Wave..... 1 Cpl and 4 men establish a bombing block in sunken
                road at T of COLOGNE TRENCH.
                1 Bomber, 2 Carriers, 2 Bayonet Men.
                1 Selected Private and 3 men work up COLOGNE TRENCH
                40 yards from T of TRENCH.
                1 Bomber, 2 Carriers, 1 Bayonet man.
                1 Sergt. and 5 men go to hedge L.6.c.3.5.
                all Bayonet men.

    Total Strength of 2nd Wave Right Platoon.
            1 Sergt
            1 Corpl
            13 Men.

3rd Wave......1 Cpl and 3 men work into the Farm buildings
about L.6.c.4.5. from the South.
1 Bomber, 1 Carrier, 2 Bayonet men.
1 Sergt.and 4 men work into the Farm buildings
about L.6.c.4.5. from the North.
1 Bomber, 2 Carriers, 2 Bayonet Men.
1 Cpl and 7 men work Northwards up Sunken Road
from T of TRENCH to junction of Road running S.E.
by E, down which they then work, bombing
dugouts if found to exist. They then work through the
Farm buildings from the East.
2 Bombers, 3 Carriers. 3 Bayonet men.

Total Strength of 3rd Wave Right Platoon.:-
    1 Sergt
    2 Cpls
    14 men.

4 Stretcher bearers with 2 Regtl Stretchers follow 3rd Wave.

Total Strength Right Platoon.:-
    1 Officer
    2 Sergts
    7 Corpls
    1 Trumpeter
    42 Men
    4 Stretcher Bearers.

Left Platoon.

1st Wave......Left Platoon Leader....Lieut KEMMIS.
    1 Trumpeter.
    3 Runners.

1 Selected Private.and 3 men block sunken road at
L.6.c.3.7. All rifle men; fire up Sunken road towards
UNNAMED FARM.
1 Cpl and 9 men work up to most Northerly Farm buildings.
2 Bombers, 2 Carriers, 6 Bayonet men.

3 men for wire cutting precede 1st Wave.

Total Strength 1st Wave, Left Platoon.
    1 Officer
    1 Corpl
    1 Trumpeter
    19 men.

2nd Wave..... 1 Sergt. and 10 men work up to the two farm buildings
L.6.c.3.6. just North of "HEDGE". After clearing
buildings, clear up between these buildings and
COLOGNE TRENCH.
2 Bombers 3 Carriers 6 Bayonet Men.

Total Strength 2nd Wave Left Platoon.
    1 Sergt
    10 men.

3rd Wave....1 Corpl and 6 men enter COLOGNE TRENCH where it crosses North
branch of road from COLOGNE FARMS to Slag Heap and work up
North to T. Trench, 90 yards.
2 Bombers, 3 Carriers, 2 Rifle men.
1 Cpl and 5 men enter at same point and work back down Sunken
Road towards Slag Heap, and then from Junction work down
Southern Arm to T of TRENCH L.6.c.4.3.
2 Bombers, 2 Carriers, 2 Bayonet men.
1 Sergt and 7 men enter COLOGNE TRENCH at same point as
above two parties and work along COLOGNE TRENCH Southwards
to Right Platoon Blocking Party at T of TRENCH
2 Bombers, 2 Carriers, 4 Bayonet Men.

In rear of 3rd Wave.

All the R.E. except 1 Sapper who accompanies Right Platoon Leader.
4 Stretcher bearers with 2 Regimental Stretchers.

Total Strength 3rd Wave, Left Platoon.-
    1 Sergt
    2 Copls
   19 Men.
    4 Stretcher Bearers.

The Raid Leader-Captain Dudgeon, follows in rear of 3rd Wave
accompanied by a Signaller who runs out a telephone line from B.3.
Advanced Hd Qrs. Another line will be laid by a second signaller
from B.3. Advanced Hd Qrs. up Sunken Road to Captain Dudgeons H.Q.
at Road Junction L.6.c.$\frac{1}{2}$.5$\frac{1}{2}$.
He has with him in addition 4 Runners and 4 men for cutting wire to
prepare road for withdrawal.

   Total Strength of Left Platoon.

    1 Officer
    2 Sergts
    3 Corpls
    1 Trumpeter
   47 Men.
    4 Stretcher Bearers.
R.E. (
    (

    With Raid Leader.

    Raid Leader
    2 Signallers
    8 Men.

   At North West Corner of Slag Heap.

    Lieut Winter Irving
    and 1 Man.

6. Co-operation on Flanks.

    2nd Cavalry Division will simulate an attack on MALAKOFF
FARM by Artillery and Machine Gun Fire.
Should the wind be favourable, smoke will be let off from the Right
flank about VILLERET.

7. Dress and Equipment.
The Khaki Serge will be worn.
All ranks taking part will wear a white band not less than four inches
wide on each arm.
All badges and marks by which the enemy might obtain identifications
will be removed. All identity discs, letters, pay books, etc.,will
be left behind.
1 P.H.G.Helmet in Satchel will be carried by each man.

Rifles with fixed bayonets will be carried, magazines will be charged
with 10 rounds, safety catches back. There will be no firing except
by the covereing parties.
Engineers will not carry rifles but will carry bayonets and bombs.
Each man taking part in the raid will take two bombs in his pockets.
100 large pattern wire cutters have been provided, the remaining men
will carry wire cutters of the ordinary pattern.
A proportion of luminous watches have been provided.
A proportion of Knobkerries are being provided.
A proportion of Electric torches has been provided.

8. COMMUNICATIONS. between Raid Leader and Platoons by Runner.
Between B.3. Subsector Adv H.Q. and Raid Leader by Telephone and runner
two lines will be laid.
Between B.3. H.Q. and B.3. Adv H.Q. by telephone and runner.

5.

9. **Headquarters.** The Raid Leader's H.Q. will be at Junction of roads leading from COLOGNE FARMS to Slag Heap.
O.C. B.3. Subsector will establish an advanced H.Q. at L.5.d.3.6.
(4th House from East end of HARGICOURT on North Side of the Road).

10. **Prisoners.** Will be handed over to a representative of the A.P.M. at North West Corner of Slag Heap.
In each of the Right and Left Platoons a small party will be detailed beforehand to deal with prisoners.
Officers, N.C.Os and men must be kept separate.

11. **R.E.** Arrangements are in charge of an Officer 4th Field Squadron, who wull accompany the raid.
Bangalore torpedoes, mobile charges and "P" Bombs will be carried.

12. **Withdrawal.** will be by time, bugle call and rocket signal, 30 minutes after Zero hour.
The Signal for the withdrawal by the bugle will be the "Trot"
The Signal for the withdrawal By Rocket Signal will be a group of 2 Red and 2 Green rockets fired from B.3. Adv H.Q.
Sufficient Rockets must be placed in position to ensure the above group as being successfully sent up.
A man will be specially detailed by O.C. B 3. Subsector to attend to this.
A group od 3 Green rockets will be fired from B.3. Adv H.Q. on the order of O.C. B.3. Subsector when all are clear.
This will signify to the Artillery and others that the withdrawal is complete.

The main route for withdrawal, and which should be used, other things being equal, will be the Sunken road running past the Slag Heap.

Alternative routes are those by which the Platoons enter COLOGNE FARMS.

Each Platoon will run out a tape from its jumping off place to where the wire in front of COLOGNE Trench is crossed. This tape will be pulled in on completion of the withdrawal.

Both Platoons on withdrawing will make for B.3. Subsector H.Q. but in case there should be a hostile barrage on the Western exits of HARGICOURT at the time of the withdrawal, cellars have been cleared near advanced Subsector H.Q. These will be marked by Red Lamps on the night of the raid.

The position of the Cellars will be reconnoitered by N.C.Os taking part in the raid previous to the night appointed.

A guide will be provided at Advanced Subsector H.Q. to point out the way to the cellars if necessary.

13. **Medical Arrangements.** An advanced Regimental Aid Post will be established atv L.5.c.9.6., in addition to the aid post at B.3. Subsector H.Q.
A.D.M.S. will provide two Regimental Stretchers yo accompany each Platoon.
Also 4 Regimental Stretchers at North West corner of the Slag heap.

14. **Code Words.** will be arranged and communicated to all ranks taking part in the raid.

15. **SYNCHRONIZATION of Watches** will be carried out just before leaving Subsector H.Q. from the watch of the Artillery Liaison Officer. This must be most carefully done.

ACKNOWLEDGE.
(sgd) G.Gould Captain
Brigade Major.....

Copies to
No.1 4th Cav Div.
2. C., R.H.A.
3. Engineer Officer accompanying the raid.
4. Major Terrot.
5. Raid Leader.
6. Right Platoon Leader.
7. Left Platoon Leader.

APPENDIX 'A'

No. 1. Group.

4 guns at L.17.a.3.9. to fire at L.6.c.5.1. to G.1.d.1.6, range 1600x – 2200x

No. 2. Group.

2 guns at L.11.c.1.9. to fire at L.6.c.5.1. to G.7.b.5.8. range 1400x to 1700x

No. 3. Group.

2 guns at L.11.a.2.2. to fire between G.7.b.2.8. and G.7.b.6.0. ranges 1650x to 1750x.

No. 4. Group.

2 guns at L.4.c.6.6. to fire at Enfilade Trench L.3.a.4.7. to G.1.b.2.8. Range 2000x to 2350x

No. 5. Group.

2 guns at F.29.c.9.4. and F.29.d.0.5. to fire at L.6.a.3.1. to G.1.d.3.6. Range 1100x to 1500x

No. 6. Group.

2 guns at L.4.d.6.7. to fire on MALAKOFF, MALAKOFF SUPPORT and TRIANGLE TRENCHES G.7.b. Range 1700x to 1900x

No. 7. Group.

2 guns at F.29.c.9.4. to fire at RUBY Emp. to Cross Roads G.1.d.3.7. Range 1200x to 1450x

No. 8. Group.

2 guns at L.10.a.8.6. to fire on MALAKOFF TRENCH, MALAKOFF SUPPORT and TRIANGLE TRENCHES. Range 2200x to 2650x.

No. 9. Group.

2 guns at L.11.b.8.6. and 8.8. near SLAG HEAP, to fire on Railway Cutting L.12.a.5.7. to G.7.b.2.4. Range 250x to 800x.

All guns to open rapid fire at Zero – 4 and continue at this rate till Zero + 15.; after which fire will slightly diminish in intensity until Zero + 30 when it will again quicken up till Zero + 35 from which hour it will gradually lessen and some guns will be withdrawn. Fire ceasing at Zero + 50.

Appendix to S.M.149. of 28-6-17.

To,
    All addressed in above No.

Captain.
Brigade Major.

SECRET.   Copy No.

            4th Dismounted Brigade ~~Operation~~ Order No. 12.
            ===

                                                    2nd July 1917.

1. The two platoons Inniskilling Dragoons that took part in
   last nights operation will be relieved tonight 2nd/3rd July
   by two platoons Inniskilling Dragoons, from Rear Area.

2. The relieving party will be moved up by motor lorry and will
   arrive at L.14 Central at 9-30 p.m.
   Guides from B.S. Subsector Hd.Qrs. will meet relieving party
   at above place and time.
   The lorries will wait and take back relieved party to
   HERMAIN.

3. The Hotchkiss Rifle teams of the King's Dragoon Guards will
   be relieved this evening by the Inniskilling Dragoons.
   Lucknow Brigade will send One L.G.S.Wagon to reach B.S.
   Subsector Hd.Qrs. at 10 p.m. to take out Hotchkiss Rifles.
   Teams will march via TEMPLEUX and will be met by their horses
   at L.7.b.3.9. (road leading to 4th Dismounted Bde Hd.Qrs.)
   at 10.30 p.m. from which point they will proceed mounted to
   camp HAMELET.

                                                    Captain
Copies to
No.1. 4th Cav Div
   2. Lucknow Bde   Brigade Major.....
   3. B.S.
   4. Inniskillings Rear.   4th Dismounted Brigade...
   5. 4th Cav Div "Q" Rear.

S E C R E T.   Copy No.
                4th DISMOUNTED BRIGADE ORDER No.13.
Reference Map 62.c.1/40000.   5-7-17.

1. 4th Dismounted Brigade will be relieved by the 102nd Infantry Bde. in accordance with attached Relief Tables.

2. 21st Northumberland Fusiliers relieving B.1. Subsector will march in from JEANCOURT.
   22nd Northumberland Fusiliers relieving B.2. Subsector will march in via HESBECOURT and L.14.central.
   23rd Northumberland Fusiliers relieving B.3. Subsector will march in via TEMPLEUX.
   102nd L.T.M.Battery will march in via TEMPLEUX.
   102nd M.G.Coy. will march in according to Subsectors being relieved.

   All details of Relief to be arranged between Officers Commanding concerned.

3. Command of Subsectors will pass on completion of the Relief, which will be reported by the code word "AFRICA".

4. 102nd Infantry Brigade will send Advance Parties to remain in the trenches for 24 hours previous to the Relief, details to be arranged between Commanding Officers concerned.

5. 176th T.M.Battery on relief by 102nd T.M.Battery will move to ROISEL and proceed on the following day in accordance with arrangements to be made between 4th Cavalry Division and 59th Division.

6. Relieving Units after being met by their guides on the day of relief will move forward by platoons at not less than 200 yds. distance.

7. Mhow and Sialkot Brigades will move mounted to their Back Areas; rendezvous for horses are given in relief table. Horses will not be brought East of a line BERNES - ROISEL before 9.30.p.m. on either night.
   Sialkot Bde. and Officer Commanding Mhow Bde. Rear Area will arrange to send up led horses in communication with Subsector Commanders concerned.

8. 4th Field Squadron and Ambala Cav. Field Ambulance are being relieved under arrangements to be made by C.R.E. and A.D.M.S. respectively.

9. Command of 'B' Sector will pass to G.O.C. 102nd Infantry Brigade at 9.a.m. on July 10th.

ACKNOWLEDGE.

                                                    G.Gould.
                                                    Captain.
                                                    Brigade Major.
Copies to :-   4th Dismounted Brigade.
No.1. 4th Cavalry Division.
   2 102nd Infantry Brigade.
   3. O.C. B.1. Subsector.
   4. O.C. B.2.   "
   5. O.C. B.3.   "
   6. S.M.G.Officer.
   7. 176th T.M.Battery.
   8. 4th Field Squadron.
   9. Mhow Bde. Rear Area.
  10. Sialkot Bde.
  11. B.S.O. 4th Dismounted Bde.
  12 & 13. B.T.Os, 4th Dismounted Bde.
  14. Ambala C.F.A.
  15 to 18 Diary etc.

RELIEF TABLE ISSUED WITH 4th DISMOUNTED BRIGADE ORDER No.13.

Night 8th/9th July.

UNITS.	RELIEVED BY.	MOVE AFTER RELIEF.	REMARKS.
17th L.T.M.Battery.	102nd L.T.M.Battery.	To ROISEL.	Leave ROISEL on following day. Relief to be completed by 6.p.m. 8th.
B.1. Subsector.	21st Northumberland Fusiliers.	St CHRIST Area.	Horses to be at L.33.a.0.9. at times to be arranged by O.C. B.1. Subsector with Sialkot Bde.
B.3. Subsector.	23rd Northumberland Fusiliers.	ENNEMAIN Area.	Horses to be at L.7.a. and b at times to be arranged by O.C. B.3. Subsector with O.C. Mhow Roar Area.
Machine Guns. B.2. Subsector.	6 Machine Guns 102nd M.G.Company.	ENNEMAIN Area.	Horses to be at L.14.central at a time to be arranged by O.C. No.11 Squadron M.G.Corps (Cav) with O.C. Mhow Roar Area.

Night 9th/10th July.

UNITS.	RELIEVED BY.	MOVE AFTER RELIEF.	REMARKS.
B.2. Subsector.	22nd Northumberland Fusiliers.	17th Lancers. to St CHRIST Area. 2nd Lancers. to ENNEMAIN Area.	Horses to be at L.14.central at times to be arranged by O.C. B.2. Subsector with Sialkot Bde. and O.C. Mhow Roar Area.
Machine Guns. B.1. Subsector.	4 Machine Guns. 102nd M.G.Company.	ENNEMAIN Area.	Horses to be at L.33.a.0.9. at a/ time to be arranged by O.C. No.11. Squadron M.G.Corps (Cav) with Mhow Bde Roar Area.
Machine Guns B.3. Subsector.	6 Machine Guns 102nd M.G.Company.	St CHRIST Area.	Horses to be at L.3.c.6.6. at a time to be arranged by S.M.G.Officer with Sialkot Bde.

Serial No: 114.

CONFIDENTIAL.

War Diary

of

Mhow Bde Head Quarters

from 1st Aug 1917 to 31 Aug 1917

WAR DIARY of INTELLIGENCE SUMMARY

Army Form C. 2118.

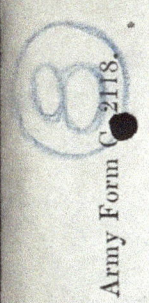

Place	Date	Hour	Summary of Events and Information	Remarks and references to Appendices
ENNEMAIN	AUGUST 1st-5th		Ordinary routine work in billets. Working party of 60 other Ranks from each of 2nd Wessex and 38th C.F.A. men employed daily in an employment of 36th Divisional Pioneers. Billeted at VENDELLES.	Uly
	6th		Working parties in 36th Divisional Area increased to a total strength of 200 each of 2nd Wessex and 38th C.F.A.	Uly
	7th		38th C.F.A. strength working down. Left one each to each of 3rd, 4th & 5th Army Schools for instruction of young officers in equitation.	Uly
	9th		One horse incidentally transferred 3rd Army Hd. Qrs. Horses sent by R.F.C. Officers for recreation purposes.	Uly
	10th		M.G. Sqn. moved up to 35th Divisional Sector. Lies in line North of LEMPIRE, to rest in camp at VILLERS FAUCON.	Uly
	11th,12th,13th		Ordinary routine.	Uly Uly
	16th 4am.		M.G. Sqn. participated in attack by 35th Div. on HARGICOURT and GILLEMONT FARM.	Uly
	19th		2nd Wessex & 38th C.F.A. men working parties were completed to a Rifle strength of 200 each and advance parties went into the line in A Sector 36th Divn. front.	Uly
	20th		Remainder of M.H.O.W. moved into the line.	Uly
	22nd		M.G. Sqn. were transferred from 36th Divn. to 38th Division around the premises at TEMPLEUX.	Uly
	26th		M.G. Sqn. participated in the attack by 38th Division on MALAKOFF F and COLOGNE troops. Attack successful.	Uly
	27th		M.G. Sqn. took part in a further attack on the COLOGNE RIDGE. Attack successful.	Uly

Army Form C. 2118.

WAR DIARY
of
INTELLIGENCE SUMMARY.
(Erase heading not required.)

Instructions regarding War Diaries and Intelligence Summaries are contained in F. S. Regs., Part II. and the Staff Manual respectively. Title pages will be prepared in manuscript.

Place	Date	Hour	Summary of Events and Information	Remarks and references to Appendices
ENNEMAIN	31.8.17		The butchers, Bakers and Sol. O.R. Funeral at but Lauren and 38th C.M. were carried out & practical activ. of the MMP Bin. in A.I. Schoolar.	

Reynold Major
Brigdlejon
Wolur-Gun Bde.

1.9.17

Serial No. 114

WAR DIARY.

of the

Head Quarters. MHOW CAVALRY Bde

From 1st Sept. 1917 To 30th Sept. 1917

Army Form C. 2118.

WAR DIARY
INTELLIGENCE SUMMARY.
(Erase heading not required.)

Instructions regarding War Diaries and Intelligence Summaries are contained in F. S. Regs., Part II. and the Staff Manual respectively. Title pages will be prepared in manuscript.

Place	Date	Hour	Summary of Events and Information	Remarks and references to Appendices
ENNEMAIN.	SEPTEMBER 1917			
	1st.		50, 1 Other Ranks from 11th 2nd Lancers and 35th Cav. m.e. relieved a similar number in A.I. Subsector.	—
	3rd.	9 a.m.	Br: Genl: Neil Haig C.M.G. and Staff relieved Br: Genl: M.F.Gage D.S.O. and Staff in command of A Sector. 34th Divisional front.	—
	4th.		100 men from 2nd Lancers & a similar number from 38th Cav. m.e. relieved like numbers in A.I. Subsector.	—
	5th.		1 Indian Officer 38th Cav. m.e. wounded. Strong Enemy patrol encountered in FISHER CRATER by patrol of 2nd Lancers who opened fire. Enemy retired towards BELLENGLISE and withdrew their wounded. Sustained some loss. Casualties, 2nd Lancers. 1. I.O.R. killed, 3 I.O.R. wounded.	—
	6th.		Casualties normal. Casualties 11th. D.R. wounded.	—
	7th. 11 th.		Situation normal. No casualties	—
	12 th.	6.30 p.m.	Advance parties from Jodhpore Bde. went into the line preparatory to relief.	—
	13 th.	5 p.m.	Balance of patrol strength of LUCKNOW Bde. arrived. 9 p.m. Relief of MHOW Bde. by LUCKNOW Bde. commenced. Relief completed without incident by 1 AM 14th.	—
	14 th.	10 a.m.	Br: Genl: L.L. Maxwell CM.G. relieved Br: Genl: Neil Haig C.M.G. in command of A Sector 34th Divisional front.	—
	16 th.		Orders received that MHOW Bde. would relieve SIALKOT Bde. in A2 Sub-sector in the night 22/23rd. Sept.	—

Army Form C. 2118.

WAR DIARY
or
INTELLIGENCE SUMMARY.
(Erase heading not required.)

Instructions regarding War Diaries and Intelligence Summaries are contained in F. S. Regs., Part II. and the Staff Manual respectively. Title pages will be prepared in manuscript.

Place	Date	Hour	Summary of Events and Information	Remarks and references to Appendices
ENNEMAIN	Sept 1917 19th–20th		Construction of huts and horse standings for hints & MLs continued.	
	21st		Advance Patrols went on to the Line	
	22nd		Balance of Cantonment following strength went into the Line - Horses stabling 3rd 100 all ranks, Lahores 270 all ranks, 38th CLIHorse 270 all ranks. Composite role up SIALKOT Bde returning to their horse.	
	27th		2 Indian O.Rs 38th CLIHorse wounded.	
	29th		11th M.G. Squadron relieves in the Line, arrived back in camp 1 am 30th	
	30th 1am		Patrol under Lt. W. Dern 38th CLIH proceeded & German line. Came under heavy fire and Lt. Dern was killed & one wounded Infantry accompanying the patrol had two men wounded. All killed and wounded brought in.	
	10pm		Relief of Indian Bm by 8th Buffs completed. Bn returned wounded BATHIES and arrived 2 am 1st Oct.	

Arnold Major
B/Lt. Major
Indian Cav. Bde.

S E C R E T.   MHOW CAVALRY BRIGADE ORDER No.14.   Copy No. 10

Reference Sheet 42.c. 1/40,000.   18-9-17.

1. Mhow Battalion, under command of Lieut-Colonel H..F.TURNER, 2nd Lancers, will relieve Sialkot Battalion in the line on 21st and 22nd September 1917.

2. The Mhow Battalion will consist of Battn. H.Q. and 3 Companies, strength as under :-

    6th Innis. Dragoons.....100 all ranks.) Exclusive of
    38th C.I.Horse..........270 all ranks.) Transport.
    2nd Lancers.............270 all ranks.)

The Establishments for Battn. H.Q., Companies and Transport are given in attached Appendix 'A'.

3. Units will submit names of officers detailed, showing appointments, so as to reach this office by midday 20th instant.

4. Medical Establishment will be detailed by D.V.O. who will forward a copy of his orders to this office for information.

5. Advance parties of 5% from each company and Battn. H.Q. will probably proceed on evening of 21st instant: Definite orders will issue later.
Remainder of Battalion will proceed on evening of 22nd instant.

Battalion will ride up, Sialkot Battn. returning on the same horses.

6. Further orders re times and rendezvous will issue later.

                                                    Captain.
                                            for. Brigade Major.
                                            Mhow Cavalry Brigade.

A.M.
Copies to :-
    No.1. 6th Innis. Dragoons.
    2. 2nd Lancers.
    3. 38th C.I.Horse.
    4. D.D.C.
    5. D.D.C.
    6. Sialkot Battn.
    7. 4th Dismounted Bde.
    8 to 10 Diary.

APPENDIX "A"
to Mhow Cavalry Brigade Order No.14.

ESTABLISHMENTS.

BATTALION HEADQUARTERS.

```
Commanding..........................Lieut Colonel TURNER, 2nd Lancers.
Adjutant............................Captain WHITMORE, 2nd Lancers.
Quartermaster.......................To be detailed by 38th C.I.Horse.
Signalling Officer..................Lieut SMITH, 2nd Lancers.
Intelligence & Sniping..............Lieut NASH, 2nd Lancers.
Transport Officer...................To be detailed by 38th C.I.Horse.
Woordie Major.......................  "  "   "   "   2nd Lancers.
R.Q.M.S.............................  "  "   "   "   6th Inniskg. Dragoons.
Qr. Mr. Dafadar.....................  "  "   "   "   38th C.I.Horse.
Clerk...............................  "  "   "   "   6th Inns. Dragoons.
Transport Dafadar...................  "  "   "   "   38th C.I.Horse.
Signalling Sergt or Cpl.............  "  "   "   "   6th Innis. Dragoons.
Signallers,6(Eight).................  "  "   "   "   "   "    "     "
Shoeing Smith.......................  "  "   "   "   2nd Lancers.
One N.C.O...........................  "  "   "   "   6th Innis Dragoons.
Cook................................  "  "   "   "   "   "    "     "
```

COMPANY.

On	Brit.	Ind.	
Commanding Officer	1	1	Major or Captain.
2nd-in-Command	1	1	Captain or Subaltern.
Platoon Commanders	3	4	Subalterns.
Bombing Officer	1	1	British or Indian.
Indian Officers	-	8	2 per Platoon.
C.S.M. or Wet Dafadar	1	1	
C.Q.M.S. or Qr.Mr's Wop.	1	1	
Sergts. or Dafadars	5	8	
Cpls L/Cpls or L/Dafrs	8	12	
Ptes or Sowars & A.L.Brs	187	208	*To include 1 Gas N.C.O. per platoon
Signallers	4	8	and Indian officers batmen.
Batmen	-	7	
Cooks	-	4	
Sweepers	-	2	
Hotchkiss Rifles	6	14	Teams included under *

TRANSPORT.

HEADQUARTERS.	Establmt.	Drivers.	Horses. Draught.	Mules. Pack.
Carts Water	1	1	2	-
G.S.Limber wagon (for Medical Dept.)	1	4	4	-
Mules Pack	7	-	-	1
British Company.				
Water Cart	1	1	2	-
G.S.Wagon	1	2	4	-
G.S.Limber Wagon	1	2	4	-
Mules Pack	-	2	-	2
Indian Company.				
Water Cart	1	1	2	-
G.S.Wagon	2	4	8	-
G.S.Limber Wagon	1	2	4	-
Mules Pack	-	4	-	4

The above Transport Establishment is that which will remain with the Battalion in the Line. Any further transport considered necessary for conveyance of kit will be returned to regiments.

S E C R E T.   Copy No.

MHOW CAVALRY BRIGADE ORDER No.15.

Reference Sheet 62.c. 1/40,000.   20-9-17.

In continuation of Mhow Cavalry Brigade Order No.14. of 19-9-17.

1. Advance parties, including their transport, of Mhow Battalion, strength as under, will rendezvous on BEAURAINS - ARRAS Road, head at point U.19.a.10.10., on Friday the 21st September 1917, at 1.p.m. and will march under senior Officer present to Crater at Western Exit of VIMY RIDGE, where they will be met at d.a.m. by one guide from each Company of Sialkot Battalion who will guide them to their sector in the line. No troops will move East of VIMY RIDGE before dark and movement East of North and South line thro' BOUVIGNCOURT by daylight will be limited to parties not larger than a troop with 100 yards distance between troops.

This party will proceed mounted and sufficient horseholders must accompany to return with horses.

No horses are to enter VIMY RIDGE.

Transport of Advance parties will proceed direct from rendezvous to G.H.Q. central/to arrive by 3.p.m.

STRENGTH OF ADVANCE PARTY.

	9th Cav.		2nd Cav.	
	O	O.R.	O	O.R.
Coy Comdr or 2nd-in-Command....................	1	-	1	-
1 Hotchkiss Rifle per Coy.......................	-	3	-	3
1 Officer and 10 men per Coy for patrols.......	1	10	1	10
Quartermasters details..........................	-	5	-	5
Bde. and Battn. Intelligence Personnel.........	-	4	-	4
Signallers and Runners..........................	-	12	-	12

2. Remainder of Battalion will proceed on 22nd September 1917, under orders to be issued by Lieut Colonel H.J.F.TRENCH, 2nd Lancers, Commanding Mhow Battalion, in accordance with instructions contained in 4th/ Dismounted Bde. Order No.4.

3. ACKNOWLEDGE.

S.E. Haway
Captain.
for, Brigade Major.
Mhow Cavalry Brigade.

20-9-17.
Issued to :-

No.1. 9th Dragoons.
   2. 2nd Lancers.
   3. 38th C.I. Horse.
   4. Lieut Col. TRENCH.
   5. R.H.Q.
   6. D.H.Q.
   7. Sialkot Battn.
   8. 4th Dismounted Bde.
   9 to 11 Diary.

A.C.

SECRET.   Copy No......

MHOW CAVALRY BRIGADE ORDER NO.16.

20th September 1917.

Reference Sheet 62.c.

In Continuation of MHOW Cavalry Brigade Order No 15.

1. The following additional personnel will go up with the Advanced party tomorrow.

    Lt. Colonel Turner Commanding Mhow Battalion.
    Quartermaster.
    Signalling Officer.
    Intelligence Officer.

2. The balance of patrol strengths

    15 O.Rs 2nd Lancers and 15 O.Rs 38th C.I.H.

    will proceed in Lorries which will be at H.Q., C.I.H. at 2 p.m. on 22nd inst, to the Crater at W exit of VENDELLES where they will be met by guides at 4 p.m.

3. Units will report as early _closely_ as possible the number of horses that will be available for bringing back men of the SIALKOT Brigade. Reports to reach this Office by 3 p.m. 21st.

4. The number of Hotchkiss Rifles taken up will be increased to

    2nd Lancers & 38th.C.I.H.   12 each.
    6th Inniskilling Dragoons.   6.

    ACKNOWLEDGE.

                                                        Davies
                                                                Captain
                                            for Brigade Major Mhow Cavalry Bde.

Issued to :-

No. 1. 6th Dragoons.
    2 2nd Lancers.
    3 38th C.I.H.
    4 Lt Col Turner.
    5 S.M.O.
    6 E.S.O.
    7 Sialkot Battalion.
    8 4th Dismounted Bde.
    9 to 11 Diary.

SECRET.   Copy No.........

MHOW CAVALRY BRIGADE ORDER No. 17.

Reference Map 1/40,000 Sheet 62c.

1.
   The Mhow Battalion and 11th M.G. Squadron will be relieved in the Line on the night 29/30th September and 30thSept/1st October.

   Horses for Relieved Units will be sent up in accordance with accompanying table A.

2. The numbers of horses required to bring back Officers and Other Ranks of Relieved Units are as under :-

   Inniskilling Dragoons...118. including 4 for Observation Post in A.1. Subsector.

   2nd Lancers...............272.

   38th C.I.Horse............222.

   No.11.M.G.Sqdn............ 42. 1 N.C.O. per gun remains in line until morning 1st October.

   All exclusive of Horse holders.

3. (a). Horses of each unit will be sent up under a British Officer. Indian regiments, in addition will send 1 Indian Officer with each of their Squadrons.

   The whole of the horses for Mhow ~~Brigade~~ Bn. will be under the command of Major GOURLIE 38th C.I.H.

   (b). Starting Point. Bridge over River COIGNON on HURBMAIN ATHIES road.

   (c). Time. 6.30. p.m.

   (d). Order of March. 2nd Lancers, 38th C.I.H, Inniskilling Dragoons.

4. All movement East of BOUVINCOURT by daylight will be by parties not larger than a troop, and at 250 yards distance.

                                                  _____ Major
                                                  Brigade Major Mhow Cavalry Bde.

28/9/17.
Copies to :-
No.1. 4th Cav Dismounted Bde.
No.2. Mhow Battalion.
No.3. 11th M.G. Squadron (forward)
No.4. Inniskilling Dragoons (rear)
No.5. 2nd Lancers   "
No.6. 38th C.I.H.   "
No.7. 11th M.G. Sqdn   "
No.8. Lucknow Bde.
No.9. 4th Cavalry Division.
No.10 to 11. Office & Diary.

TABLE "A".

Date	UNIT	RENDEZVOUS.	TIME	ROUTE.	REMARKS.
Sept. 29th.	11th Bn.&7th Transport (8 Load.) (Wagons)	Transport Lines O.S.R. Central.	8. P.m.	CAMP-ST.ELOI-DICKEBUSCH-ROUTES COURT-LANCOURT-JUNCTION.	Guides will meet.
"	11th Bn.Reserves.	East entrance to VRERLINGHE.	8. P.m.	do do	Guide will meet.
29th.	LANCOUR BATTALION.	E.10.d.4.4.	9. P.m.	HATEBURY - BURGHS.	Not to enter VRERLINGHE before 9 p.m.
"	8TH Battalion.	B. 4. Central.	9. P.m.	LOUE-x-READING-WALKER-FLANSUS-VRERLINGHE.	To follow LANCOUR through VRERLINGHE. 4 horses for Battalion commanding O.P. in A.1. to join LANCOUR at ST.VRERLINGHE. A Staff Officer will meet horse parties at VRERLINGHE on night 29th/1st.

JOINER. Lancer horses will accompany LANCOUR to VRERLINGHE and move thence in rear of LANCER Battalion horses.

CONFIDENTIAL

WAR DIARY
of
HEADQUARTERS
MHOW CAVALRY BRIGADE

from 1-10-17 to 31-10-17

114.

Army Form C. 2118.

WAR DIARY
OF
INTELLIGENCE SUMMARY.
(Erase heading not required).

Headquarters Mhow Cav Bde

Instructions regarding War Diaries and Intelligence Summaries are contained in F. S. Regs. Part II. and the Staff Manual respectively. Title pages will be prepared in manuscript.

Place	Date	Hour	Summary of Events and Information	Remarks and references to Appendices
ENNEMAIN OCTOBER 1917	3rd		1 Troop Inniskilling Dragoons reported from 5th Army School. M.G. Squadron moved into ATHIES in relief btn near their work of building limbers billets.	—
	4th		2 Troop Inniskilling Dragoons reported from 3rd and 4th Army Schools.	—
	6th		2nd Lancers less Hd. Qrs. moved into ATHIES.	—
	9th		Hd. Qrs. 2nd Lancers joined remainder of regt. in ATHIES.	—
	12th		1 Officer + gunner "A" Bty. R.H.A. moved to ATHIES to examine billets + stablings.	—
	15th		"A" Bty. R.H.A. lent van from the line but remain at Voyennes.	—
	19th		"A" Bty. R.H.A. occupy their billets in ATHIES.	—
	23rd		Scout Squadron of Inniskilling Dragoons reported from Cavalry Corps.	—
	29th		Br. Ford. Will Stay Currys reported from sick leave.	—
			Throughout the month work in buildings billets. a little training was carried out from the 7th inst. Spreading of all limits was carried and reported very good.	—

Woodall Major
Brett Major
Indian Cavalry Brigade

Confidential

WAR DIARY.

4 DIV

of

Headquarters
Mhow Cav Bde

from 1-11-17. to 30-11-17

3 FEB 1918

WAR DIARY
or
INTELLIGENCE SUMMARY.

Army Form C. 2118.

Headquarters
Meerut Cavalry Brigade

Place	Date	Hour	Summary of Events and Information	Remarks and references to Appendices
ENNEMAIN NOV. 1917.	1st to 14th		Routine work; troop, squadron and regimental training.	
	15th		Pioneer Bn. found with command of Lt.Col. Bell S.O. 29th Cldh. and moved to MISERY.	
	19th		Bde. moved. Kit ready to move at 2½ hours after Zero hour in 20 lb. kit.	
	21st	3am	Bde. moved. Transport near FINS arriving there at 6.30 a.m.	
	22nd		Bde. moved to MASNIERES and MARCOING. Orders not that had until midnight that 22nd cancelled and Bde. to return by 2 p.m. return to ENNEMAIN next morning.	
FINS	23rd	9.30am	Bde. marched in Cross at short notice. Orders rec'd 8.p.m. return to ENNEMAIN arriving 1 p.m.	
"	24th		Bde. at 1 hours notice later cancelled & later put on again. Orders rec'd to move to VILLERS FAUCON morning of 25th.	
ENNEMAIN	25th	5.30am	Bde. marched VILLERS FAUCON arriving 9.15 a.m. Orders rec'd return to ENNEMAIN at 1.45 p.m.	
			Bde. marched 1.55pm and arrived 4.55pm.	
	26th		Bde. at short notice.	
	27th		Bde. informed that the Bde. will shortly be taking over a portion of the line.	
	29th	12.30pm	Advance parties went up by lorry for 24 hours attachment before taking over from the 72nd Inf. Bde. U.Col. Paterson S.O. i/c party. The MHH Bn. proceeded later in the afternoon.	
	30th	6.30am	Remainder of company proceeded mounted to point East of TEMPLEUX. Followed at 7.15am by B Sqn. 11th. M.G. Sqn. and at 8.30 am. by the remainder of Bde. and 38th Ct. Horse. At 10.35am. when one-r'd to saddle up and move out to central the Bde. East of ESTREES-EN-CHAUSSÉE immediately this received to ENNEMAIN and picketed middle ready for mounted action. Intense machine and pick-up in lorries for D.L.H. C.L.H. and moved there later. At 12.10p.m. Bde. less D.L.H and S Puree by MHH'D Sqn., were concentrated East of ESTREES. At 2.20 p.m. 2 K. moved/amend north of ST EMILIE, S from 2K. and S from 11 Hr. M.G. Sqn.	

Army Form C. 2118.

WAR DIARY
or
INTELLIGENCE SUMMARY.
(Erase heading not required.)

Instructions regarding War Diaries and Intelligence Summaries are contained in F. S. Regs., Part II. and the Staff Manual respectively. Title pages will be prepared in manuscript.

Place	Date	Hour	Summary of Events and Information	Remarks and references to Appendices
		7.45 p.m.	Joined the Brigade at 6 p.m. Preliminary orders issued that 55th. Division were preparing a minor line through LEMPIRE – MALASSIS FME. GAUCELETTE FME. MHW Cav. Bde. detail Kieufrei line to cov. of attack.	
		11.30 p.m.	Intimation received that an attack on LEMPIRE – VAUCELETTE FME. line was considered likely early in morning of 1st. MHW Cav. Bde. stand to ready to move on notifying orders after 5.30 a.m.	

Myuell Major
Bdr. Major
Indian Cav. Bde.

4.12.17

SECRET.   MHOW CAVALRY BRIGADE ORDER No.17.   Copy No. 17

Reference 1/40,000 Sheets 62c and 57c.   19th November 1917.

1. The Brigade will move on Z day (at a time to be notified later), to a forward concentration area immediately N.E. of FINS, i/a with attached March Table.

   Starting Point.:- Divisional Officers Club ATHIES. U.12.b.9.9.
   ROUTE:- DOINGT - ST DENIS - NURLU - EQUANCOURT - N.of FINS.

   Rate of March.:- 5 miles per hour.

2. At Zero + 2½ hours, units will be ready to move at short notice, (saddles packed and men dressed).
   Following will be notified from Bde. H.Q. to all concerned.:-

   (a) Zero hour.
   (b) "X time" (the hour at which the head of the Brigade Column is to pass the Starting Point.)

3. Except for an interval of 200 yards between each regiment, or similar unit, the column will be closed up.
   Whenever possible squadrons will move off the roads, while wheels move on the roads. (Attention is drawn to G/81/1, re march discipline.)

4. "A" Echelon in order of units will be brigaded in rear of the Bde. under command of Lieut BLEAKLEY, Inniskilling Dragoons. 'A.1' leading, followed by 'A.2', Cyclists under the senior cyclist N.C.O. Inniskilling Dragoons, will move in rear of 'A.1' and must keep closed up.

5. Horse rugs will be carried on horses as far as, but not beyond, the forward concentration area.

6. Major PRICHARD, att. 38th C.I.H. will join Divl. H.Q. (W.l.c.sheet 57c.) on arrival at forward concentration area, reporting to Camp Commandant and General Staff.

7. No secret documents, except maps, Station code calls and code names will be taken beyond the forward Concentration area.

8. The following will remain in the present area under Major LANCE, 19th Lancers, who will be at Divnl. H.Q. at ATHIES. :-
   (a) Surplus Officers and Dismounted men.
   (b) "B" Echelon (except that of C.F.As.)

9. The Pioneer Battn. will return to MISERY on Zero + 1 day.

10. Ambala C.F.A. will move under orders to be issued by A.D.M.S.

11. Reports to head of Bde. during march.

                                                G. Gould.
                                                       Major.

Issued to Signals, at 5.p.m., to:-
Copy No.
   As per normal distribution.
A.H.

MARCH TABLE.

ISSUED WITH MHOW CAVALRY BRIGADE ORDER No.17.

*****

ORDER OF MARCH:-

   Brigade Headquarters.
               50 yards.

2nd Lancers.
               200 yards.

No.11. M.G.Squadron.
               200 yards.

38th C.I.Horse.
               200 yards.

Inniskilling Dragoons.
               200 yards.

    Echelon 'A.1'. Under Command of Captain GRAY. 11th M.G.Sqdn.

    Led Horses, under Lieut PRATT. Inniskilling Dragoons.

    L.G.S.Wagons, in order of Units.

    Cyclists, under senior cyclist N.C.O. Inniskilling Dragoons.

       200 yards.

Echelon 'A.2', under Command of Lieut PEASE, Inniskilling Drags. (in order of Units.)

Followed by Mobile Veterinary Section.

****

A.H.

Secret. Mhow Cav Bde Order No. 18.
Reference Sheet 62 C. S.E/3. . . 20-11-17

1. "X" hour is 2.30 am.
2. Camp parties will parade at Officers Club at ATHIES at 2.30am and proceed to Y roads 300x N of FINS. V.6.d.1.1. under command of senior officer proceeding. They will there report to Staff Captain. Sketch map attached (for S.Cav.B. & Mh.Sqd.) Parties will consist of 1 B.O., 1 N.C.O. with 6 men.
3. After leaving this area no bugle calls will be sounded.
4. 2nd Lancers will provide one Troop to maintain connection with Divisional Troops.

Issued at 12.30 am
Normal Distribution
AH.

S. G. Gould
Major
Brigade Major
Mhow Cav Bde

SECRET.   MHOW CAVALRY BRIGADE ORDER No.20.   Copy No. 5
Reference Map 1:40000, sheets 62c and 57c.   24-11-17.

1. The Brigade will march ~~tomorrow~~ today 25th instant in accordance with the following instructions :-

2. Brigade Starting Point :- Officers Club at ATHIES.

    Time. :- 5.45.a.m.

    Order of March :- As for last march up.

    Route.:- PRUSLE X roads S.12.c.7.1. - CARTIGNY - TINCOURT - LONGAVESNES - X roads E.15.a.0.3.

3. An interval of about 200 yds will be maintained between regiments and similar units.
    Squadrons will move off the roads when possible.

4. O.C. 2nd Lancers will detail one troop to precede Bde. H.Q.

5. (a) "A" Echelon in order of units will be brigaded in rear of the Brigade under command of Lieut BLEAKLEY, Inniskilling Dragoons. "A.1" leading, followed by "A.2". Cyclists under senior Cyclist N.C.O. Inniskilling Dragoons, will move immediately in rear of "A.1".

    M.V.Section will march immediately behind "A.2", as far as O.12.c.7.1., where it will join Sialkot M.V.Section and move forward with it at 7.25.a.m.

    (b) "A" Echelon will be Divisionalised at O.12.c.7.1. and march under command of Major TERROT, D.S.O. Inniskilling Dragoons.

    (c) At the same point cyclists will be formed into a Divisional party by the A.P.M. and will march as a formed body under the senior N.C.O., leaving A.12.c.7.1. at 7.30.a.m.

6. A Horse Ambulance will march in rear of Inniskilling Dragoons.

7. Major PRICHARD, att. C.I.H. will join Divisional H.Q. on arrival in forward concentration Area.

8. Horse rugs will not be taken.

9. Surplus officers, Dismounted men and "B" Echelon will remain in the present area, as before.

10. Reports to Head of Brigade during march.

11. Rate of march 5 miles an hour.

12. Brigade will water at TINCOURT compatible with fighting troops arriving in concentration area by 9.a.m.

    ACKNOWLEDGE.

                                                    Major.
                                              Brigade Major.

Issued to Signals at 1.15.a.m.
Normal distribution.

CONFIDENTIAL.

WAR DIARY.

of

Headquarters, Mhow Cavalry Brigade.

fro, 1-12-17.   to 31-12-17.

WAR DIARY / INTELLIGENCE SUMMARY

Army Form C. 2118.

4 DIV
Headquarters
Mhow Cav Bde

Place	Date	Hour	Summary of Events and Information	Remarks and references to Appendices
ST. EMILIE	Dec 1st	1.45am	Warning order received that Division, less LUCKNOW Bde and "A" Echelon, will be in a position of readiness west PEIZIERE at 6.15am. Mhow Cav Bde to move via 13.d. at Duty's mo. OU. Ellis to take place in front of Bde but being required to reinforce LEMPIRE - VAUCELETTE line.	
		2.50am	5th Cav. Div. Order No. 22 read 5th Cavalry Division with LUCKNOW Bde attached to attack VILLERS-GUISLAIN and GAUCHE WOOD at 6.30 am. Tanks co-operating. 4th Cav. Div. less LUCKNOW Bde. to cover & west of PEIZIERE with object of trying to stop the advance of tanks and seizing VILLERS-GUISLAIN Ridge. MHOW Bde. detailed to move to 4th Bell Sp. MHOW Bde to move on the Enemy's through line up line just East of PEIZIERE and keep line given with 5th Tank attack. As soon as a suitable opportunity presents itself MHOW Bde is moving forward and seize and establish itself in the VILLERS RIDGE, measures to be taken to watch the Right flank.	
		5.30am	Mhow Bde. moved off.	
		6.30am	Bde. concentration lead west of PEIZIERE. Situation and probable plan position explained to Commanding Officers.	
Wood 33		7.15am	Reports received from Tank officer that in spite of Lucknow Bdes were much entitled but were supporting infantry in VAUCELETTE ME.	
		8.15am	Mhow Bdes received from Lt. Col. Lapage to endeavor to push forward towards upper 6 Victors supported by the artillery.	

Army Form C. 2118.

WAR DIARY
or
INTELLIGENCE SUMMARY.
(Erase heading not required.)

Instructions regarding War Diaries and Intelligence Summaries are contained in F. S. Regs., Part II. and the Staff Manual respectively. Title pages will be prepared in manuscript.

Place	Date	Hour	Summary of Events and Information	Remarks and references to Appendices
PEIZIERE W 30 b 5.3 (Sheet 57c)	Dec 1st	8.20AM	Situation explained to O.C. Regiment. Division informed that Bde was moving off at once & a request made that 5th Cav Div might co-operate by attacking VILLERS-GUISLAIN	DMcM
		9.35AM	2nd Lancers, "C" Sqdn INNISKILLING DRAGOONS, & Machine Guns seen moving forward N.E. of 14 WILLOWS, on the way to their 1st objective TARGELLE, QUAIL & PIGEON RAVINES. At the same moment leading Squadron Inniskilling Dragoons, followed closely by two more Squadrons & M.G. moved down the PEIZIERE-VILLERS-GUISLAIN Road on the way to their objective VILLERS HILL at X.10 (sheet 57c)	DMcM
		9.40AM	Headquarters & 2 Squadrons Inniskilling Dragoons returned having come under heavy M.G. fire. No one returned of the leading Squadron or the M.G. Section.	DMcM

WAR DIARY or INTELLIGENCE SUMMARY

Army Form C. 2118.

Place	Date	Hour	Summary of Events and Information	Remarks and references to Appendices
PEIZIERE	Dec 1st		Division informed of situation of 2nd Lancers etc that G.O.C. Mhow Bde was meeting two Squadrons 38th C.I.H. in support of them and was himself following with the remaining two Squadrons via road through X26 - X27 - X22 (sheet 57c)	
		10.10AM		
		10.15AM	He about two Squadrons left their horses in EPEHY & proceeded on foot but were held up at X27 by heavy M.G. fire.	
		10.20AM	G.O.C. removed his B.H.Q. to F16a.5, nothing could be seen of 2nd Lancers except led horses at about X27 b.9.9	
		10.30AM	Situation report received from 2nd Lancers, in Sunkenroad X28central — X22c, both held by 1 Company 418th Regt. (R.I.R).	
		11 A.M.	2nd Lancers retired to get touch with Infantry to hold on, told that 1 Sqn C.I.H. was being sent to support them & also that the Minishlings had had to withdraw. 4th Cav Div informed of the above.	
		11.30AM	G.O.C. Mhow Bde conferred with G.O.C. 166th Inf Bde and arranged to test him two dis-mounted Squadrons 38th C.I.H. to assist him in the attack on the MEATH-CATELET line at 1 P.M. Officers commanding these two squadrons went to confer with O.C. 1/5- King's Own	

WAR DIARY
or
INTELLIGENCE SUMMARY.
(Erase heading not required.)

Army Form C. 2118.

Place	Date	Hour	Summary of Events and Information	Remarks and references to Appendices
EPEHY	Sept-	11.55 AM	Message received from 2nd Lancers that their hind was from X 28 a 9.9 on right (in touch with Infantry) to X 22 c 9.4 on left. Left flank in the air. Enemy attacking from left rear.	
		12 noon.	4th Cav Div + Infantry of 116 Inf Bde informed & arrangement for Cavalry Divisions to co-operate in attack	
		12.45 pm	Communication with 2nd Lancers established by Lamp. Information received that Col. Turner 2nd Lancers had been killed, that M.G. reinforcements were required. These reinforcements were unable to get through	
		1 P.M.	The Sqdn C.I.H. which had been sent to reinforce 2nd Lancers was obliged to withdraw to Infantry strong post.	
		2 P.M.	Verbal messages received to 2/I of 1st attack of 1 PM ejected with heavy loss, that the Enemy were strongly entrenched & had many M.G.s in position.	
		2.15 P.M.	Order received from 4th Cav Div. Lucknow Bde to attack TRAPERIE from West and the whole of Mhow Cav Bde to attack Trapezoidal from South. Sialkote Bde to act as a Mounted Reserve and take advantage of any success obtained.	

Army Form C. 2118.

WAR DIARY
or
INTELLIGENCE SUMMARY.
(Erase heading not required.)

Instructions regarding War Diaries and Intelligence Summaries are contained in F. S. Regs., Part II. and the Staff Manual respectively. Title pages will be prepared in manuscript.

Place	Date	Hour	Summary of Events and Information	Remarks and references to Appendices
F P E H7	Dec 1st	2.30 PM	4th Cav Div informed of future of attack in conjunction with Infantry and that with total available forces in his hand, the G.O.C. where P.B.S felt he was unable to attack his empinial objective with any hope of success.	
		3.10 PM	G.O.C. 165th Inf Bde informed G.O.C. 165th Inf Bde that he was being relieved by 110th Inf Bde and that he would arrange with the latter to relieve Cavalry Posts	
		3.40 PM	O.C. 2 Aynaham C.I.H., who co-operated in Infantry attack, ordered to remain in position where he was, until relieved by Infantry that evening.	
		6 PM	Information recd that 165th Inf Bde were dealing with situation at KILDARE.	
		6.58 PM	Permission obtained from 165th Inf Bde to withdraw the 3 advanced Sqns O.I.H.	
		8.40 PM	Orders received for Bhow Bde to be withdrawn from their post as a reserve	
			if required to concentrate at E17 (Sheet 62 D)	
	Dec 2nd	6 AM	Brigade arrived at concentration area E 17	
		7.45 AM	Orders recd for Bhow B.C. 8pm a dismounted Bn, to act as a Reserve to 4th Cav Div	

Army Form C. 2118.

WAR DIARY
or
INTELLIGENCE SUMMARY.
(Erase heading not required.)

Instructions regarding War Diaries and Intelligence Summaries are contained in F. S. Regs., Part II. and the Staff Manual respectively. Title pages will be prepared in manuscript.

Place	Date	Hour	Summary of Events and Information	Remarks and references to Appendices
ST EMILIE	Dec 2nd	12.15 P.M	Intimation received that 7th Cav Div would relieve 4th & 5th Cav Divs in the line that night 2nd/3rd Dec.	SMc
		11.10 PM	Orders received to move back to Athies next morning.	
	3rd Dec	9 AM	Brigade moved off	DMc
		1 PM	Arrived in Lillelot.	
ENNEMAIN	7th Dec	11.50 P.M	Orders received that Cav Corps would take over the AMP91 COURT— VADENCOURT. Sector from 10 am 8th inst. 4th Cav Div to act as a Mobile Reserve. To be prepared to move up mounted to act mounted or dismounted. In the latter case on the Dismounted Organisation.	DMc
	8th		Orders received that from 6 pm 9th inst. till 5 pm 12th inst. MHW Bde would be 1 hours notice and ready to move to relieve the Southern protection of the Cavalry Corps Front.	McG

A 5834 Wt W4973/M687 750,000 8/16 D. D. & L. Ltd. Form C.2118/13.

Army Form C. 2118.

WAR DIARY
INTELLIGENCE SUMMARY.
(Erase heading not required.)

Instructions regarding War Diaries and Intelligence Summaries are contained in F.S. Regs., Part II. and the Staff Manual respectively. Title pages will be prepared in manuscript.

Place	Date	Hour	Summary of Events and Information	Remarks and references to Appendices
ENNEMAIN Decr.	9th.		Following reinforcements arrive from Rouen:— Inniskilling Dns. B.O.Rs. 112. 2nd. Lancers B.O.s.1. B.O.Rs.1. J.O.s.2. I.O.Rs. 85. Central India Horse I.O.Rs. 54. Machine Gun Sqn. B.O.s.1. B.O.Rs. 52.	
	12th.	6 p.m.	When Cav. Bde. taken off horse lines 1 B.O. 2 S.I.O.Rs. 2nd Lancers 25 I.O.Rs. 38th C.I.Horse proceeded d'ERVILLY for work with Infy. & F.E. Cav. Corps.	
	13th.		Following reinforcements arrived:— Inniskilling Dns. 126. 2nd Lancers 5 G. M.G.Sqn. 82. 57 B.O. B. arrived as reinforcements for M.G.Sqn.	
	14th.		Military arrived awarded to 4 men M.G.Sqn. 3 men Inniskilling Dns. 2 men Bohopal Troops.	
	15th.		A reinforcement of 1 B.O. arrived for M.G.Sqn.	
	18th.		Following awards given for Gallantry: Decr. 1st. Inniskilling Dns. 2 Military Crosses, 1 D.C.M. 2nd Lancers 1 Bar to D.S.O. 3 Military Crosses, 2 I.D.S.M. 38th Central India Horse 2 Military Crosses. 1 D.S.M. 9 I.D.S.M. 2 Military Crosses.	
	19th.	1.0 M	Remount arrived as follows:— Bhopals 3. Inniskilling Dns. 6 S. 2nd Lancers 131. 38th. C.I.Horse 16. M.G.Sqn. 2.	
	23.0.		Reinforcements:— 2nd Lancers 1 B.O. 38th C.I.Horse 17. I.O.Rs. Reinforcements arrived as follows:— 1 Officer, 25 B.O.R. Inniskilling Dns.	
	23.0.		"	
	25 th.		Bde. found two parties of 300 each for work under Cav. Corps in Intermediate line.	
	26 th.		"	
	29 th.		1 party of 300 men	
	31st.		Following reinforcement arrived:— 2nd Lancers 7 I.O.Rs. 38th C.I.Horse 1 I.O.S.& I.O.Rs. Bhopals 1 party of 300 men (made into CRE Cav Corps.) An advance party of 1 B.O. Lancers & 3 men from each regt. moved up towards new VENDELLES.	

[signature] Major
B.G. Major
[signature] Gen Bde.

SUMMARY OF OPERATIONS, MHOW CAVALRY BRIGADE,

November 30th to December 2nd 1917.

****

Nov. 30th.
10.35.a.m.   Brigade ordered to saddle up and concentrate at P.30.d.

The Brigade were on their way to relieve the 72nd Infantry Brigade in the Centre Sector, 24th Divisional Front. Inniskillings returned to ENNEMAIN and packed saddles, ready for mounted action. Lances and swords were sent up in wagons for 2nd Lancers and 38th C.I.Horse and issued later.

12.10.p.m.   Brigade, less 2nd Lancers, H.Q. and 8 guns 11th M.G.Sqdn. and advance parties from all units, in the trenches, concentrated in P.30.d.

2.20.p.m.   Brigade moved off under orders to proceed to camp between LONGAVESNES and VILLERS-FAUCON.

3.10.p.m.   Orders received to proceed as fast as possible to camp S.W. of SAULCOURT E.14.b. (62.c.)

3.40.p.m.   Orders received to concentrate as quickly as possible in Square E.18. just North of St.EMILIE.

4.15.p.m.   G.O.C. and Brigade Major reported at 4th Cavalry Division H.Q. E.22.b.5.0., Brigade moved on to E.18.

6.0.p.m.   2nd Lancers and H.Q. & 8 Guns 11th M.G.Squadron joined the Brigade North of St.EMILIE.

6.45.p.m.   G.O.C. rejoined Brigade in E.18.

7.0.p.m.   Brigade Report Centre moved to E.24.c. Southern exit of St.EMILIE.

7.45.p.m.   Intimation received that 55th Division preparing reserve line through LEMPIRE - MALASSISE Fme.- X.26 - VAUCELETTE Fme.
Mhow Cav. Brigade detailed to reinforce line in case of attack.
Brigade Major proceeded to EPEHY to get in touch with 166th Infantry Bde. holding centre of line. Returned 9.45.p.m.

9.5.p.m.   Order received to get in touch with 165th Infantry Bde. in St.EMILIE.

11.30.p.m.   Intimation received that an attack on LEMPIRE VAUCELETTE Line is considered likely early on morning of 1st.
Mhow Cav. Bde. ordered to be ready to move on receipt of orders after 5.30.a.m.

Decr. 1st.
1.45.a.m.   Warning order received that Division, less Lucknow Bde. and 'A' Echelon, will be in position West of PEIZIERE at 6.15.a.m.. Mounted Pack Sections to join Brigade at Rendezvous. All this to take place in event of Brigade not being required to reinforce LEMPIRE - VAUCELETTE Line at 5.30.a.m.

2.50.a.m.   4th Cavalry Division Order No.22. received.
5th Cavalry Division, with Lucknow Bde. attached, to attack VILLERS GUISLAN and GAUCHE WOOD at 6.30.a.m.
Tanks co-operating.
4th Cavalry Division, less Lucknow Bde, to assemble West of PEIZIERE with object of taking advantage of the advance of the Tanks and seizing VILLERS GUISLAN Ridge (X.10. Sheet 57.c.).

Mhow Bde. allotted 1 troop 4th Field Squadron.
Mhow Bde. to reconnoitre crossings through a line of our wire just E of PEIZIERE and to keep close liaison with the Tank attack.

P.T.O.

	As soon as a suitable opportunity presents itself MHOW Brigade to move forward and seize and establish itself on the VILLERS Ridge about X.10., measures to be taken to watch the Right flank.
4.0.a.m.	Mhow Brigade Order No.22. issued on above.
5.30.a.m.	Brigade moved off to concentrate West of PEIZIERE. G.O.C. and B.M. proceeded to meet Divisional Commander at E.4.d.8.5.
6.45.a.m.	G.O.C. rejoined Bde. West of PEIZIERE. Brigade Report Centre established W.30.b.5.3. Situation and probable plan of action explained to Commanding Officers.
7.30.a.m.	Reports received from officers reconnoitring wire that there were exits by the PEIZIERE - VILLERS GUISLAN Road and by 14 Willows road F.1.b.
8.10.a.m.	Reports received from Tank Liaison Officers that no Tanks arrived at rendezvous and that consequently Lucknow Bde. were unable to attack but were supporting Infantry in VAUCELETTE Fme.
8.15.a.m.	Order received from 4th Cav. Divn. "You are to endeavour to push forward towards your objective supported by the Artillery........."
8.20.a.m.	Commanding Officers arrived at Bde. H.Q. and situation explained. 2nd Lancers with 2 Machine Guns ordered to try and seize TARGELLE, QUAIL and PIGEON ravines. Inniskilling Dragoons and 4 Machine Guns to follow as soon as 2nd Lancers were seen approaching their objective and endeavour to seize and hold the VILLERS GUISLAN Ridge about X.10.
8.39.a.m.	Division informed the Brigade was moving forward at once, and a request made that 5th Cav. Divn. might co-operate and attack VILLERS GUISLAN. Artillery warned that Brigade was moving forward.
9.35.a.m.	2nd Lancers seen moving forward N.E. of the 14 willows. At the same moment the leading Squadron of the Inniskilling Dragoons moved off down the PEIZIERES - VILLERS GUISLAIN road closely followed by the more squadrons (One squadron had accompanied 2nd Lancers).
9.40.a.m.	Headquarters and 2 Squadrons Inniskilling Dragoons returned, having come under very heavy M.G.fire. No one returned of the leading squadron.
10.10.a.m.	Following report sent to 4th Cav. Divn. :- "2nd Lancers are believed to be in or about PIGEON Ravine, one Squadron Inniskillings is with them. I am now sending 2 squadrons C.I.H. in support of them and am following with remaining two squadrons via road running through X.26. - X.27. - X.22. 3 Machine Guns will also accompany me."
10.15.a.m.	2 Squadrons C.I.H. left their horses in EPEHY and proceeded forward dismounted, they could only reach X.27.central when they were held up by machine Gun fire.
10.20.a.m.	G.O.C. went to F.1.b.4.5. but nothing could be seen of the situation except led horses of the 2nd Lancers about X.27.b. 9.9. Brigade Report Centre then moved to Railway embankment near by.
10.50.a.m.	Following from 2nd Lancers received :- "2nd Lancers and Capt. MONCRIEFF's squadron in fortified sunken road X.22.c., also 4 Machine Guns. lately held by 1 Coy 418th Regt.

P.T.O.

                (2). Herewith shoulder straps and papers of a prisoner. (sent to 4th Cav. Divn.)
                (3). Enemy who retired from this position went North.
                (4). Infantry in touch on our Right.
                (5). Enemy shelling Little PRIEL Fme. which is believed empty."

              Sent off 10.30.a.m.

1.0.a.m.   2nd Lancers asked if they were able to connect up with Infty. and hold out.
Informed that 1 Sqdn. C.I.H. dismounted was being sent to their support, and also that Inniskillings had had to withdraw.

11.15.a.m.   Division informed that 1 Sqdn. C.I.H. dismounted was being sent to assistance of 2nd Lancers; that it was impossible to get through mounted. That 166th Infty. Bde. were arranging to advance at 1.0.p.m. and that C.I.H. had been asked to inform 2nd Lancers of this and to tell them to hold out until then. That one troop C.I.H. was being sent mounted by a more southerly route to try and get in touch with the 2nd Lancers.

11.30.a.m.   G.O.C. Mhow Cav. Bde. conferred with G.O.C. 166th Infty. Bde. and arranged to lend him two dismounted squadrons C.I.H. to assist him in his attack on the MEATH.- CATELET line at 1.p.m.

11.45.a.m.   Officers Commanding these two squadrons went to confer with O.C. 1/5 Kings Own.

11.55.a.m.   Following received from 2nd Lancers. :-

"Am connected with Infantry on Right about X.28.a.9.9. AAA Left flank about X.22.c.9.4. AAA Enemy M.G. 800 yds from left flank between us and you AAA Left flank in air and enemy attacking from left rear.

12.Noon.   Message received from G.O.C. 166th, which informed his Infty that the Cavalry would only assist him to get his objectives and that he must arrange to take over the whole of his new frontage and release the Cavalry.

12.3.p.m.   Telephonic conversation with 4th Cav. Divn. informing them of arrangement to co-operate with the Infantry in their attack.

12.7.p.m.   Conversation confirmed.

12.45.p.m.   Message received from 2nd Lancers by lamp to effect that Colonel TURNER had been killed or wounded in advance, and that M.G.reinforcements were required.

12.50.p.m.   O.C. 11th M.G.Squadron informed and a reinforcement of Machine Gunners sent up.
They were unable to get through and remained with the Sqdn. C.I.H. who had been sent to reinforce 2nd Lancers.

1.0.p.m.   Message received from above sqdn. C.I.H. that they were held up and unable to advance, the enemy were coming down on their left and they were going to fall back on the Infantry strong post if necessary.

2.0.p.m.   Verbal message received to effect that attack in conjunction with Infantry had failed with heavy loss and that the enemy were strongly entrenched and had many machine guns in position

2.15.p.m.   Order received from 4th Cav. Divn. giving enemy's apparent main line of resistance. Our Horse Artillery continuing to bombard RAPERIE till 3.p.m. At which hour Lucknow Bde. to attack RAPERIE from the West and Mhow Bde. to endeavour to obtain possession of some of their original objectives and RAPERIE from the South with the whole Brigade dismounted. One Battery East of EPEHY to come under orders of Mhow Bde. Sialkot Bde. to act as a mounted reserve and take advantage of any success obtained.

2.20.p.m.	G.O.C. Mhow Bde. informed O.C. 38th C.I.H. of the attack at 3.p.m. and directed that the two squadrons in advance about X.27.central should co-operate in this attack and would be supported by 1 Sqdn. C.I.H. O.C. Inniskilling Dragoons was informed that in case of success of this attack his two squadrons would be required.
2.30.p.m.	Division informed of failure of attack in conjunction with Infantry and that total available force in hand of G.O.C. consisted of two weak squadrons Inniskilling Dragoons; 1 Sqdn. C.I.H. and 2 Machine Guns. Further that the enemy had been found to be extremely strong in machine guns and that with the small force available he felt he was unable to attack his original objectives with any hope of success.
2.30.p.m.	Message received from M.G.reinforcements that he was about .27.central with the leading dismounted Sqdn. C.I.H.
3.0.p.m.	Message received from 2nd Lancers that their line ran X.28. central to X.22.c.9.4.. German strong points at X.22.c.5.9. and X.21.c.8.0., Left flank very much in air, attack developing from Left.
3.10.p.m.	165th Infantry Bde. were informed by G.O.C. 166th that 2 Sqdns Cavalry were in posts about X.27.central. That he was being relieved by 110th Infty. Bde. that night and would ask this Bde. to relieve those Cavalry Posts and throw out a string of posts to join up with troops, believed Cavalry, in KILDARE Post and near ADELPHI. He also informed 165th that Mhow Bde. were unable to communicate with Cavalry in KILDARE and ADELPHE. That G.O.C. Mhow approved his suggestion and wished 165th in inform troops in KILDARE and ADELPHI and tell them to send their horses back to EPEHY.
3.10.p.m.	Officer Commanding the two squadrons that co-operated in the Infantry attack at 1.p.m., was ordered to send back the M.G. reinforcement with him. And that he would remain in his present position until relieved by the Infantry in the evening.
3.25.p.m.	Following received from 2nd Lancers. :- "Sqdn. of C.I.H. not arrived. AAA Some pressure on my Left flank and Left rear. AAA Total strength 2nd Lancers and T.F. about 200, position as before". Sent off 3.10.p.m.
6.0.p.m.	Intimation received from 166th Infty Bde. that 165th were dealing with situation at KILDARE.
6.5.p.m.	Permission obtained from 166th Bde to withdraw three advanced sqdns of 38th C.I.H.
7.0.p.m.	3 Sqdns. C.I.H. rejoined remainder of regiment in Square E.6.d. (62.c).
8.40.p.m.	Orders received fro Mhow Bde. to be withdrawn from the line after handing over positions to the Infantry and then to bivouac in E.17. and be prepared to act as a reserve if required.
9.15.p.m.	Major KNOWLES D.S.O. 2nd Lancers reported at Bde. H.Q. that 2nd Lancers and 1 Sqdn. Inniskilling Dragoons had been relieved and had moved into Camp in E.6.d.
2nd Dec. 1.0.a.m.	Intimation received of expected heavy Enemy attack on sector GONNELIEU - LA VACQUERIE. Troops warned to be on the alert.
6.0.a.m.	Brigade Report Centre established at ST EMILIE.
9.45.a.m.	Orders received to form Mhow Bde into a Dismounted Battn. to act as a Reserve to 4th Dismounted Bde. In the event of its being required, to proceed to Southern exit of EPEHY and thence to Railway cutting in X.25.a. - W.24.d.

P.T.O.

COPY.   (Supplied by Major S.E. Harvey 21/3/27).

OPERATIONS CARRIED OUT BY MHOW CAVALRY BRIGADE
ON DECEMBER 1st 1917.

The following order was received by the Brigade at
2.50 a.m. on the morning of December 1st 1917 :-

"4th Cavalry Division Order No. 22.   1. 12. 17.

Reference 1/40,000 Sheets 62.c. and 57.c.

1.   The enemy's line is approximately (Sheet 57.c) X.29.
VAUCELETTE FARM - R.31.
      5th Cavalry Division (with Lucknow Brigade attached)
is to attack VILLERS GUISLAN and GAUCHE WOOD /to-day/ at 6.30 a.m.,
co-operating with 14 Tanks. At 6.30 a.m. 6 tanks are
to cross a line from VAUCELETTE FARM to CHAPEL HILL
in their advance on VILLERS GUISLAN, and 8 tanks a North
and South line through W.12.Central (57.c.) for the
attack on GAUCHE WOOD.

2.   4th Cavalry Division (less Lucknow Brigade) will
assemble West of PEIZIERE as below with the object of
taking advantage of the advance of the tanks and seizing
VILLERS Ridge (X.10) (Sheet 57.c.).

      Mhow Brigade plus one troop Field Squadron. W.30.a.
                                                   and b.
      R.H.A. Brigade. W.29.b.) Sheet 57.c.
      Sialkot Brigade. W.29.a.)
                       and c.)
      Field Squadron (less 1 troop) E.5.a.

3.   G.O.C. Mhow Brigade will arrange :-

      (a) To have reconnaissance made of crossings through
           a line of our wire just East of PEIZIERE.
      (b) To keep close liaison with the Tank Attack.

4.   (a) As soon as a suitable opportunity presents itself, Mhow Brigade will move forward to seize and establish itself on the VILLERS Ridge, about X.10. Measures
must be taken to watch the right flank.

     (b) R.H.A. Brigade will support the advance to and
occupation of the above objective from about X.19.a. and
c. (57.c.).

     (c) Sialkot Brigade will, under Divisional Orders,
be moved forward as required.

5.   Pack Mounted Sections, C.F.A. will join Brigades
forthwith. C.F.A's (less Pack Mounted Sections) will
be with Divisional "A" Echelon, which will remain in
present area till further orders.

6.   Signal communications will be established as soon
after the advance of Mhow Brigade as possible to the
Ridge N. of PEIZIERE.

7.   At 6.0 a.m. Divisional Advanced Report Centre will
open near 5th Cavalry Division Report Centre in E.4.d.
(62.c.).

ACKNOWLEDGE.

issued at 2.0 a.m.

On this, orders were issued for the Brigade to move off at
5.30 a.m. and concentrate in the low ground N. and N.W. of
PEIZIERE.
The Brigade was concentrated in this area by 6.30 a.m. and from
this hour onwards were under pretty heavy fire, (H.E., timed
H.E. and Shrapnel). Some casualties occurred to men and horses.

The G.O.C. then explained to Commanding Officers the plan of
action he proposed in accordance with 4th Cav.Div.Order No. 22,
which was for the 2nd Lancers with 2 machine guns to gallop the
TARGELLE QUAIL and PIGEON Ravines and form a defensive flank
East and South East.

The Inniskilling Dragoons, as soon as the 2nd Lancers were
seen approaching their objective, were to advance down the
valley between QUAIL Ravine and the BEET FACTORY and establish
themselves on the VILLERS - GUISLAIN Ridge. Six machine guns
were placed at their disposal and also one Field Troop R.E.
38th C.I. Horse and 3 machine guns in reserve.

At 7.30 a.m. reports were received from the officers reconnoit-
ring the wire that exits existed on the PEIZIERE & VILLERS
GUISLAIN Road and also on the road running North East from
EPEHY.

At 8.10 a.m. The Tank Liaison Officers reported that the Tanks
had not arrived at their rendezvous and that consequently
Lucknow Brigade, who with the 5th Cav.Div. were to have attacked
VILLERS GUISLAIN and GAUCHE WOOD were not carrying out an
attack but were supporting our Infantry at VAUCELETTE Fme.
On this information it appeared that there was no chance of
using Mhow Brigade to seize the VILLERS GUISLAIN Ridge, since
the advance to this objective was to have been made on a suitable
opportunity presenting itself on the advance of the tanks and
the attack on GAUCHE WOOD and VILLERS GUISLAIN by the 5th
Cavalry Division (with Lucknow Brigade).

At 8.15 a.m. however an order arrived from the 4th Cav.Div.
as follows :- "You are to endeavour to push forward towards
"your objective supported by the Artillery....."
Commanding Officers came to Brigade H.Q. and the fresh situation
consequent on the non-arrival of the Tanks was explained.
It was decided that 2nd Lancers should advance by the road
running north-east from EPEHY this being less exposed to fire
from the direction of Villers Guislain during the earlier
stages of the advance.
One squadron of the Inniskilling Dragoons to follow by the
same route as the 2nd Lancers, the remaining 3 squadrons to
advance by the PEIZIERE - VILLERS GUISLAIN road and the valley
between the BEET FACTORY and QUAIL Ravine as soon as the 2nd
Lancers were seen to be approaching TAGELLE Ravine.

At 8.38 a.m. the 4th Cavalry Division were informed that the
Brigade were moving forward at once and that the Artillery had
been warned, and a request was made that the 5th Cavalry Divn.
might co-operate and attack VILLERS GUISLAIN.

About 9 a.m. the 2nd Lancers with 2 machine guns followed by
"C" Squadron Inniskilling Dragoons, moved off through PEIZIERE
and EPEHY villages, the hostile shelling in these two villages
at this time was extremely heavy.

The action of the Inniskilling Dragoons, less 1 squadron, but
plus four machine guns and a Field Troop R.E., may now be
dealt with :-
At 9.35 a.m. the 2nd Lancers were seen moving forward N.E. of
the 14 Willows: the Inniskilling Dragoons had been waiting for
this and the leading squadron, under Capt. BRIDGEWATER, immediately moved forward over the railway bridge and down the

PEIZIERE - VILLERS GUISLAIN Road. The Squadron under Capt.
MONCRIEFF which accompanied the 2nd Lancers was to have been
the leading squadron of the regiment but owing to strong enemy
forces on their left flank neither this squadron nor the 2nd
Lancers were able to enter the valley between QUAIL Ravine and
the BEET FACTORY. Consequently Capt. BRIDGEWATER'S Squadron
was leading the regiment and had four machine guns with it,
whereas it should have been the second squadron and the 4 machine
guns should have brought up the rear of the regiment, but by
mistake came in behind the leading squadron.
The leading squadron advanced at the gallop and soon came under
heavy machine-gun fire, from the flanks.
The remaining two squadrons following in line of troop columns
in extended order some 600 yards behind the leading squadron
likewise came under heavy machine-gun fire. In spite of this
however, all three squadrons, the machine gun section and
Field Troop R.E. most gallantly continued towards their objective.
The leading squadron, greatly depleted in numbers, continued
as far as the BEET FACTORY when a large force of the enemy were
seen to come in from all sides and surround them.
On seeing this and realizing the situation Lt.-Col. PATERSON,
D.S.O. commanding the regiment, ordered the two squadrons and
the Field Troop R.E. to retire on PEIZIERE, which operation
was successfully carried out.
Many acts of devotion and gallantry were carried out during
this retirement.
The losses were heavy, 6 officers and 96 rank and file of the
Inniskilling Dragoons being killed, wounded or missing.
Of the Section of Machine guns complete with personnel, not a
man returned.

The part taken by the column composed of the 2nd Lancers with
two machine guns and "C" squadron Inniskilling Dragoons with
two machine guns may be considered under three headings :-

(a) The advance to the German wire and occupation of the trench
and sunken road known as KILDARE Trench from X.22.c.9.1. to
X.28.central.

(b) The holding and defence of this position.

(c) The withdrawal after dark.

The 2nd Lancers with 2 machine guns ("C" squadron leading under
Major G. KNOWLES, DSO.,) followed by "C" squadron Inniskilling
Dragoons with two machine guns, moved off through PEIZIERE
and EPEHY at 9 a.m. and debouched from the latter village by
the road in F.1.b.
From this point the advance was made at the gallop, 'C' squadron
Inniskilling Dragoons being to the left rear of the 2nd Lancers
and somewhat on the flank.
The formation adopted was column of squadrons in line of Troop
Columns extended.
As the column moved forward at the gallop it soon came under
very heavy machine-gun fire from the front (KILDARE Trench),
from a German outpost position on the Right flank about
X.27.c.8.0. and from an old British Strong Point and trench
occupied by the Germans on the left flank about X.27.b.5.9.
The German outpost on the right flank almost immediately
retired, but reoccupied their position on being passed by.
The two leading squadrons galloped KILDARE Trench, some horses
passing through a gap in the wire, others actually jumping it.
This was a narrow belt of wire put up the night before by the
Germans. A few men led by Lieut. BRAODWAY crossed KILDARE
Trench, got through the wire on the other side and followed in
pursuit of the hostile Garrison who had started to retire as
the leading squadron reached the wire. Lieut. BRAODWAY

had already killed two Germans with the sword when he was treacherously killed by a revolver shot by a German officer, who raised one hand in token of surrender keeping the other behind his back. This German officer was immediately killed by a lance thrust from a man following Lieut. Broadway. This small party then returned to the position occupied by the remainder of the regiment and "C" Sqdn. Inniskilling Dragoons.
The position occupied being from X.22.c.9.1. to X.28.central, 'C' Squadron Inniskilling Dragoons being on the left flank. 15 Germans were killed with the "Arme blanche" and 20 to 30 knocked over by rifles and machine-gun fire when retiring from the position. Three light machine guns were left in the position by its retiring garrison, estimated at from 50 to 100 men of the 418th Regiment. Two prisoners were captured.

Lt.-Col. H.H.F. TURNER, commanding 2nd Lancers, was killed just after crossing the first belt of wire, west of KILDARE Trench. The horses of the two leading squadrons 2nd Lancers and of the leading troop of 'C' squadron Inniskilling Dragoons were got under cover in KILDARE LANE. There was no room for the remainder and they had to be sent back to PEIZIERE suffering heavily on the way from machine-gun fire.

The position was now as follows :-

A german position had been captured and was occupied by about 200 men 2nd Lancers, 36 men Inniskilling Dragoons, 4 machine guns, 11th M.G. squadron and in addition there were 169 horses in the position, which greatly interfered with the movement of the garrison and the evacuation of the wounded.

The holding and defence of the position gained.

Lieut.-Col. H.H.F. Turner, 2nd Lancers, having been killed, the organization and defence of the position devolved on Major G. Knowles, DSO., 2nd Lancers.
He disposed his force as follows:- From right to left. D. A. B. C. Squadrons, 2nd Lancers, "C" Squadron Inniskilling Dragoons, two machine guns on either flank, one of each subsection facing forward and the other to the rear.
'D' Squadron, 2nd Lancers, pushed out a post to the right flank and got into touch with the 1/6th King's Liverpool Regt. This afterwards proved of great value in getting up ammunition and bombs, evacuating wounded and eventually facilitating the withdrawal at night.
The infantry assisted materially in the evacuation of the wounded. On the extreme left flank 'C' Squadron Inniskilling Dragoons occupied KILDARE POST and a sap-head running out a short distance from it. This sap head was commanded on three sides from a Ridge under 100 yards distant, and the whole trench was enfiladed to the south from this spur.
To hold this, the flank nearest the enemy, a post with a machine gun was pushed out on to the ridge. The machine gun officer, Lieut. R. OAKLEY, and all the men soon became casualties. The machine gun had to be withdrawn, and it was not possible after this to leave the sap head. Owing to lack of space the sap head could only be occupied by two machine guns, two Hotchkiss Rifles and a few men. The enemy soon crawled up and enveloped this flank on three sides.
Fortunately several boxes of ammunition and bombs were found in the position, formerly a British one, and the machine guns, with a party filling belts, were able to check the repeated attempts of the enemy to crawl through the scrub and rush the sap head.

Unsuccessful in this, the enemy bombed his way down the communication trench from Limerick Post, this trench led into the main trench 50 yards south of the sap head.

A counter-bombing party was organized, bombs were fortunately at hand, also many German bombs, which after being experimented with were used. This party /was most gallantly led by a Corporal of the Inniskilling Dragoons who killed the leading German; bombs were, at the same time, thrown with much good effect that one German was blown off his feet above the level of the parapet and the remainder were in such a hurry to leave the trench that they came into the open under the fire of one of the sap head machine guns and were shot down. The enemy did not again attempt to approach the position by this trench.

Further attempts were made to reach the sap head from the ridge, but all were frustrated.

Had the enemy been able to gain the sap head the whole length of untraversed trench would have been enfiladed and the position would have been untenable. It was thanks to the machine guns and the magnificent way in which they were served and the fortunate finding of a considerable supply of ammunition in the position, that this did not occur.

Meanwhile the machine guns on the right flank had been firing short bursts on the ridge running east of LITTLE PRIEL FARM, and also on the ridge to the right rear on which small parties of the enemy were seen.

Shortly after reaching the position a considerable body of Germans was seen moving round to the left rear. Major SALKELD, 2nd Lancers, took his squadron out in skirmishing order to delay their advance and give time for the remainder of the garrison to organise the defence of both sides of the sunken road (KILDARE TRENCH).

The large party of Germans first seen moved northwards and disappeared, but a smaller party of about 60 was encountered and followed up at the double for about 300 yards until they took refuge in the western portion of KILDARE TRENCH and LIMERICK POST.

Some ten men of this party were seen to fall as the result of rifle fire.

Machine-gun fire was opened on the squadron from the position entered by the enemy and Major Salkeld withdrew his squadron about 100 yards and awaited developments.

The firing line of the enemy shortly advanced against this squadron, but withdrew on being fired on, losing a few men.

The squadron was then withdrawn to the sunken road bringing in some wounded from the original mounted advance of the regiment.

The casualties in Major Salkeld's squadron in this skirmish were 4 killed and 6 wounded.

During the morning preparations were made by Major Knowles, DSO., for a further advance, a track being cut in the wire on the western side of the position for this purpose.

Any thought of a further advance had, however, to be abandoned owing to the forced retirement of the 3 squadrons Inniskilling Dragoons from LINNET RAVINE and the precarious position of the left flank. The Germans brought heavy machine-gun fire to bear on the position most of the day and barraged the rear communications with H.E. Nothwithstanding this and also heavy machine-gun fire from both flanks on the way out and back, a sowar of the 2nd Lancers brought in two messages describing the situation to Bde. H.Q. He had three horses shot under him, but nevertheless was ready, and wished, to return to his regiment. Later Lieut. SMITH was able to establish Signal communication with Bde. H.Q.

The withdrawal from the position.

6.

Orders to withdraw from the position were received from G.O.C. 165th Infantry Bde. by Capt. WHITWORTH, 2nd Lancers, who twice went through a very heavy barrage of H.E. to give this Bde. information as to the state of affairs in KILDARE TRENCH.

The withdrawal was rendered difficult owing to the congested state of the sunken road, 169 horses were in it, some of them wounded, and owing to the narrowness of the road only one horse at a time could be led out, as the only exit was from the southern end of the position. The covering of the retirement was entrusted to "E" Squadron Inniskilling Dragoons, who most ably carried out their task. Very lights were fired frequently from the sap head and succesive covering positions were taken up until all the wounded and horses had been withdrawn.

Major Knowles, DSO., was wounded during the advance to the position, but notwithstanding this conducted the organization and defence of the position. He has since been evacuated.

No praise is too high for the conduct of all ranks during the whole operation.

The total casualties were :-

	KILLED.			WOUNDED.		
	B.O's	I.O'S	I.O.R's.	B.O's.	I.O's.	I.O.R's.
2nd Lancers	2	1	5		1	1	42

				MISSING.		
				B.O's.	I.O's.	I.O.R's.
-do-				1	1	48

	Killed.		Wounded.		Missing.	
	B.O's.	O.R.	B.O's.	O.R.	B.O's.	O.R.
'C' Sqdn. Inniskilling Dragoons	-	1	-	5	-	5
Section 11th M.G.Squadron.	-	2	1	9	-	1

Operations by 38th C.I. Horse on Dec. 1st 1917.

At 10.10 a.m. G.O.C. Mhow Bde. decided to send two squadrons 38th C.I. Horse to the support of the 2nd Lancers and 'C' Sqdn. Inniskilling Dragoons.

Two squadrons moved off through PEIZIERES and EPEHY closely followed by Bde H.Q. and the remainder of the Central Indian Horse. Just as the leading squadrons had moved off a Non-commissioned officer of 'C' Squadron Inniskilling Dragoons came in with a report of the situation: on this the two leading squadrons were halted in EPEHY, and an officers' patrol was sent off to try and find a more southerly route than fallen tree road by which it might be possible to go mounted to the assistance of our troop in KILDARE Trench. The patrol reported having come under heavy machine-gun fire and that it would be impossible to advance mounted. On this "D" squadron, dismounted, under command of Lieut. PAGE was sent off with the object of gaining touch with the troops in KILDARE trench and connecting up their left flank with the Infantry posts in rear.

The right half squadron advanced up to a little south of C.20 Cen. where they were held up by heavy-machine-gun fire and unable to advance further, they were also unable to retire and had to remain here till after dark.

The left half squadron advanced up to about X.26.b.8.0

where they took up a position.

About 11.45 a.m. a mounted patrol of two men was sent to ascertain if the Western portion of KILDARE Trench was occupied by the enemy. This patrol galloped up to the trench and crossed it, pretending not to see the Germans, who let them go by. They then turned about and galloped back under heavy machine-gun fire and rifle fire. They reported that the trench was strongly held by the Germans and that they had seen at least one machine gun and what looked like several automatic rifles.

At 11.30 a.m. G.O.C. Mhow Bde. conferred with G.O.C. 166th Infantry Brigade and arranged to lend him two dismounted squadrons of the Central India Horse to assist him in an attack he was making on the MEATH - CATELET line at 1 p.m.

Captain Daunt and Lieut. Woodhouse Commanding A and C Squadrons then went to confer with O.C. 1/5th King's Own Regt.

The attack took place at 1 p.m. after very slight artillery preparation, the objective of these two squadrons being the Western portion of Kildare Trench.

The attack was made over the open, a small trench in front of Kildare Trench was entered and its occupants driven out and back to the main trench in rear. The attack was then held up by heavy machine-gun fire and no further advance was possible.

Of the six British officers with A and C Squadrons and half of D Squadron which also joined in the attack, Captain Cameron, M.C. and Lieut. Pinney were killed and Lieuts Woodhouse, Page and Milner were wounded.

At 2.15 p.m. an order was received from 4th Cavalry Division ordering Lucknow Bde to attack the Raperie from the west and MHOW Bde to endeavour to obtain possession of some of their original objectives and the Raperie from the south with the whole brigade dismounted. One battery east of Epehy to come under the orders of MHOW Bde.

4th Cavalry Division were informed that the total available force in the hand of G.O.C. Mhow Cav. Bde. consisted of two weak squadrons Inniskilling Dragoons, 1 squadron C.I.H. and two machine guns. G.O.C. Mhow Cav. Bde then informed Lt.-Col. Browne, commanding 38th C.I.Horse of the attack planned for 3 p.m. and directed that the two squadrons in advance about X.27.central should co-operate in this attack and that they should be supported by 1 squadron C.I.H. O.C. Inniskilling Dragoons was informed that in case of success in this attack, the remains of his two squadrons would act mounted.

At 3 p.m. no attack appeared to develop on the left flank and as the 2 advanced squadrons of the Central India Horse were under heavy machine gun fire and unable to advance. The squadron of the Central India Horse in the hands of the G.O.C. was not sent forward.

At 6.5 p.m. permission was obtained from G.O.C. 166th Infantry Bde to withdraw the three advanced squadrons of the Central India Horse. The withdrawal was successfully carried out, but before retiring an Indian officer and some other ranks had been buried and all other killed and wounded brought in.

Too much cannot be said of the spirit and conduct of all ranks of the Central India Horse throughout the day.

12.15 p.m. Intimation received that 1st Cavalry Division would
            relieve 4th and 5th Cav.Divns. in the line that
            night.

11.10 p.m. Orders received to move back to Athies area next morning.

3rd Dec.

9 a.m.   Brigade moved off.

1 p.m.   Arrived in billets.

****

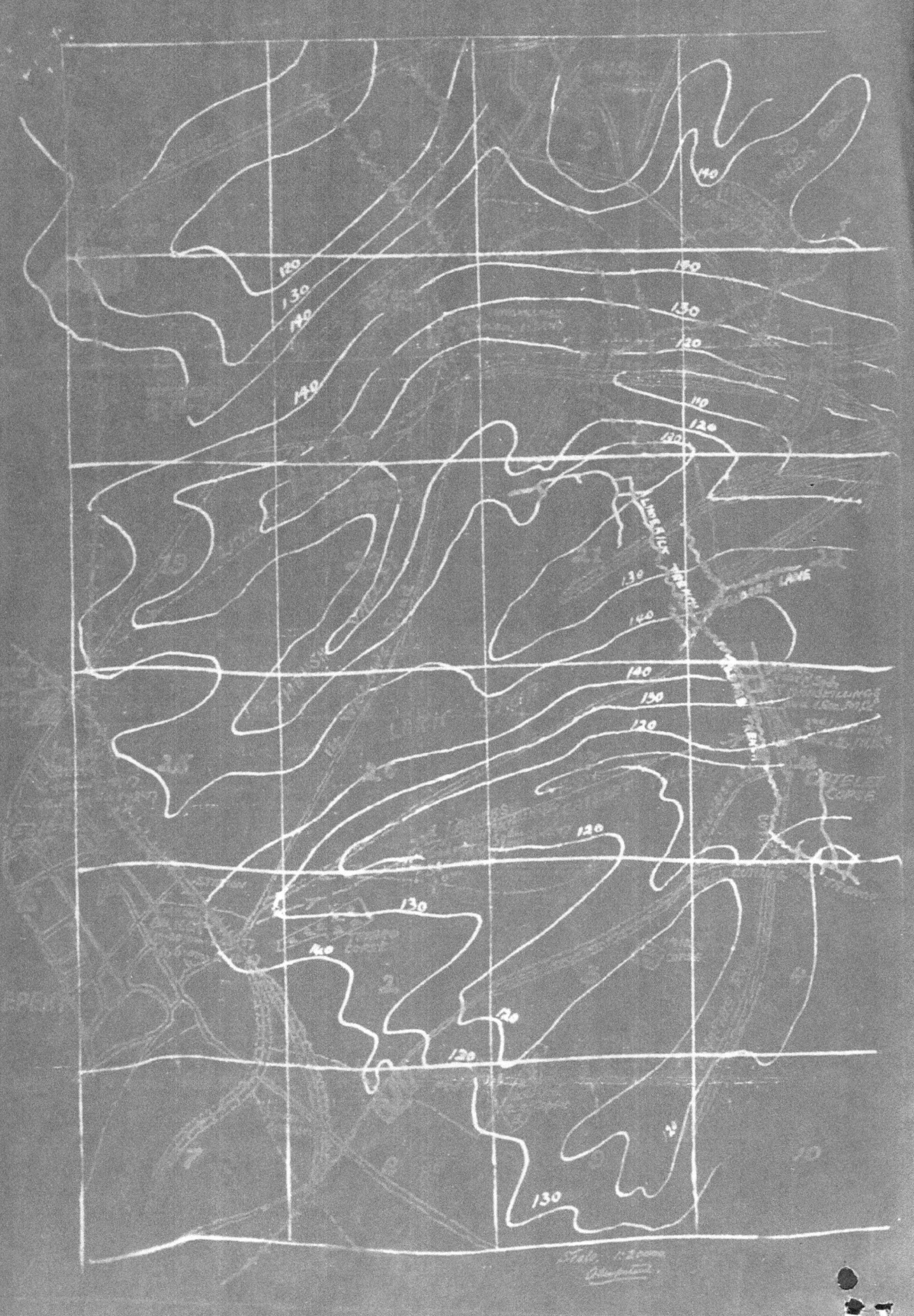

CONFIDENTIAL.

WAR DIARY.

of

Headquarters.

MHOW CAVALRY BRIGADE.

from 1-1-18.   to 31-1-18.

****

4 DIV

Army Form C. 2118.

WAR DIARY
INTELLIGENCE SUMMARY.
(Erase heading not required.)

Headquarters Indian Cavalry Bde

Place	Date	Hour	Summary of Events and Information	Remarks and references to Appendices
ENNEMAIN. JANY. 1918.	1st.	6 am	Party of 4 B.O.s = 250 men moved up to Camp near VENDELLES for 3 days for work under C.R.E. Cavalry Corps.	W/w W/w
	2nd.	6.30 am	Party 3 B.O.s and 400 men proceeded by lorry for work near JEANCOURT.	W/w W/w
	3rd.	7.30 am	Party of 2 Officers - 150 men Inniskilling Drs. proceeded by lorry for work near JEANCOURT.	W/w W/w
		12.30 pm	" " 2 B.O.s. 31. O.s. 150 men 2nd Lancers " " " " " BIHECOURT.	S.C.H.
	4th.		Similar parties to above from 38th C.I.H. & Inniskilling Drs. went up for work.	
	5th.		Similar parties from 2nd Lancers and 38th C.I.H. for same work.	S.C.H.
	6th.		Similar parties from 2nd Lancers and Inniskilling Drs to same work and in addition 1 B.O. + 50 men from 2nd Lancers and 2.B.O.s + 50 men from 38th C.I.H proceeded by lorry to HERVILLY to work at dug outs under R.E. Tunnelling Coy.	S.C.H.
	7th.		Parties similar to those found on 4th and 5th insts went up for work from 38th C.I.H.	S.C.H.
	8th.		and Inniskilling Drs	S.C.H.
	9th.		Similar parties to those found on 7th inst. went up from 2nd Lancers + 38th C.I.H.	S.C.H.
			Similar parties from Inniskilling Drs and 2nd Lancers	S.C.H.
	10th.	7.30 am	Party of 1 B.O. and 150 men found by 38th C.I.H. for work at JEANCOURT was dismissed as roads were impassable owing to Snow, to barrier.	
		11.30 am	1.B.O. + 150 men from Inniskilling Drs proceeded by lorry for work near BIHECOURT.	S.C.H.
	11th.		Party of 1 B.O. + 150 men found by each of 2nd Lancers + 38th C.I.H. for work as above	S.C.H.

Army Form C. 2118.

WAR DIARY
INTELLIGENCE SUMMARY.
(Erase heading not required.)

Headquarters Mhow Cavalry Bde

Instructions regarding War Diaries and Intelligence Summaries are contained in F. S. Regs., Part II. and the Staff Manual respectively. Title pages will be prepared in manuscript.

Place	Date	Hour	Summary of Events and Information	Remarks and references to Appendices
	12th	7am	Draw Scheme in function. Similar working parties from Inniskillings D'ns and 2nd Lancers proceeded mounted to same places. horses remaining in forward area until party returned at 5 p.m.	S/H
	13th	7am	Inniskilling D'ns & 38th C.I.H. each found 100 men plus horseholders to work at BIHECOURT.	S/H
		2.45pm	Dn Corps Commander inspected medal ribbons to Cross NCOs & men H.Q. Car D'nd ENNEMAIN	S/H
	14th	7am	2nd Lancers & 38th C.I.H. each found 100 men who proceeded by lorry to work at BIHECOURT.	S/H
			Officer 25 R.S & Inf'y went with line under Dismounted Division.	S/H
	15th	7am	Inniskillings found 200 men for work at BIHECOURT again. Horses back.	S/H
		7am	2nd Lancers found 150 men & a 38th C.I.H. 100 men who proceeded mounted to BIHECOURT.	S/H
	16th	7am	38th Lancers Capt'n proceeded mounted for work near BIHECOURT.	H/H
	19th	7am	200 men 2nd Lancers proceeded mounted for work near JEANCOURT, Inniskilling Gun Carried Hotchkiss Rifle firing Ect near LIECOURT. 40 men Inniskillings to man M.G.S'n went & HERVILLY.	H/H
	20th	7am	Similar party went to BIHECOURT found by 38th Q.H. one. 2nd Lancers carried out Hotchkiss Rifle firing near LIECOURT.	H/H
	21st	7am	100 men Inniskilling D'ns & 100 men 2nd Lancers proceeded mounted for work near JEANCOURT. 38th Qtr.	H/H
			carried out Hotchkiss D'n. firing 100 mtr. 38th Q.H. one proceeded mounted for work near BIHECOURT.	H/H
	22nd	1pm	100 men Inniskilling D'ns 100 mtr.	H/H
	23rd	7am	200 men 2nd Lancers proceeded by lorry to work near BIHECOURT.	H/H
	24th	7am	100 men Inniskilling Dn, 100 men 2nd Lancers proceeded by lorry to work near Jeancourt.	H/H
		1pm	350 men 38th C.H.one proceeded by lorry to work near BIHECOURT.	H/H
	25th	9am	Draught Inds Cond'n and Dism'td. Regim'l Cmdrs. went up & reconnoitred the line preparatory to taking over the entire relief Cavalry Corps front.	H/H

A 5834 Wt.W4973/MC87 750,000 8/16 D. D. & L. Ltd. Form/C2118/13.

WAR DIARY
INTELLIGENCE SUMMARY.
(Erase heading not required.)

Army Form C. 2118.

Headquarters Milton Gar. Bn.

Place	Date	Hour	Summary of Events and Information	Remarks and references to Appendices
ENNEMAIN	26th.	2pm	1 Offr. 25 men working in relief of working party 1 B.O. 25 men Duchesne 3 Pkt. H.Q. proceeded to HERVILLY in relief of Inniskilling party from Inniskilling Bns. on Intermediate Line.	Ml.
	27th.	6am	Above party proceeded to work on Intermediate Line.	
		2pm	Milton Bde. Trench party at 210 N.C.O's and men per regt. under O.C. L Patrison Bt. O. proceeded to Coy. H.Qrs. French Relief. 2 Officers 235 men both Infy. Bn. accompanying them.	Ml.
	28th.	8.30pm	Relief of Bde. returned by Gadbrit in Intermediate Line and moved into Front Line, relief completed 10.55pm.	Ml. Ml.
	29th.	6.30a.t.	Trench routine.	

Wheeler Major
B.M. Major
Milton Garrison Brigade

CONFIDENTIAL.

WAR DIARY
of
H.Qr. Mhow Cavalry Bde

~~1st Ind~~ Cav Div
4 Cav Div
Box 867

From. 1st February 1918. to 28th Bebruary 1918.

Army Form C. 2118.

WAR DIARY
INTELLIGENCE SUMMARY.
(Erase heading not required.)

Instructions regarding War Diaries and Intelligence Summaries are contained in F.S. Regs., Part II. and the Staff Manual respectively. Title pages will be prepared in manuscript.

4 CAN DIV   BOX 867
ADD 1st IND CAN DIV

Place	Date	Hour	Summary of Events and Information	Remarks and references to Appendices
CENTRE SECTOR CAV. CORPS FRONT	Feb.			
FEBRUARY			Remainder HET RAM and Jemadar JANG BAHADUR SINGH 2nd Lancers wounded. 1.1.0.R. 38th. C.I. Horse killed.	Ely.
	2nd.	11.30pm	MHow Dismounted Brigade relieved by SIALKOT Dismounted Brigade. 1.1.0.R. 2nd Lancers wounded.	Ely.
	4th.		Remilda MUKAND SINGH 2nd Lancers wounded.	Ely. Ely.
	6A.		I. Indian O.R. 38th Q.I.M. wounded.	Ely.
	8th.		MHow Dismounted Bde. relieved SIALKOT Dismounted Bde. in front line. 1 Inniskilling Dns. on Right. 2nd Lancers in Reserve, 38th C.I.Horse on the Left. Relief completed 10.30 pm	Ely.
	11th.		I.O.R. Inniskilling Dns. killed.	Ely. Ely.
	11th. 9am		General Briel Hg. Corps. and Staff relieved by Br. Genl. Beatty, & Staff.	Ely.
CROIX CELES AREA	12th.		Inniskilling Dns. relieved in front line by 17th. Lancers.	Ely.
	13th.		Orders received for relief of French partie. Indian cyts. between block area but Inniskilling Dns. to remain for fyfry.	Ely.
	14th.		3. O.Rs Inniskilling Dns. killed. 1.O.R wounded all accidentally.	Ely. Ely.
	15th. 7pm		2nd Lancers & C.I.H. French partie rejoined the Brigade.	Ely.

Army Form C. 2118.

WAR DIARY
or
INTELLIGENCE SUMMARY
(Erase heading not required.)

Instructions regarding War Diaries and Intelligence Summaries are contained in F.S. Regs., Part II. and the Staff Manual respectively. Title pages will be prepared in manuscript.

Place	Date	Hour	Summary of Events and Information	Remarks and references to Appendices
COURCELLES AREA. 1Bde.			40 men from each 2nd Lancers C.I.H. left for Ind. Ad. Base Depot. 75 men rejoined from 238th. Travelling Coy. HERVILLY.	
	22nd.	4.20 p.m.	3 B.Os. 1 B.O.R. 3 I.Os. 110 I.O.Rs. 4 followers 2nd Lancers, 2 B.Os. 1 B.O.R. 3 I.Os. 101 I.O.Rs. 3 followers 38th.C.I.Horse. 11 I.O.Rs. M.V.S. left by train for TARANTO.	
	23rd.	4.20 p.m.	10 I.O.R. 2nd Lancers, 1 B.O. 10 I.O.R. 36th.Cav. " "	
	24th.	4.20 p.m.	1 B.O. 25 I.O.R. 2nd Lancers. 2 B.Os. 1 B.O.R. 36th.Cav. & 4 I.Os. in each. can. left by train for TARANTO.	
	26th.	5 a.m.	11th. M.G.Sqn. completed proceed by march route to join 1st.Cav. Div.	
	28th.	1 p.m.	1 B.O. 2 I.Os. 58 I.O.Rs. 2nd Lancers, 6 I.Os. & 91 I.O.R. 38th.C.I.Horse left for TARANTO. Dismantling Bde. proceed to VAUCHELLES LES DOMART area to come under orders of AMBALA Cav. Bde.	

E. Gwladys "n"
Bt.Lt.Major
Mhow Cavalry Brigade

1.3.18.

Army Form C. 2118.

WAR DIARY
or
INTELLIGENCE SUMMARY.
(Erase heading not required.)

Instructions regarding War Diaries and Intelligence Summaries are contained in F.S. Regs., Part II. and the Staff Manual respectively. Title pages will be prepared in manuscript.

4 DIV / H.Q. Mhow Cav Bde.

Place	Date	Hour	Summary of Events and Information	Remarks and references to Appendices
POIX	MARCH 1918 1st		R.H.H.R. moved from COURCELLES to POIX.	
		11am	Remy entrained SALEUX for TARANTO 1 S.O., 21 O.Rs. 36 I.O.Rs. 2nd Lancers 31 O.S. + 36 I.O.Rs. 38th C.I.H. one.	Mr.
	2nd	11.30am	1 S.O., 57 O.Rs. & 7 animals Ambth Cav. Fd. Amb. & 4 BGR. Personals MHOW M.V.S. Lift.	Mr.
	3rd		SALEUX for TARANTO. 11 horses from 2nd Lancers + 52 horses from 38th C.I.H. transferred to Lucknow Bde. to complete them prior to departure for MARSEILLES.	S.C.H.
	4th		12 horses transferred from Divl. H.Q. to 2nd Lancers to replace above.	S.C.H.
	6th		33 horses transferred from Bde H.Q. & Signal troop to 2nd Lancers.	S.C.H.
	26th		2nd Lancers entrained SALEUX for MARSEILLES.	S.C.H.
	27th		38th C.I.H., details of Bde. H.Q. and M.V.S. entrained SALEUX for MARSEILLES.	S.C.H.

S.C. Hamed Capt.
for Bde Major.
Mhow Cav. Bde.

G.S.B.

1917
4TH CAVALRY DIVISION
MHOW CAVALRY BRIGADE

'A' BATTERY R.H.A.

JAN - NOV 1917

(DEC MISSING)

SERIAL NO. 4

Confidential
War Diary
of

"A" BATTERY, ROYAL HORSE ARTILLERY.

FROM 1st JANUARY 1917 **TO** 31st JANUARY 1917

Confidential

Army Form C. 2118.

WAR DIARY
or
INTELLIGENCE SUMMARY.
(Erase heading not required.)

January. 17.

Instructions regarding War Diaries and Intelligence Summaries are contained in F. S. Regs., Part II. and the Staff Manual respectively. Title pages will be prepared in manuscript.

Place	Date	Hour	Summary of Events and Information	Remarks and references to Appendices
Molliens-aux-Bois	1st		Cleaned up, battery preparatory to march.	MyH
	2nd		Adjutant de Leoube joined.	
Molliens-aux-Bois	3rd		Marched to LONGPRÉ via VILLERS BROCAGE – BERTANGLES – ST SAUVEUR and thence down left Bank of SOMME. Horses under cover.	MyH
LONGPRÉ	4th		Marched out at 9 a.m. and continued along S bank of SOMME, turning S near LIERCOURT, thence via HUPPY to TOEUFLES. Horses mostly in the open.	MyH
TOEUFLES	5th	9.30 a.m.	Marched to SALLENELLE via ACHEUX - FRANLEU - ARREST and PENDÉ	MyH
			Billets taken over from "Q" Bty. Dr Mudd joined. Dr Gorringe joined.	MyH
SALLENELLE	8th		Took over 13 hrs at WOINCOURT and returned 18 hrs	MyH
"	12th		Dr Billings to hospital	MyH
"	13th		Dr Ludlow Joined Gun D carry to hospital.	MyH
"	14th		Dr Kingdon to hospital	MyH
"	15th		2/Lt Crofton + 2/Lt Hayley went for a course at RHA School.	MyH
"	26th		Br Branch to hospital.	MyH

My Howard R/H Capt "D" Bty (The Chestnut Troop) to O.C. "D" Bty.

SERIAL No. 4.

Mhow Bde
4th Can Div

"A" Battery, Royal Horse Artillery

1st to 28th February 1917.

WAR DIARY or INTELLIGENCE SUMMARY

Army Form C. 2118.

FEBRUARY 1917

Place	Date	Hour	Summary of Events and Information	Remarks and references to Appendices
SALLENELLE	1/2/17	—		
Do Do	2 & 3		2nd Lieut J C Ellis, having been attached to Divisional Infantry staff at S[?]H.Q. H.Q, his name was struck off the strength of the Bty [?] Bty R.F.A. to "A" Bty R.H.A. [?]	
Do Do	6		O.C. Wed posted from Bty R.F.A.	
" "	26	1.50 am	Others received to be in readiness to march owing to retirement of Germans in front of 4th Army [?]	
" "		7 AM	Shells from Sallenelle & [?] opened up with Puchevitz Pass at [?] MOYENNEVILLE and from there marched to HAVERNAS and billeted [?]	
HAVERNAS	27		Remained in billets at Havernas.	
ALBERT	28	9 am	heads from HAVERNAS & I am with Puchevitz Posts & [?] bivouacked at Prisoners of War Camp on Western outskirts of ALBERT. [?]	

Wt. W10791/1773 500,000 1/15 D.D. & L. A.D.S.S./Forms/C. 2118.

Serial No: 4.

"A" Battery, R.H.A.

From 1st to 31st March, 1917.

Army Form C. 2118.

WAR DIARY
or
INTELLIGENCE SUMMARY.
(Erase heading not required.)

March 1917

Instructions regarding War Diaries and Intelligence Summaries are contained in F. S. Regs., Part II. and the Staff Manual respectively. Title pages will be prepared in manuscript.

Place	Date	Hour	Summary of Events and Information	Remarks and references to Appendices
ALBERT (PRISON CAMP)	1st		2nd Lieut Ford Commissioned and posted to 161st Division	MW
"	2nd		Capt Ransom admitted to Hospital	MW
"	3rd		Marched to BONNEVILLE at 2 pm via TALMAS and HAVERNAS	MW
"	4th		In billets. Horses under cover. Attached LUCKNOW Bde. H.Q. at CANAPLES.	MW
BONNEVILLE	5th			
"	9th		Marched about 9 am to St OUEN via CANAPLES.	MW
St OUEN	10th		Dr Bullock admitted to hospital. Cpl Rendle posted to D.A.C. Lts Crofton and Hayley went forward to reconnoitre	MW
"	15th		Orders at 10 am to move to AVELUY. Arrived about 9 pm	MW
"	17th		Marched at 5 am leaving B Echelon with regt, kits etc. Marched via MIRAUMONT, IRLES encountering difficulty in valley 1 mile NW of IRLES. Thence along GREVILLERS road	
AVELUY	18th		cutting across country to ACHIET-LE-GRAND. Erased railway at ACHIET-LE-GRAND. Concentrated with LUCKNOW Bde at LOGEAST WOOD. At 5 pm Brigade moved to GOMMIE COURT and at 6.30 am battery came into action just W of ERVILLERS. Captain Howard & Lt West reported from B.C's Overseas course and RHA School respectively.	MW

1577 Wt.W10791/1773 500,000 1/15 D. D. & L. A.D.S.S./Forms/C. 2118.

Army Form C. 2118.

WAR DIARY
or
INTELLIGENCE SUMMARY.
(Erase heading not required.)

Instructions regarding War Diaries and Intelligence Summaries are contained in F.S. Regs., Part II. and the Staff Manual respectively. Title pages will be prepared in manuscript.

Place	Date	Hour	Summary of Events and Information	Remarks and references to Appendices
	19th		Remained in action near ERVILLERS till about 3pm when Battery advanced to action near MORY copse. Heavy rain.	M/A
	21st		Lt Evans left to join 20th Divison. Lt Newth joined. 1 Horse died	M/A
	22nd		Wagon line moved back to ERVILLERS. 1 horse died	M/A
ERVILLERS	23rd		Dungeoned as Cerestro - Spenet - Hervergeles	M/A
"	25th		1 horse died.	M/A
"	27th		1 horse died	M/A
"	29th		1 horse died	M/A
"	30th		Travelling Horse Transport arrived with horse rugs. 1 horse died	M/A
"	31st		2 horses died	M/A

M N Nosend Capt. RHA.
Chestnut Troop RHA
for OC.

Serial No. 4

CONFIDENTIAL

WAR DIARY OF

"A" Battery R.H.A.

From 1-4-17. to 30-4-17.

"A" Battery R.H.A.

WAR DIARY
or
INTELLIGENCE SUMMARY

Army Form C. 2118.

April 1917

Place	Date	Hour	Summary of Events and Information	Remarks and references to Appendices
ERVILLERS	1st		Battery in action between ERVILLERS & ST LEGER. Wagon lines at ERVILLERS	MGH
"	4th		At 9.0 pm guns were moved up to a position near ST LEGER	MGH
"	9th		Orders received at 1.30 am to withdraw from action & rendezvous with RHA Bde E of ERVILLERS. Heavy snow storms. At 7.0 am orders were received to return to wagon lines	MGH
"	10th		Marched at 3.30 am to same rendezvous as previous day. At 8.0 am battery moved on to MORY. Orders were received at 5.0 pm to return to wagon lines.	MGH
"	11th		Remained at wagon lines till 8.0 pm when guns returned into action at old position near ST LEGER. 18 horses evacuated.	MGH
"	15th		Moved to MIRAUMONT via ACHIET-LE-GRAND. Tents. Horses in the open.	MGH
MIRAUMONT	15th			
MAILLY-MAILLET	16th		Marched at 11.0 am to MAILLY-MAILLET. Billets. Some horses in stables.	MGH
SARTON	19th		Marched to billets at SARTON	MGH
"	23rd		25 horses evacuated to Mobile Veterinary Section	MGH
"	25th		55 remounts joined the battery.	MGH

M.G. Hinton
Capt. R.H.A.
for Major Cmdg A "Battery" R.H.A.

Serial No. 4.

"A" Battery, Royal Horse Artillery.

From 1st May to 30th June 1917.

Army Form C. 2118.

A.06.9 W.A.
Vol I

WAR DIARY
or
INTELLIGENCE SUMMARY.
(Erase heading not required.)

Instructions regarding War Diaries and Intelligence Summaries are contained in F. S. Regs., Part II. and the Staff Manual respectively. Title pages will be prepared in manuscript.

Place	Date	Hour	Summary of Events and Information	Remarks and references to Appendices
SARTON	1st		Horses in 9 long stables. Men billeted in village.	
	9th		Gr Quick rejoined from hospital	MyN
MEAULTE	12th		Moved at 10 am to MEAULTE via ACHEUX & MBERY	MyN
COURCELLES	13th		Marched at 10am via MERICOURT & PERONNE to COURCELLES. bivouac	MyN
"	15th		Draught of 15 men joined including QMS McColgan.	MyN
St CHRIST.	17th		Marched to Join Mhow Bde at St CHRIST. bivouac	MyN MyN
"	19th		Moved from St CHRIST to BOUCLY. bivouac	MyN MyN
BOUCLY	20th		3 guns moved into action near HEBECOURT.	
"	21st		3 guns went into action One section (Rt) being detached in a position	MyN
			a few hundred yards from the remainder.	MyN
"	22nd		Dr Buttock Joined	MyN
"	23rd		98 Remounts Joined	MyN
"	29th		6 Remounts Joined	MyN
"	29th		Dr Smart re-joined from 3rd DAC.	MyN MyN
"	30th		Gnr Webb wounded. 9 horses Joined from DAC.	

My Strange
Cap't.
for OC "A" Sty R170
RHA

Serial No: 4.

"A" Battery, Royal Horse Artillery.

From 1st to 31st July 1917.

Army Form C. 2118.

THE
CHESTNUT TROOP,
R.H.A.
Month......6......
Dated....1-7-17

WAR DIARY
or
INTELLIGENCE SUMMARY.
(Erase heading not required.)

Instructions regarding War Diaries and Intelligence Summaries are contained in F. S. Regs., Part II. and the Staff Manual respectively. Title pages will be prepared in manuscript.

Place	Date	Hour	Summary of Events and Information	Remarks and references to Appendices
BOUCLY	1st		Draft of 9 men joined. MGA	
"	6th		One Dr transferred, one joined. MGA	
"	25th		B.S.M. Hodges to Hospital. Sgt Tripp commissioned & posted to 1st Div Arty. MGA	
"	26th		Centre Section guns moved into action with R Section about 10 pm MGA	
"	27th		Three Signallers joined. MGA	
"	28th		S/N Higgins joined. MGA	
"	29th		S/N Stayley promoted a/Capt & posted to 30th Div. MGA	
			Left Section moved into action with remainder of Battery about 10 pm MGA	

MG Ansard
M/Sgt Capt RHA

Commndg. The Chestnut Troop, R.H.A.

Major, R.H.A.

Serial No: 4.

"A" Battery, Royal Horse Artillery.

From 1st to 31st August 1917.

A.Bty. RHA
Army Form C. 2118.

WAR DIARY
or
INTELLIGENCE SUMMARY.
(Erase heading not required.)

Place	Date	Hour	Summary of Events and Information	Remarks and references to Appendices
CARPEZA Copse	1st		Battery in action covering Mhow Bde till 6th then 35th Div. Wagon lines at BOUCLY.	MGH
	6th		Sgt Rotherham Commissioned & posted to 30th Div Artillery	MGH
	10th		Centre Tr moved from CARPEZA Copse to "D" Bty RCHA's position at VADENCOURT.	MGH
VADENCOURT	11th		Remainder of Battery moved to VADENCOURT arriving at new position about 3 am	MGH
	12th		Bty Wagon Lines remained at BOUCLY.	MGH
	16th		Br Grogan rejoined from DAC	MGH
	18th		Letter received from WO stating that 2nd Lt C. Neville was struck off the strength owing to ill health.	MGH
	28th		Lt Tr moved to a new position near VADENCOURT	MGH

M.H.Napier Major RHA
Capt. Chestnut Troop RHA
Comdg A Bty RHA

Army Form C. 2118.

"A" Bty, R.H.A.

WAR DIARY
or
INTELLIGENCE SUMMARY.

(Erase heading not required.)

Place	Date	Hour	Summary of Events and Information	Remarks and references to Appendices
VADENCOURT	1st		4 guns in action near Chan. Left section detached about 800" away.	
	5		No 1 gun moved into action near PONTRU Sniping.	
			Centre Section joins Left Section. No 2 gun made new pit and remains in old position.	
	11th			
	8.		Wagon line moved from BOUCLY to CAULINCOURT near CAULINCOURT.	
	22.		2/Lt Jackson joined from base.	
	28		Lt Johnston lent from "B" Bty R.H.A.	
	30		2/Lt Jackson posted to "O" Bty RHA	

31-8-18

"A" Bty. R.H.A.
Serial No. 4

WAR DIARY
or
INTELLIGENCE SUMMARY
(Erase heading not required.)

Army Form C. 2118.

Place	Date	Hour	Summary of Events and Information	Remarks and references to Appendices
VADENCOURT	5.9.17		2nd Lieut CASTELLI joined the Troop from England – in.	
"	23.9.17		Bty Comdr Xn returns to the Main Battery Position line	
"	24.9.17		MAIN took over Command of B22 Bde Right Group R.F.A, 34th Division the Group Commander having proceeded on leave – line	
"	26.9.17		A Schneider having been shelled their gun was moved to another position line	

Mn Carton Trick R.H.A
the Chestnut Troop R.H.A.

"A" Bty. R.H.A.

Army Form C. 2118.

(4)

WAR DIARY
or
INTELLIGENCE SUMMARY.

(Erase heading not required.)

October 1914

Place	Date	Hour	Summary of Events and Information	Remarks and references to Appendices
VRAIGNCOURT	1st		Battery in action. B subsection detached about 900' from Bty. Position. "A" Subsection forward near PONTRUE for sniping. About 100 rounds fired by "B" Sub per day.	Nil
	12th		A/I withdrew from action to wagon lines at COUVIGNY Fm.	Nil
	13th		Centre & Rt. Subs withdrew to wagon lines. Battery position dis handed Mft over to "A" Bty. 108 Bde.	Nil
	15th		B.S.M. Hodges R commissioned & posted to 56th D.A.	Nil
ATHIES	16th		Party of 30 men marched to ATHIES to prepare stables for Bty. Mft	Nil
	19th		Battery marched from COUVIGNY Fm to ATHIES. Mft	
	26th		All guns except "A" Subsection marched to 7th Corps range N.D. PERONNE to Calibrate. Heavy rain.	Nil

N.Y. Bryant. R.H.A.
Capt. for Major Rotter
Commanding "A" Bty R.H.A.
1-11-

Army Form C. 2118.

A Bty. R.H.A.

WAR DIARY
INTELLIGENCE SUMMARY.
(Erase heading not required.)

November 1917.

Place	Date	Hour	Summary of Events and Information	Remarks and references to Appendices
ATHIES	1st – 13th		In billets and stables at ATHIES.	Nil
VAUX WOOD	14th		Orders received to move to bivouac at MOISLAINS in VAUX Wood. Route DOINGT Mt ST QUENTIN. Troop arrive at bivouac about 8.30 p.m.	Nil
	16th		Guns & Wagons marched at 6pm via ETRICOURT, FINS, GOUZEAUCOURT to position just South of BEAUCAMP. Guns & ammunition dumped and camouflaged & guard of two men left. Battery returned to VAUX Wood about 3 am.	Nil
	17th		Lines of fire laid out. 18 wagon loads ammunition dumped during night making a total of about 900 rounds per gun.	Nil
BEAUCAMP	19th		Troop marched at 6pm via FINS to wagon lines near QUEENS CROSS. Detachments rode up to gun position. 2Lt Huggins with 86th Inf Bde 29th Div & Lt Johnston to do FOO & Liason respectively.	Nil
	20th	6.20am	Bombardment & attack opened.	
		7.20	Major Duffey, 2Lt Crofton went forward with party of Sappers to prepare route of advance for Troop via VILLERS PLOUICH and thence along HIGHLAND RIDGE.	
		10 am	Orders received at Wagon lines for Troop to advance. Slight Check in VILLERS PLOUICH due to congestion & also at bridge over rl. Nord Canal.	Nil

Army Form C.2118.

WAR DIARY
of
INTELLIGENCE SUMMARY.

NOVEMBER. 17

R/ Sheet 57.c 1/40,000

(Erase heading not required.)

Place	Date	Hour	Summary of Events and Information	Remarks and references to Appendices
	20th	12 noon	Troops came into action in position about L.32.c. MGM	
		12.30 p	Orders received to advance. Troops moved about 1pm, delayed by Tilly & by Trenches & cutting wire, and came into action about 2.30 pm in position about L.27.b. Q.85 on own left. Information being received that enemy still occupied RUMILLY, Troops moved under cover of ridge to about L.27.a. (Wagon lines (G.L. & FBW) at RIBECOURT 1st Line & Col Dr at near VILLERS PLOUICH	
	22.?		Troops took over position of 111th Battery SE of MARCOING about L.28.b. Horsy Snow Storm. Wagon lines remained at RIBECOURT. MGM	
MARCOING	25th		Rear lines moved back near DAC at 1st gun position MGM	
BEAUCHAMP	28th	6 p	Troops pulled out of action & returned via MARCOING & RIBECOURT to Van Hoya lines. MGM	
ATHIES	29th	9 am	Moved at 9 am via FINS, DOINGT, to dle billets at ATHIES arriving 2.30 pm. MGM	
VILLERS FAUCON	30th	9 am	Orders received to saddle up at once & rendez-vous at ESTREES.	
		12 noon	March with 16th RHA Bde via TINCOURT to bivouac at VILLERS-FAUCON. arriving about 9 pm.	
		7 pm	Information received that enemy had broken through as far as EPEHY & GOUZEAUCOURT Troops to march at 9 am.	

MG. Anson RHA Chief. H.Q.
Capt. Cust. Chief. H.Q.

(In amplification of Bde.O.O.No.1.)   Copy No.

APPENDIX 2

S E C R E T

MHOW Brigade Operation Order No.2.   28th September 1916

1. From today all map references will be to sheet 57c.1:40000, unless otherwise stated.

2. With reference to Bde.O.O.No.1.para 8, for "at Zero plus 1 hour" substitute "When the Infantry have reached their 2nd.Objective (Brown line given to all concerned)".

3. The Liaison Officer 2nd.Lancers (Lt.COMMELINE) will report to advanced H.Q.110th.Infty Bde. at Zero hour and will arrange mounted D.R.service between himself and H.Q.2nd.Lancers. He will keep O.C.2nd.Lancers informed of progress of Infantry and will particularly report immediately the Infantry have reached the Brown line. O.C.2nd.Lancers will repeat all reports to MHOW Bde. and to O.C.6th.Dragoons.

4. In addition to mounted D.R.service a line is being laid between Adv. H.Q.110th.Infty.Bde. and WATERLOT Fms., and Lt.Commeline will only use his mounted D.Rs. if this telephone communication is cut.

5. On receiving the report that Infantry have reached Brown Line, O.C.2nd. Lancers will order Major KNOWLES to move with his squadron to forward position selected in about S.12.b. and Major KNOWLES will himself report to Adv.H.Q.110th.Inf.Bde. and remain with them until the ultimate Inftry objective is reported captured, when he will decide the most favourable moment to advance. (xxxxxxxxxx Bde.O.O.No.1.para 12) Major KNOWLES will not advance from his forward position until the Inftry.have captured their ultimate objective beyond both LES BOEUFS and GUEUDECOURT.

6. When O.C.2nd.Lancers orders Major KNOWLES' squadron to forward position about S.12.b., O.C.6th.Dragoons will order Captain MONCRIEFF's squadron to move to their forward position about S.12.b.

7. When Major KNOWLES has reached Adv.H.Q.110th.Inf.Bde. he will employ Lt.COMMELINE to reconnoitre a route for his advance, and will ensure that mounted D.R.service is still existing between himself and Os.C. 2nd.Lancers and 6th.Dragoons. He will then also be in communication by direct telephone line and by visual signalling. One station to be arranged by him at the forward position of his squadron-One station to be arranged by Brigade Signal Troop near N.E.corner DELVILLE Wood, and one station at WATERLOT Fms. to be arranged by O.C.6th.Dragoons.

8. When Major KNOWLES decides to advance he will report by telephone "Am Advancing", he will use both Mounted D.R.and visual if telephone is cut and his report will be addressed MHOW Bde.,repeated 6th.Dragoons and 2nd.Lancers. When Major KNOWLES advances his visual station will be replaced by Signallers from Captain MONCRIEFF's Squadron.

9. Captain MONCRIEFF will arrange with his Liaison Group, which goes with Major KNOWLES, that he is informed immediately when it is possible for him to advance to GUEUDECOURT. He should not necessarily wait for a report that crossings are passable but should endeavour to time his movement to cross immediately after Major KNOWLES' Squadron 2nd.Lancers.

10. Immediately Captain MONCRIEFF decides to advance he will report "Am Advancing" addressed MHOW Bde.repeated 6th.Dragoons,2nd.Lancers by telephone, from H.Q. xxxxxx 110th.Inf.Bde., if possible, and if not by both Mounted D.R. and by visual.

11. On receipt of above message (para10) O.C.6th.Dragoons will at once advance with the remainder of his regiment, moving as close in rear of Captain MONCRIEFF's squadron as he considers advisable, and O.C.2nd. Lancers will follow 6th.Dragoons. O.C.6th.Dragoons will report to MHOW Bde. by telephone or by duplicated mounted D.R., the time at which he leaves his position about S.23.d., If message given in para 10 is not received by O.C.6th.Dragoons by 5.30.p.m. the movement detailed in para 11 will not take place.

4th Cav. Dv.
Mhow Cav. Bde

Diary Dec '17 of "A" R.H.A. is missing

to withdraw to this road.

The day therefore ended with the 127th Brigade on the Ribécourt - Beaucamp road with a right defensive flank back to the 125th Brigade on the Flesquières - Beaucamp Road.

Attack by 5th Division [1]

---

[1] The 5th Division still had four battalions in each brigade.

The objective that the 5th Division had first to gain was a trench which ran in a north-north-east direction and included Beaucamp and the high ground south of it. Though this was the first main objective of the division, it will be called here the second objective, because it was a prolongation of the second objective of the corps further north. The capture of this line entailed an advance of 1500 yards for the left brigade, but of only 500 yards for the right brigade (see map). An intermediate objective was therefore fixed for the left brigade on the western edge of Beaucamp, and this brigade was timed to arrive here at the same time that the right brigade reached the second objective. The left brigade would then pivot on its right and advance on the second and third objectives, the right brigade standing fast on the second objective which was to be

1917-18
4TH CAVALRY DIVISION
MHOW CAVALRY BRIGADE

2ND LANCERS

JAN 1917-MAR 1918

TO EGYPT   4 CAV DIVISION
            10 CAV BDE

SERIAL NO. 179

Confidential

War Diary

2ND LANCERS (GARDNER'S HORSE).

FROM 1st JANUARY 1917 **To** 31st JANUARY 1917

Army Form C. 2118

2nd Lancers

WAR DIARY
or
INTELLIGENCE SUMMARY.
(Erase heading not required.)

Instructions regarding War Diaries and Intelligence Summaries are contained in F. S. Regs., Part II. and the Staff Manual respectively. Title pages will be prepared in manuscript.

Place	Date	Hour	Summary of Events and Information	Remarks and references to Appendices
	9 Jan 17		Lieut R.P.L. RANKING, 5th Cavalry, reported his arrival at 6 p.m.	
	11		Pioneer Company left at 4.45 a.m. for work with the 1st ANZAC Corps near	
	26		MONDICOURT. 1 British Officer (Capt. ROBERTSON) and 20 O.R.) sent in chief to abysin party near MONDICOURT	
	28		CAPT D. E. WHITWORTH rejoined from M.G. SQDN at 12.30 P.M.	

H.M.Turner Lieut-Colonel
Commanding 2nd Lancers

T2134. Wt. W708—776. 500000. 4/15. Sir J. C. & 8.

SERIAL No. 179

CONFIDENTIAL.

WAR DIARY.

of

2nd Lancers. I.A.

From 1-2-17   To 28-2-17

Army Form C. 2118

WAR DIARY
or
INTELLIGENCE SUMMARY. 2nd Lancers

(Erase heading not required.)

Place	Date	Hour	Summary of Events and Information	Remarks and references to Appendices
LAUCHERET	3 Feb	10 a.m.	Relief party 21 I.O.R. and 1 B.O.R. under LIEUT E.W.D. VAUGHAN left for MONDICOURT in lorries. KEW	
LANGUEDOC	4 Feb	11 a.m.	A similar party to the above without an officer rejoined from the M.H.U.W. PIONEER BATTN at MONDICOURT. KEW	
"	13 Feb	10 a.m.	Relief party of 1 B.O., 2 B.O.R., & 20 I.O.R. left for Pioneer Coy in a lorry. KEW	
"	14 Feb	3 p.m.	A party, similar to the above, rejoined. KEW	
"	27 Feb	1 p.m.	LIEUT H.G. MONKS I.A.R.O. rejoined from No 11 M.G. Squadron KEW	

M J Wench
Lieut - Colonel
Commanding 2nd Lancers

WAR DIARY. Serial No. **179**.

Confidential

2ND LANCERS. (G.H.)

FROM 1-3-1917 TO 31-3-17.

Volume XIII.

Army Form C. 2118

WAR DIARY
or
INTELLIGENCE SUMMARY.
(Erase heading not required.)

2nd Lancers

Instructions regarding War Diaries and Intelligence Summaries are contained in F. S. Regs., Part II. and the Staff Manual respectively. Title pages will be prepared in manuscript.

Place	Date	Hour	Summary of Events and Information	Remarks and references to Appendices
LANCHERES	9/3/17	9 a.m.	A relief party of 3 I.O., 20 I.O.R. under Lieut E.W.D. VAUGHAN left in lorries for the Pioneer Coy at MONDICOURT.	
	10/3/17	4.30 p.m.	A party of 3 I.O., 1 B.O.R, 14 I.O.R. under 2nd Lieut. G.A.C. HEARCER rejoined from the Pioneer Coy.	
	12/3/17 1 p.m.		Lieut N.H. BROADWAY reported his arrival from ROUEN.	
	13/3/17 7 a.m.		Lieut P. BANERJEE I.M.S. left for the Pioneer Coy to relieve M.O. of C.I.H.	
	17/3/17 4 a.m.		Pioneer Coy - 4 B.O., 2 B.O.R., 5 I.O., 261 I.O.R. - returned in lorries from MONDICOURT.	
PT LAVIERS	19/3/17 11 a.m.		Marched from LANCHERES to PT LAVIERS.	
ST OUEN	20/3/17 11 a.m.		Marched from PT LAVIERS to ST OUEN	
AVELUY	21/3/17 9.45 a.m.		Marched from ST OUEN to AVELUY. The Regiment bivouacked at Square W.16.3 (Ref Sheet 57 D 1/40,000) at 8.20 p.m. B Echelon halted at HERISSART.	
	22/3/17		In bivouac at AVELUY. 2 Lieut B.C. WALLER left for Dismounted Men at MIANNAY.	
MIRAUMONT	29/3/17 10.45 a.m.		Marched to camp in bivouac to mile N.E. of MIRAUMONT.	

H.A. Turner Lt Col -
C.O. 2nd Lancers

Serial No. 179.

CONFIDENTIAL.

WAR DIARY OF

2nd Lancers

From 1-4-17.   to   30-4-17.

Army Form C. 2118.

WAR DIARY
of 2nd LANCERS
INTELLIGENCE SUMMARY.

(Erase heading not required.)

April 1917

Instructions regarding War Diaries and Intelligence Summaries are contained in F. S. Regs., Part II. and the Staff Manual respectively. Title pages will be prepared in manuscript.

Place	Date	Hour	Summary of Events and Information	Remarks and references to Appendices
	APRIL			
MIRAUMONT	1st-4th		The Regiment furnished daily working parties of 1 B.O., in the vicinity of IRLES.	B/W
-,,-	5th		T. Capt. D.E. WHITWORTH appointed Adjutant vice Capt. D.S. DAVISON, resigned.	B/W
-,,-	9th	2 p.m.	Received Mhow Bde's O.O. No 3 ordering the Bde to march to MORY to co-operate in an attack by 5th Army on BULLECOURT.	B/W
-,,-		10 p.m.	Received Mhow Bde's O.O. No 4 giving time of starting - 1.30 A.M.	B/W
MIRAUMONT	10th	1.30 a.m.	Marched to B.23 (Sheet 57.c). 'A' Echelon to BIHUCOURT. 'B' Echelon to SPAM H.Q.	B/W
		7.30 a.m.	Returned to camp at MIRAUMONT in accordance with Mhow Bde B.M. 2.	B/W
		6.45 p.m.	Received Mhow Bde's B.M. 3. ordering Bde to return to B.23 (Sheet 57.c.), starting 2.45 A.M.	B/W
	11th	2.45 a.m.	Marched to B.23. arriving 5 a.m. Echelons moving as before.	B/W
		4.05 p.m.	Returned to camp at MIRAUMONT in accordance with a verbal order from Mhow Bde.	B/W
	12th	10 a.m.	Ordered to stand at 2 hours notice of moving (B.M. 1 Mhow Bde).	B/W
	13th	10.30 a.m.	Marched to billets at ORVILLE.	B/W

F Bennett Major
for Commdt 2nd Lancers 1/5/17

Serial No. 149

C O N F I D E N T I A L.

WAR DIARY.

2nd Lancers.

from 1st May 1917.   to 30th June 1917.

Army Form C. 2118.

WAR DIARY
or
INTELLIGENCE SUMMARY. 2nd Lancers

(Erase heading not required.)

Instructions regarding War Diaries and Intelligence Summaries are contained in F. S. Regs., Part II. and the Staff Manual respectively. Title pages will be prepared in manuscript.

Place	Date	Hour	Summary of Events and Information	Remarks and references to Appendices
TEMPLEUX	May 23rd	11 pm	2. L. Dismounted Regt arrived in bivouac at a Quarry 1050" N.E. of TEMPLEUX. £u	
--	24th	10 p.	Provided working parties in the Intermediate Defence Line £u.	
--	25th	--	--- do ---	
--	26th	10 pm	Provided working parties in the Intermediate Defence Line £u.	
--	--	2 AM	2 Troops "C" Sqdn under Lt. E. VAUGHAN and Jem DHAPRA SINGH took over 2 Posts from Lts 36½ C.I.H. in B.2. Sector. £u	
--	28.	7 AM	Quarry Shelled by 8.5" gun. 1 I.O.R. slightly wounded. £u	
--	--	9 h.	"A" Sqdn marched to a position in Reserve to A.2. & Sector about 2 miles N. of LE VERGUIER. £u. The 2 Troops "C" Sqdn were relieved by 36½ C.I.H. £u.	
GD PRIEL WOOD	29th	3 AM	Lt. Col. H.H.F. TURNER took over command of the above Sector & was known as B.1. Subsector. £u	
--	--	9 pm	B. C. & D Sqdns under Major H.K. SALKELD marched from TEMPLEUX to B.1. Subsector and came into Reserve about 2 miles N. of LE VERGUIER £u	
--	30th	1 am.	"A" Sqdn relieved 2 posts of 17th Lancers 800" S.E. of PERVAISE F.M. £u	

Ghurstry Major
for O.T.I. 2nd Lancers

Army Form C. 2118.

WAR DIARY
or
INTELLIGENCE SUMMARY. 2nd Lancers

(Erase heading not required.)

Instructions regarding War Diaries and Intelligence Summaries are contained in F. S. Regs., Part II. and the Staff Manual respectively. Title pages will be prepared in manuscript.

Place	Date	Hour	Summary of Events and Information	Remarks and references to Appendices
	MAY			
URVILLE	1st–14th		In billets &c.	
—	15th		Marched to HEILLY. &c.	
HEILLY	16th		" " LA NEUVILLE (nr BRAY) &c.	
BRAY	17th		" " ST CHRIST &c.	
ST CHRIST	19th		2 B.O., 2 B.O.R, 1 J.O. & 115 I.O.R. 2 followers rejoined from 4th Cav. Div. D.M. Baltn. &c.	
ST CHRIST	22nd	12 Noon	Advanced party of 2 B.O & 19 J.O.R. proceeded to HERVILLY to take over from the Reserve Baltn of 176 F. Bde. &c.	
ST CHRIST	23rd	12 Noon	8 R.O. 1 M.O 12 B.O.R 9 I.O. 282 I.O.R. rode to Hervilly & then proceeded on foot to TEMPLEUX LE GUÉRARD &c.	
ST CHRIST	27th		24 I.O.R. 2 G. Pack Horses proceeded to join present party at TEMPLEUX &c.	
			Uneventful day.	

C O N F I D E N T I A L.

WAR   DIARY

of

2ⁿᵈ Lancers

from 1st June 1917.   to 30th June 1917.

Army Form C. 2118.

WAR DIARY
of
INTELLIGENCE SUMMARY
(Erase heading not required.)

2nd Lancers

Instructions regarding War Diaries and Intelligence Summaries are contained in F.S. Regs., Part II. and the Staff Manual respectively. Title pages will be prepared in manuscript.

Place	Date	Hour	Summary of Events and Information	Remarks and references to Appendices
GD PRIEL WOOD	1st June	10am	1 I.O.R. wounded by enemy anti-aircraft M.G. fire. SPW	
		9pm	Digging party of 50 men making new communication trench to ground front. SPW	
	4th	1pm	2nd Lancers Dismounted Regt relieved by 365 jawabs horse, and marched to HERVILLY where they were put at disposal of 4th Cav. Div. for digging etc. SPW	
HERVILLY		10am	Horses and details at ST CHRIST marched to camp at HAMELET where they arrived 2 p.m. Regtal HQ opened at the same place. SPW	
	5th	4pm	2nd Lancers Dismounted Regt at HERVILLY relieved by Mhow Row Dismounted Regiment Regt — to which 2nd Squadron 1 B.O. + 2 I.O. , 89 I.O.R. — and returned 6pm to camp at HAMELET. SPW	
	15th	7pm	2nd Lancers Dismounted Cav under command of Major G. KNOWLES D.S.O. (Strength 7 B.O. 7 B.O.R. and 312 I.O.R.) marched from camp HAMELET and relieved 6th Cav Dismounted Cav in the trenches at VILLERET at 11 p.m. SPW	
	16th	3am	1 B.O. 1 B.O.R., 2 I.O.S., + 87 I.O.R. rejoined from Mhow Row Dismounted Regiment Cav on the latter's relief by the Sialkote Bgde. SPW	
	17th	9am	2nd Lancers dismounted patrols marched to camp at ATHIES SPW	
ATHIES	22nd		Major J. BENNETT relieved Lt 2nd L Command in B.3. trenches at HARGICOURT SPW	

Army Form C. 2118.

WAR DIARY
or
INTELLIGENCE SUMMARY
2nd Lancers

(Erase heading not required.)

Instructions regarding War Diaries and Intelligence Summaries are contained in F. S. Regs., Part II. and the Staff Manual respectively. Title pages will be prepared in manuscript.

Place	Date	Hour	Summary of Events and Information	Remarks and references to Appendices
ATHIES	June 28th	7 p.m.	A party of 2 B.O., 2 B.O.R., 4 I.O. and 51 I.O.R. proceeded to relieve an equivalent number of the 2d Lancers Dismounted Coy at VILLERET Rly.	
	29th	4.30 a.m.	A party of 1 B.O., 4 B.O.R., 4 I.O. & 35 I.O.R. returned from Dismounted Coy at VILLERET Rly.	
		8.30 a.m.	Maj Scarth having been relieved as 2nd in command I.O.3 redactor rejoined at ATHIES Rly	
		9.30 a.m.	Lt Col H.H.F. Turner & Capt D.E. Ashwood proceeded to take over command of 15² redactor Rly	
		2.30 p.m.	Lieut H. Banister proceeded to relieve the 2nd in 15² redactor Rly	
		4 p.m.	A party of 1 B.O., 1 B.O.R., 1 I.O., 9-34 I.O.R. proceeded to relieve an equivalent number of the 2nd Lancers Dismounted Coy at VILLERET Rly.	
	30th	5.30 a.m.	A party of 3 B.O., 3 B.O.R., 3 I.O., 34 I.O.R. returned from Dismounted Coy VILLERET Rly.	

Inverell Major
for O.C. Lancers

Serial No: **149.**

CONFIDENTIAL.

WAR DIARY

of

2nd Lancers. G.H.

from 1st July 1917 to 31 July 1917

(Volume XIII.)

Army Form C. 2118.

WAR DIARY
or
INTELLIGENCE SUMMARY.
(Erase heading not required.)

2nd Lancers

Place	Date	Hour	Summary of Events and Information	Remarks and references to Appendices
ENNEMAIN	JULY 1st	12.30 am	'A' Sqdn's Platoon of the 2.L. Company at VILLERET relieved 'D' Sqdns Platoon, the Regiment, less the 2.L. Company, being at ENNEMAIN	
"	2nd	11 p.m	2 men of 'C' Sqdn killed by premature burst of shell at COTE WOOD.	
"	3rd	10.65	2 men of 'A' Sqdn killed by shell fire in a communication trench at VILLERET	
"	10th	4 a.m	The 2.L. Company was relieved by 2 Cny 22nd Northumberland Fusiliers. The above were the the relieved malachite rifles	
			all the details of the relief were carried out without of hitch. The 2.L Coy on relief marched by Platoons independently to HERVILLY, where horses sent from ENNEMAIN arrived there, and proceeded mounted to ENNEMAIN camp. All (with) except in by 7.30 a.m.	
	23rd	8 am	Dismounted Working Party under command of Lieut F.T.Cunneline left camp to march with Mhow Dismounted Coy to VENDELLES. Strength 1 B.O. 1 B.O.R, 1 I.O, 57 I.O.R and 1 cook	
	30th	12 Noon	Lt J.A NASH proceeded to join 'A' Batty R.H.A. for 8 days stay course of instruction in gunnery	

H.M. Wilson Lieut Colonel
Comdg 2nd Lancers

C O N F I D E N T I A L.

W A R   D I A R Y.

2 N D   L A N C E R S. (G. H.)

F R O M   1-6-1917   to   31-8-1917.

(VOLUME XIII).

Serial No: 179.

Army Form C. 2118.

WAR DIARY
of the
INTELLIGENCE SUMMARY &c.
(Erase heading not required.)

2nd Lancers

Instructions regarding War Diaries and Intelligence Summaries are contained in F. S. Regs., Part II. and the Staff Manual respectively. Title pages will be prepared in manuscript.

Place	Date	Hour	Summary of Events and Information	Remarks and references to Appendices
1917				
Aug	4.	9 am	A relief party of 1 I.B.O.R, 1 B.O.R, 30 & 28 I.O.R proceeded to VENDELLES to relieve a similar number of the 4th Cav. Div. working party. And	
	8	10 am	A party of 1 I.B.O, 1 B.O.R, 4 I.O & 2 & 35 I.O.R proceeded to VENDELLES to relieve similar dismounted working party And	
	12	9.30 am	A party of 29 I.O.R proceeded to VENDELLES to relieve the remainder of the dismounted working party which went up to 23rd July 1917. And	
	19	8 am	7 B.O, 6 B.O.R, 71 I.O. and 68 I.O.R. left ATHIES for VENDELLES to bring up the working party already at that village to Trench Strength as a Dismounted Coy. &c.	
		12 Noon	3 I.O. & 17 I.O.R. rejoined at Camp ATHIES from the working party at VENDELLES &c.	
	20	1 pm	2 I.O.S. 27 I.O.R under command of R.M. GANPA DAT relieved a similar party in the trenches. The left. party arrived Camp ATHIES at 6.30 p.m. &c	
		6.30 p		
	23	4 p	Lieut G.A.C. HEARSEY and Jem: DEVI CHAND left ATHIES for the Mhow Batt. &c	
	31	6.30 p	2 I.O. 48 I.O.R and 2 Signallers left ATHIES to relieve a similar party of the Mhow Batt. The relief was complete at 12 midnight when the relieved party started for ATHIES. &c	

CONFIDENTIAL.

WAR DIARY.

2ND LANCERS (G.H.)

FROM 1-9-1917 TO 30-9-1917.

(VOLUME XIII).

Serial No. 149

Army Form C. 2118.

WAR DIARY or INTELLIGENCE SUMMARY.

2nd Lancers

(Erase heading not required.)

Instructions regarding War Diaries and Intelligence Summaries are contained in F.S. Regs., Part II. and the Staff Manual respectively. Title pages will be prepared in manuscript.

Place	Date	Hour	Summary of Events and Information	Remarks and references to Appendices
ATHIES	Sept 5th	8 am	Lt BROADWAY, Lt WALLER, Lt MONK'S & Lt PECK Jem GURDITTA and 60 IOR having relieved Ress DIWAN SINGH and a similar party the Batt'n returned to ATHIES.	
	8th	9 am	Capt. JACKSON, 1 B.O., 1 I.O., and 16 I.O.R. having been relieved in the trenches by Ress KET RAM and 16 I.O.R. returned to ATHIES.	
	10th	9 am Pt to	Ress MUKAND SINGH Br, Jem BHAPUR SINGH and 20 IOR having been relieved in the trenches by Jem DHARA SINGH and 15 IOR returned to ATHIES.	
	11th	9 am	Ress ABDUL LATIF having proceeded to the trenches with 20 IOR relieved a similar party also returned to ATHIES.	
	14th	4 am	The 2.L. Cy of the MHOW BATT under command of Major J.F. BENNETT having been relieved in the trenches by a Cy of the LUCKNOW Batt'n returned to ATHIES.	
	21st	1 pm	Advance parties of the MHOW BATT'n left for the trenches near LE VERGUIER	
	22nd	5 pm	2.L. Cy of Mhow Batt'n under command of Major H.F. SALKELD relieved a Cy of the Suffolk Batt'n in the trenches near LE VERGUIER. Strength 1 Cy 7 B.O., 8 I.O. 254 I.O.R.	
	30th	10 p.m.	The above company was relieved by a Cy of 8th Batt'n Buffs and returned mounted to ATHIES	

[signed] J.M. Turner
Lieut. Colonel
Cmdt. 2nd Lancers

Confidential

War Diary
of
2nd Lancers

from 1-10-17 to 31-10-17

179.

Army Form C. 2118.

WAR DIARY
or
INTELLIGENCE SUMMARY. 2nd Lancers

(Erase heading not required.)

Instructions regarding War Diaries and Intelligence Summaries are contained in F. S. Regs., Part II. and the Staff Manual respectively. Title pages will be prepared in manuscript.

Place	Date	Hour	Summary of Events and Information	Remarks and references to Appendices
ATHIES	OCT 1st 6th 7th		In camp ATHIES. (½ mile S. of village) Men employed in making permanent horse standings for the mule Bty.	
"	8th		The Regiment moved into ATHIES village. Standings not yet completed. Bty.	
"	8th 3½		Regiment employed in making horse standings and mule filters, and in training. Bty.	

J.M. T----- Lieut. Colonel
Commdt. 2nd Lancers

Confidential

WAR DIARY
of
2nd (Bengal) Lancers.

from 1-11-17 to 30-11-17

(179)

Army Form C. 2118.

WAR DIARY
or
INTELLIGENCE SUMMARY. 2nd Lancers

(Erase heading not required.)

Instructions regarding War Diaries and Intelligence Summaries are contained in F. S. Regs., Part II. and the Staff Manual respectively. Title pages will be prepared in manuscript.

Place	Date	Hour	Summary of Events and Information	Remarks and references to Appendices
ATHIES	Nov 1917		Lieut PECK, Lieut HARDY, 1 I.O. & 15 I.O.R. left to form part of nucleus of 4th Cav Div Pioneer Batt at MISERY. &c.	
	15th		Lieut PRITCHARD, 1 I.O. & 5th I.O.R. left for above Pioneer Batt. &c.	
	21	9 a.m.	Marched with Bde to a camp at BOIS DESSARTS M.9 of FINS where the Divn was in Reserve for operation W. of CAMBRAI. &c.	
	23	9 a.m.	Returned from above camp to ATHIES &c.	
	25	5.20 a.m.	Marched to a position of readiness between GUREVOURT and LONGAVESNES &c.	
		2 p.m.	Marched back to ATHIES. &c.	
	30	6 a.m.	Trench party of 260 under command of Major K. ROBERTSON accompanied by Capt. G.A. DIKE, all mounted, marched to TEMPLEUX to take over a portion of the trench line in that vicinity. &c.	
		11 a.m.	Regtl H.Q. and details remaining in ATHIES returned to rendezvous on low ground and hence to (roads) just E. of ETRECHE en cuirasses (see trench details in a separate file) &c.	
		1 p.m.	Arrived at above rendezvous. &c.	
		2.30 p.m.	Marched with Bde towards VILLERS FAUCON &c.	

Army Form C. 2118.

WAR DIARY
or
INTELLIGENCE SUMMARY. of 2nd Lancers

(Erase heading not required.)

Place	Date	Hour	Summary of Events and Information	Remarks and references to Appendices
ST EMILIE	Nov 1917 30	7pm	The Brigade bivouacked just N. of ST EMILIE where the 2nd Lancer Band party rejoined the Regiment. A' Echelon Transport at this time reached the vicinity of VILLERS FAUCON where it was parked also.	

Bennett Major
Commanding 2nd Lancers

CONFIDENTIAL.

WAR DIARY.

of

2nd Lancers

fro, 1-12-17.　　　　　　　to 31-12-17.

Army Form C. 2118.

WAR DIARY
of
INTELLIGENCE SUMMARY. 2nd Lancers

(Erase heading not required.)

Instructions regarding War Diaries and Intelligence Summaries are contained in F. S. Regs., Part II. and the Staff Manual respectively. Title pages will be prepared in manuscript.

Place	Date	Hour	Summary of Events and Information	Remarks and references to Appendices
ST EMILIE	Dec 1	4.15 am	Warning Brigade Order No 77 received. JW	
		8.30 am	Moved off & marched to position NJ PEIZIERE JW	
		6.30 am	Concentrated with brigade N of PEIZIERE from heavy shelling and casualties to men & horses. JW	
		3 pm	Ordered to gallop thro' THIGELLE QUAIL & PIGEON RAVINES from a position flank E & SE. Two machine guns attached (57°) JW	
		4 pm	Moved to more N of big copse named NE from EPEHY – moved via PEIZIERE & EPEHY villages Ref. 62° c 57°. JW accompanied by two M.Gs & two squadrons Inniskilling Dragoons ; remainder & reserve of squadrons in line of troop column. JW As column moved forward at gallop it came under very heavy machine gun fire from front [KILDARE Trench] right flank (German outpost about X 27 c 8.0) left flank an old British strong point about X 27 b.5.9. away captured by Germans. JW KILDARE LANE was reached about 50 of the enemy being accounted for. Two being captured & three light M.Gs. JW	

WAR DIARY
INTELLIGENCE SUMMARY.

2nd Lancers

Army Form C. 2118.

Place	Date	Hour	Summary of Events and Information	Remarks and references to Appendices
	22/3/18	9 am	Position occupied was from X.11.c.9.1 to X.28 central /W	
			There being no return for the horses, 2 troops operations on this position /W	
			they had to return to PEIZIERE suffering heavily on the way. /W	
		10 am	Right flank got in touch with our Infantry about X.28 central, left flank	
			to occupied KILDARE POST on its head /W	
		Dusk	Enemy tried to envelop left flank but were driven off after counterattack	
		4pm	upon right flank at intervals /W	
			Several times during the day Germans barraged the position & brought	
			heavy M.G. fire to bear but no attack developed /W	
		6.30pm	Relieved by Infantry; withdrew horses with difficulty via EMPIRE Rd	
			returned, camping in E.6.a. /W	
	23/3/18	3 am	Moved to neighbourhood of ST EMILIE & joined Dismounted Brigade	
			in reserve /W	
		11 am	Relieved by 1st Can. Div /W	
		9 am	Moved back to billets in ATHIES /W	
	23/3/18		Supplies dropped, remaining horses of Cavalry Corps sent in /W	

Maj R. Parr
2 Lancers
Ppennett

CONFIDENTIAL.

WAR DIARY.

2ND LANCERS (G.H.)

FROM 1/3/1918 to 30/3/1918.

(1 month)

(VOLUME XIII).

4 DIV MHOW CAV

Army Form C. 2118.

Instructions regarding War Diaries and Intelligence Summaries are contained in F. S. Regs., Part II. and the Staff Manual respectively. Title pages will be prepared in manuscript.

WAR DIARY
or
INTELLIGENCE SUMMARY.
2nd Lancers

(Erase heading not required.)

Place	Date	Hour	Summary of Events and Information	Remarks and references to Appendices
ATHIES	January 1918 1-6		In billets ATHIES	
"	6th		2/Lt G. MALLAM 1 I.O. 50 O.R. left for HERVILLY to join No 4 Working Party. &c.	
"	13th		2/Lt C.E.L. HARRIS relieved 2/Lt MALLAM above &c.	
"	19th	6 p.s.	Above party rejoined from HERVILLY	
"	26th	7 p.s.	22 O.R. rejoined from 4th Cav. Entrenching Battn. HERVILLY &c	
"	"	9 am	2/Lt C.E.L. HARRIS, 1 I.O. and 26 O.R. left for No 4 Working Party HERVILLY. &c	
"	27th	1 pm	2 Lt. D. dismounted Regt under command of Capt D.S. DAVISON, strength 3 B.O. 8 I.O., 3 B.O.R., 227 I.O.R., 7 Followers, left to take over trenches at COTE WOOD 2 miles E. of TEMPLEUX LA FOSSE &c.	
"	28th	9 am.	2 Lt R.P.L. RANKING and 1/Lt E. ST J. KING having rejoined from courses left to reinforce 2.L. Dismounted Regt. 2/Lt C.E.L. HARRIS also joined 2.L. Dismounted Regt from No 4 Working Party HERVILLY &c.	
"	28th	3 p.s.	4 I.O.R. returned from Dump Guard JEANCOURT &c	
"	29th	12 noon	13 I.O.R. joined No 4 Working Party HERVILLY &c.	

J Bennett Lieut. Colonel
Commanding 2nd Lancers

WAR DIARY or INTELLIGENCE SUMMARY

Army Form C. 2118.

Place	Date	Hour	Summary of Events and Information	Remarks and references to Appendices
ATHIES	1·2·18	1 p.m.	Jem JOT RAM with three other ranks left to join the party in the trenches. HB	
N.E. of VILLERET	"	1 p.m.	Ress. HET RAM and Jem JANG BAHADAR SINGH were both wounded by the same bullet, which passed through Cpl. HET RAM's abdomen and him into the thigh of Jem JUNG BAHADAR SINGH who was standing behind him in the trench. HB	
ATHIES	4·2·18	9 a.m.	1st Regiment, less the trench party, marches to GUILLAUCOURT. HB	
N.E. of VILLERET	"	7.30 a.m.	Sr. NIHALA (No. 2514) wounded by M.G. fire. HB	
GUILLAUCOURT	5·2·18	8 a.m.	The Regiment less the trench party, continued march to rear. Billets of the night — H.Q. and 'A' Sqn. at GUIGNEMICOURT; 'B','C', + D' Sqns at CLAIRY. HB
GUIGNEMICOURT	5·2·18	6 a.m.	Threct billets:- H.Q., 'D' Sqn. + Right 'C' Sqn. at FRESNOY-au-VAL; Left 'C' Sqn. at MONT-ENDY; 'A' Sqn. at BUSSY; 'B' Sqn. at MOYENCOURT. HB	
N.E. of VILLERET FRES NO HB	5·2·18	7.45 p.m.	Ress. MUKAND SINGH M.C. wounded by shell-fire. HB	
FRESNOY au VAL	9·2·18	3 a.m.	Jem: KARAM SINGH and Ten Indian Other Ranks left for the trenches. HB
"	10·2·18	8 p.m.	Lieut. H. BANISTER and one B.O.R. and an I.O.R. and likewise. HB	
"	13·2·18	5 p.m.	2nd Lieut KING rejoins from the trenches. HB	
"	14·2·18	11 a.m.	No. 1447 Dfr. SAHIB SINGH I.O.M. wounded by shell-fire. HB	
FRESNOY au VAL	15·2·18	7 p.m.	The trench party of 5 British Officers; 8 Indian Officers; 5 B.O.R; 224 I.O.R.; and

4 DIV
Army Form C. 2118.

WAR DIARY
or
INTELLIGENCE SUMMARY. 2nd Lancers.
(Erase heading not required.)

Instructions regarding War Diaries and Intelligence Summaries are contained in F.S. Regs, Part II. and the Staff Manual respectively. Title pages will be prepared in manuscript.

Place	Date	Hour	Summary of Events and Information	Remarks and references to Appendices
FREJNOY-en-VAL	15/2/18		2 followers rejoined from reinforcement Wg	
"	18/2/18 11am		Jem: HARI SINGH and 37 I.O.R's rejoined from Nott working Party W	
"	22/2/18 12noon		The first party for the East via TARANTO, consisting of 3 British Officers: 1 B.O.C. 10 D.I.O.R. & 4 followers; Major H.Y. SALKELD, D.S.O. being in command, left 4 in Motor Lorries 1.R.	
"	23/2/18 3pm		Ten Indian Other Ranks left for the East via TARANTO. W	
"	24/2/18 12.15pm		Lieut L.J. PECH M.C. and a party of 4 Indian Officers and I.O.R's and 5 followers, entrained to East 1R via TARANTO W	
"	25/2/18 11am		A further party of 2 Indian Officers & 5 I.O.R's under the command of 2nd Lieut LAWLER left en route for the East 1R via TARANTO 1R.	

Grants
Major
Commanding 2nd Lancers.

Army Form C. 2118.

WAR DIARY
or
INTELLIGENCE SUMMARY. 2ⁿᵈ Lancers

March 1918

(Erase heading not required.)

Instructions regarding War Diaries and Intelligence Summaries are contained in F. S. Regs., Part II. and the Staff Manual respectively. Title pages will be prepared in manuscript.

Place	Date	Hour	Summary of Events and Information	Remarks and references to Appendices
	MARCH			
FRESSNOY AU VAL	1st		2/Lt G.L. MALLAN 2 I.O., 34 I.O.R. 2 Fll. entrained for TARANTO en route for EGYPT.	See
SALEUX	20th		2ⁿᵈ Lancers entrained in 3 trains for MARSEILLE.	See
MARSEILLE	23rd		Arrived MARSEILLE. Marched to MONT FURON Camp	See
	30th		Major K. ROBERTSON and 2 I.O. & BOR 3 I.O. 179 I.O.R. 52 horses embarked on H.M.T. "MINOMINEE" for EGYPT.	
			2/Lt G.J. SILVER & 32 Mules entrained on H.M.T. "PANCRAS" for EGYPT	See

J Bennett Lieut- Colonel
Commanding 2ⁿᵈ Lancers

1st May 1918

1917-18
4TH CAVALRY DIVISION
MHOW CAVALRY BRIGADE

6TH INNISKILLING DRAGOONS

JAN 1917 - FEB 1918

FROM 1 CAV DIV MHOW CAV BDE
TO 7 CAV BDE 3 CAV DIV

SERIAL NO. 73

Confidential
War Diary
of

6TH INNISKILLING DRAGOONS.

FROM 1st JANUARY 1917. TO 31st JANUARY 1917.

Army Form C. 2118.

6th Pram Falling Dragon

WAR DIARY
or
INTELLIGENCE SUMMARY.
(Erase heading not required.)

Place	Date	Hour	Summary of Events and Information	Remarks and references to Appendices
ESGARBOIN	Jan. 1		Capt. Dilich.	
	" 3		3. O.R. rejoined from No.5 Base Depôt as reinforcement.	Appx.
	" 7		10. O.R. " " " " " " " in Africa.	Appx.
	" 9		The following troops received commissions as under in Infantry Batts.	Appx.
			L.R. Jones. O.R. Sergt. E.L. Forces.	Appx.
			Amounting Pioneer Bn" A/t. Dilich, and 2nd Ales Batts. for digging Latrine at	
	12		The following troops received commissions as under in Infantry.	Appx.
			J. DeHardin. 1st Potts. Q Menoward.	
			O/R. N.H. Buchty joined regt from England.	
			P. O.M. Cunningham, rejoined as Captain with effect from 04/10/16.	Appx.
	24		3127. A.M. Hall joined from Lon. England, reinforcements.	Appx.
			9013. joined from No.5. Bn. Base as reinforcements.	

Army Form C. 2118.

6th Inniskilling Dragoons

WAR DIARY
INTELLIGENCE SUMMARY.
(Erase heading not required.)

Place	Date	Hour	Summary of Events and Information	Remarks and references to Appendices
Escarbotin	29 Jan.		Lieut S.C. Cridland-Owen joined from England reinforcement. 60 O.R. joined regt. from R.S. General Base Dept.	App

30/1/12

H. de Pass Lieutenant
6th Inniskilling Dragoons

SERIAL No 73.

WAR DIARY

OF

THE INNISKILLING DRAGOONS.

FOR

FEBRUARY 1917.

VOLUME.   SERIES.

Army Form C. 2118.

WAR DIARY

—OF—

INTELLIGENCE SUMMARY. 6th Inniskilling Dragoons

(Erase heading not required.)

Instructions regarding War Diaries and Intelligence Summaries are contained in F. S. Regs., Part II. and the Staff Manual respectively. Title pages will be prepared in manuscript.

Place	Date	Hour	Summary of Events and Information	Remarks and references to Appendices
ESQARBOTIN	1. FEB	/	WINTER BILLETS.	P/Wb.
	5 FEB.		INSPECTION OF TRANSPORT BY OC A.S.C.	P/Wb.
	11	—	CAPTAIN C.J.B. BRIDGEWATER JOINED REGT FROM ENGLAND & ASSUMED COMMAND OF "D" SQDN.	P/Wb.
			2/LT H.L. VILLIERS (ATTACHED R.F.C.) KILLED IN AIR COMBAT.	P/Wb.
		4	9.O.R. JOINED REGIMENT FROM No 5. BASE, ROUEN. REINFORCEMENTS	
		22	2/LT J. REYNOLDS: 2/LT A.W. FAIRBURN: 2/LT S. DE MOYSE-BUCKNELL: 2/LT J.B. McGRAW. JOINED REGIMENT FROM ENGLAND. REINFORCEMENTS TAKEN ON STRENGTH.	P/Wb.

—x—

R.H. Wostlus
Adjutant,
The Inniskilling Dragoons.

Serial No: 113.

Confidential

INNISKILLING DNS

WAR DIARY.

MARCH 1917

From 1st to 31 March 1917

[Stamp: ORDERLY ROOM — 1 APR 1917 — INNISKILLING DRAGOONS]

WAR DIARY
or
INTELLIGENCE SUMMARY.
6th Inniskilling Dragoons

Army Form C. 2118.

(Erase heading not required.)

Instructions regarding War Diaries and Intelligence Summaries are contained in F. S. Regs., Part II. and the Staff Manual respectively. Title pages will be prepared in manuscript.

Place	Date	Hour	Summary of Events and Information	Remarks and references to Appendices
ECOREVIN	1 March 19		HALTED.	App.1a
	2 - 9		HALTED	App.1b
	10	-	REINFORCEMENTS 3 O.R. & S/Sergeant Jones from R.S. East Base Depot.	App.1c
	11 - 17		HALTED.	App.1d
	18		ORR'S MEMORIAL SERVICE. In memory of 2 late Capt. L.C.A. Orr. Maj. Gen. Mulcahy from Command attended.	App.1e, App.1f
	19		The following telegrams were despatched to the Equerry to H.R.H. the Duke of Connaught, London. "ALL RANKS SEND DEEPEST SYMPATHY IN YOUR GREAT LOSS" Telegram received from H.R.H. Duke of Connaught's Equerry. "HIS ROYAL HIGHNESS MUCH APPRECIATES YOUR KIND MESSAGE" Orders received at 10.15 am to move to new area, at 10 am.	App.1g, App.1h, App.1i, App.1j
DROCAT	19		HALTED DROCAT for the night, arrived 5.35 p.m.	App.1k
	20		March at 9.45 am to St LEGER, arrived 1.59 p.m. Halted for night	App.1l
St LEGER	21		Marched at 9.30 am to AVELUY, 1000 yds E of ALBERT (Somme), about 16 miles, arrived 4.30 p.m. Camped in field proved W of AVELUY.	App.1m, App.1n
AVELUY	22-		Halted.	App.1o

2353 Wt. W2344/1454 700,000 5/15 D.D.& L. A.D.S.S./Forms/C. 2118.

Army Form C. 2118.

WAR DIARY
or
INTELLIGENCE SUMMARY.

(Erase heading not required.)

6th Inniskilling Dragoons.

Instructions regarding War Diaries and Intelligence Summaries are contained in F. S. Regs., Part II. and the Staff Manual respectively. Title pages will be prepared in manuscript.

Place	Date	Hour	Summary of Events and Information	Remarks and references to Appendices
AVELUY	25	HALTED	Received clothing party 107 men 1 Officer, for repairing roads.	Ap/10
"	24	"	ditto	Ap/10
"	25	"	ditto	Ap/10
"	26	"	"	Ap/10
"	27	"	6th W. Parade w/t arms. heavy Enemy shells between MIRAMONT & IRLES. about 13 Kilos.	Ap/10
"	28	"	Dent Laity & 20 OR to ACHIET-LE-PETIT to join horses Bank.	Ap/10
"	29	"	Stokeswich then rejoined order for full transit.	Ap/10
"	30	"	Following day carried & Sqdn	Ap/10
"	31	"		

[signature] Lieut & Adjutant
6th Inniskilling Dragoons

[signature]

Serial No. 73.

CONFIDENTIAL.

WAR DIARY OF

6th Inniskilling Dragoons

Mhow Bde

From 1-4-17. to 30-4-17.

6th Inniskilling Dragoons

WAR DIARY
or
INTELLIGENCE SUMMARY.
(Erase heading not required.)

Form C. 2118.

Instructions regarding War Diaries and Intelligence Summaries are contained in F. S. Regs., Part II. and the Staff Manual respectively. Title pages will be prepared in manuscript.

Place	Date	Hour	Summary of Events and Information	Remarks and references to Appendices
AVELUY	APRIL 1st		Halted. Sent 110 horses & horseholders to convey Siallor Bryg; dismounted men to forward concentration front	Appx O
—	2nd		Halted. Dismounted party under Capt. Burtle & Lt. B. Reynoldson proceeded to ACHIET LE PETIT and were struck off the strength of the regiment	Appx O
MIRAUMONT	3rd		Marched at 9 a.m. to new camp. Arrived 11 a.m. Fine weather	Appx O
—	4th		Halted. Rain & snow till 2 p.m. Camp very muddy. Fatigue of 30 men drawing rifles	Appx O
—	5th		Halted. Fine day. C.O., Adjt. and Intelligence Officer made reconnaissance to 1 mile S. of CROISILLES. Squadron reconnaissances also took place and working party cleaning roads.	Appx O
—	6th		Halted. Good Friday. Working party. Bad weather.	Appx O
—	7th		Halted. Gas rations issued. Reconnaissance of proposed new camp at MORY. Working party	Appx O
—	8th		Halted. Easter Sunday. Church service. Working party. Fine day	Appx O
—	9th		Halted. 5 O.R. arrived from Base as reinforcements	Appx O
—	10th		Left camp 1.30 a.m. for concentration ground at MORY. Arrived 5 a.m. Practice over cancelled & Brigade returned reaching MIRAUMONT at 10.15 a.m. The still standing awful weather all day. Battery arr and many had some storms	Appx O

Army Form C. 2118.

6th Inniskilling Dragoons

WAR DIARY
or
INTELLIGENCE SUMMARY.
(Erase heading not required.)

Place	Date	Hour	Summary of Events and Information	Remarks and references to Appendices
MIRAUMONT	April 11th		Left Camp again at 2.45 am for MORY, arriving 5.45 am. On hearing that BULLECOURT had been taken, the 5th Cavalry Brigade were ordered off at 9.15 am to take objective, the high ground N.E. of BULLECOURT. The Inns. Brigade moved up in support, the Inniskilling's leading. It was killed after advancing 1 mile and shortly afterwards the news arrived that BULLECOURT had been retaken by the enemy. The Scottish Brigade were then withdrawn & Inns. Brigade ordered to cover position S. of MORY at 4.45 pm. Inns. Brigade returned to old Camp at MIRAUMONT arriving 7 pm. Weather very bad all day.	See Appendix No. 1
	12th		Halted	Helio
AUTHIE	13th		Marched at 10.30 am to AUTHIE. Weather fine & fine - arrived in rest arriving 3.30 pm.	Helio
"	14th		Halted. Iall men in billets & most horses under cover	Helio
"	15th		Halted - Sunday Horse inspection during morning	Helio
"	16th		Halted. Bad weather	Helio

Army Form C. 2118.

WAR DIARY
or
INTELLIGENCE SUMMARY.
(Erase heading not required.)

6th Inniskilling Dragoons

Instructions regarding War Diaries and Intelligence Summaries are contained in F. S. Regs., Part II. and the Staff Manual respectively. Title pages will be prepared in manuscript.

Place	Date	Hour	Summary of Events and Information	Remarks and references to Appendices
AUTHIE	APRIL 17th		Halted. Bad weather. Squadron Training	Herp?
"	18th		"	Herp?
"	19th		"	Herp?
"	20th		Batt. Wether. Armourer-Sergeant inspected arms	Herp?
"	21st		" "	Herp?
"			Fine. Horse inspection	Herp?
"	22nd		Fine. Church Service	Herp?
"	23rd		Fine. Regimental Parade in drill order	Herp?
"	26th		Fine. Signalling scheme.	Herp?
THIEVRES	25th		Scott's Brigade took over regimental area and Regt. marched into THIEVRES during the morning. FAMECHON which was also allotted to Regt. was not	
			utilised to-day owing to the troops there not receiving orders to go	Herp?
"	26th		FAMECHON vacated and B. Squadron billeted there. Fine grazing	Herp?
"	27th		Halted. C Squadron horses dampitted. All received suspension destroyed. Fine grazing	Herp?
"	28th		Halted. Fine. grazing	Herp?
"	29th		Halted. Fine grazing. Sunday.	Herp?
"	30th		Halted. B. Squadron Inspected by G.O.C. Brigade	Herp?

H. Dejas 2/Lt.
Inniskilling Dragoons

SECRET.   MHOW. CAV. BDE. OPERATION ORDER No.3.   9-4-17.
Reference Sheets 1:40.000, 57c and 51b
1. The Fifth Army is attacking at zero (on date to be notified later) in accordance with the plan already circulated.
2. The Brigade will move to a position of readiness in square B.28 South of MORY. <u>Starting Point</u>. Eastern Extremity of C.I.H. LInes.
   <u>Time</u>. Will be notified later.
   <u>ROUTE</u>. IRLES — CROSS ROADS in G.22.c.9.0. — 5 roads junction BIHUCOURT —SAPIGNIES — thence by Cavalry Track to square B.28.
<u>Order of March</u>. Bde. Head Qtrs. 38th C.I.Horse., Pack Mounted Section., M.G. Squadron, 2nd. Lancers, Inniskilling Dragoons.
3. O.C. 38th C.I.Horse will detail 1 troop under a British Officer to clear the road by which the Brigade is moving.
4. Fighting Troops of Lucknow Brigade will follow Mhow Brigade, starting one hour after head of Mhow Brigade passes starting point.
5. A1 Echelon under Lt. Peck, 2nd Lancers, will follow Lucknow A1 Echelon which will follow in rear of Lucknow Brigade Fighting Troops. Officers Led Horses in order of units will march at the head of A1 under Lt. Hilder, Inniskilling D Dragoons.
   A2 Echelon under Lt. Dudgeon Inniskilling Dragoons, will follow Lucknow Brigade A2 Echelon. M.V. Section will march in rear of cyclists with Echelon A2 'B' Echelon under B.T.O. will move under orders of O.C.A.S.C.
6. All cyclists less those with 'B' Echelon, will march under the senior cyclists N.C.O. of Inniskilling Dragoons in rear of Echelon A2.
   At least 2 cyclists per unit will be left with 'B' Echelon during operations.
7. All units will water at the SAPIGNIES water point, and water bottles and water carts must be filled at this place, as there is little water beyond.
8. On arrival at position of readiness all units will off saddle.
9. At position of readiness, Brigade Report Centre will be near the MORY — FAVREUIL road and gallopers will report here immediately on arrival.
::
                                                              0/80.
Memorandum.
   Reference above. Squadrons will parade on there own lines and move off in the following order. Head quarters, 'D', 'C' 'B' 'A' Squadrons.
   'A1. 6 Limber Wagons will parade under Lt. Prideaux-Brune, near their own standings. Officers' Led Horses under 2/Lt. Hilder, will parade at the head of A1.
   'A2. Mess Cart. Doctors' Cart, Water Cart, (Cyclists under Cpl. Larcombe) will parade under Lt. Dudgeon, near the guard room tent.
   O.C. 'B' & 'C' Sqdns, will each detail a cyclist to remain with 'B' Echelon.
   'B' Echelon Transport will await orders from the B.T.O. Brigade.

To/ Four Squadrons.
    Headquarters.
    Transport.   Sd/ R.M. WOOTTEN.
    Quartermaster.   Lieutenant & Adjutant.
    Medical Officer.   Inniskilling Dragoons.
    N.C.O. i/c Cyclists.
                                    Issued by D.R. 2.55 p.m.

Serial No. 73.

WAR DIARY
OF
INNISKILLING DRAGOONS.

For May 1917 & June 1917.

ORDERLY
5 - JUN 1917
INNIS

WAR DIARY or INTELLIGENCE SUMMARY

Army Form C. 2118.

(Erase heading not required.)

Place	Date	Hour	Summary of Events and Information	Remarks and references to Appendices
THIEVRES	1 Nov 1917		Regiment halted.	
	2nd to 3rd		Reinforcements arrived from No. 5. Gen. Base Depôt Rouen. 19 B.O.R.	
	8		Regiment halted.	
	9	11	Brigadier's attack. West Yeo, Inniskilling Dragoons, rejoined regiment from H.Q. 3rd Army.	
	10	11	Regiment halted.	
	11		Holiday. Bn. Parade.	
	12	12 P.M.	Regiment halted. to Saddle.	
	13	15 A	Regiment moved to MERICOURT-L'ABBÉ met New Brigade, en route to ST. CHRIST. halted by night.	
MERICOURT	14		Regiment halted up. Regiment moved, continuing to march to BRAY. halted by night.	
BRAY	14		Regt. went on to ST. CHRIST. arriving about 10-15 a.m. Camp situate between ST CHRIST & BRIE	
CAMP. C.M.C.	15	9.04	Regiment halted. Scout reported to Captain V.O.M. De Cerjat (Capt. A Sct. 4th Bde Cyclists Brigade)	
ST. CHRIST	31		Reinforcements arrived from No 5 Gen Base. Horse. B.O.R. 5 Riding horses & Chargers & Pelou Officers Ponies	
	22		Coach of Brownstones Regiment furnished by right, for Brigade advance Party moved up.	
	25		Main Party moved up. Party consisted of 15 B.O., 315 B.O.R., met & marched at HARCOURT.	
	3 Dec		Rear Main halted at St. Christ.	
HARCOURT	24		Letter received by Scouts Rgt. from 6th Staffords. at 1 a.m. everything quiet. Senior are subordinate one one sent put out	
St Christ	24			

Army Form C. 2118.

WAR DIARY
or
INTELLIGENCE SUMMARY.

(Erase heading not required.)

Instructions regarding War Diaries and Intelligence Summaries are contained in F. S. Regs., Part II. and the Staff Manual respectively. Title pages will be prepared in manuscript.

Place	Date	Hour	Summary of Events and Information	Remarks and references to Appendices
HARCOURT	25th		Scouts Out. Line put out knive improved.	
ST CHRIST	26th		Gen. Staff. Head.	
HARCOURT	27th		Scouts Out. Patrols went out but not no enemy. Post relieved.	
ST CHRIST	27th		Gen. Staff. Kosha.	
HARCOURT	27th		Scouts Out. 9 Other Ranks 5 wounded.	
ST CHRIST	28th		Rev. into Camp.	
HARCOURT	28th		Scouts Out. Listed Artillery action. Otherwise quiet.	
ST CHRIST	28th		Gen. Staff. Camp.	
HARCOURT	29th		Enemy put to this advance post on left of battalion, but was driven back and explained fire.	
ST CHRIST	29th		Rev. Three Rivers.	
HARCOURT	30th		Patrol sent out to B. Sudan, and not strong enemy patrol who retired. A relief of enemy presented to us.	
ST BLUE	30th		Rec. Trois Camp.	
HANCOURT	31st		9 H.R.'s wounded. Heavy shelling all day	
ST CHRIST	31st		Rev. Trois to Camp.	

(sgd) _____
Lieutenant
Commanding Bn/Coys.

C O N F I D E N T I A L.

WAR   DIARY

of

6th Inniskilling Dragoons

from 1st June 1917.   to 30th June 1917.

Army Form C. 2118.

6th Inniskilling Dragoons

WAR DIARY
INTELLIGENCE SUMMARY.
(Erase heading not required.)

Instructions regarding War Diaries and Intelligence Summaries are contained in F.S. Regs., Part II. and the Staff Manual respectively. Title pages will be prepared in manuscript.

Place	Date	Hour	Summary of Events and Information	Remarks and references to Appendices
St. CHRIST, HARGICOURT	JUNE 1st 1917	1 to 3.30	REAR TROOPS. HALFED CAMP. INNISKILLING COY TRENCHES.	R.Mils. R.Mils.
St. CHRIST	JUNE 4		REAR TROOPS. Moved to forward concentration trench with horse transport in bivouack to HAMELET, 3 kilos	R.Mils.
"	"		W. of ROISEL. TIME 9.a.m. INNISKILLING Coy were relieved by K.D. Gds at HARGICOURT, at 1 A.M.	R.Mils.
"	"		and returned to camp HAMELET, rejoined rear troops.	R.Mils.
HAMELET	JUNE 5th 1917		SQUADRON TRAINING. Standing to as emergency brigade. Major C.R. Ferrot awarded D.S.O. action in Holiday Honours. Party of 1.30 & 83 O.R proceed to HERMLY - H kilo SE of	R.Mils. R.Mils.
"	"		ROISEL, as Dismounted Reinforcement Coy.	R.Mils.
"	6/6/17		SQUADRON TRAINING. In horse lent by D.D.R for recruit reason in war. Recruiting Coy Candids for instruction prior to proceeding to Recruits and reserve Btns of Btty at HARGICOURT.	R.Mils. R.Mils.
"	"	10	SQUADRON TRAINING.	R.Mils.
"	"	10 K	"INNISKILLING Coy" proceeded to trenches at HARGICOURT, 10 kilo N.E of ROISEL, at 6.4.45 p.m. to	R.Mils.
"	"		stand (to) of until 2nd Brigade, and relieved K.D Gds at 1 A.M 14th Casualties 1 O.R Killed	R.Mils.
"	"		1 O.R Wounded. Strength of Sqdn. 3 H Officers & other Rank. Major O.R. Ferrot D.S.O. in/Command.	R.Mils.
"	"	14	REAR TROOPS. Proceeded to march to CAMP AT ENNEMAIN 15 kilo S of PERONNE, Horse camp kind at Voyeux. TIME 9.A.M. arrived ENNEMAIN 10-50 A.M.	R.Mils.
HARGICOURT	"	14	Our Guns on Bertois front.	R.Mk.

WAR DIARY or INTELLIGENCE SUMMARY

Army Form C. 2118.

(Erase heading not required.)

Instructions regarding War Diaries and Intelligence Summaries are contained in F. S. Regs., Part II. and the Staff Manual respectively. Title pages will be prepared in manuscript.

Place	Date	Hour	Summary of Events and Information	Remarks and references to Appendices
EMMEMAIN	JUNE	18h.	REAR TROOPS HALTED CAMP	R.Mbo.
HARGICOURT	"	"	TRENCH PARTY. Sechi trenches Bust.	P.Mbo.
EMMEMAIN	"	19h.	REAR TROOPS hailed Camp.	P.Mbo.
HARGICOURT	"	"	TRENCH PARTY. Capt Roman relieved Capt Moreuil, who returned to regt. Lt Bridges returned to	R.Mbo.
"	"	20h to	take over command of trenching party. Lt Dunn relieved Lt Van Tuyl. Lt Verne proceeded on leave.	P.Mbo.
EMMEMAIN	"	29h.	party. REAR TROOPS Resting Camp.	P.Mbo.
HARGICOURT	"	22	Raiding Party of 133 officers & men proceeded to HERMLY + held S.E. ROSEL 1st train 5 before	R.Mbo.
"	"	"	In road on Sechi trench. Major L.R. Robert 2.50 in command. This party were relieved	P.Mbo.
"	"	"	by K.R.R.C. 90 on Sechi trench.	P.Mbo.
"	"	23	No casualties on any Sechi trench resting to present.	P.Mbo.
"	"	24h.	Major M. Leroch returned to head qrs from Hermly to take over command of D.S. Squadron	P.Mbo.
"	"	"	Capt. Lt Cox found him as adjutant. Quart. or Sergt. Carring Carty rejoined.	P.Mbo.
EMMEMAIN	"	25h.	REAR TROOPS. Halted Camp. Colonel for H.R.H. DUKE OF CONNAUGHT. K.P. K.T. K.C.B. G.V.O. K.C.	P.Mbo.
"	"	"	Colonel-in-Chief. H.O.R. Cuirassiers. turn from Base depot.	R.Mbo.
HARGICOURT	"	30	Trench Party. Casualties, 1 O.R. (Reis) 2 O.R. wounded by shell. Lt Regnault took over duties	P.Mbo.
"	"	"	as Signalling Officer from 2Lt Longueil Simmo who rejoined Rear Troops.	R.Mbo.

T2134. Wt. W708-776. 500000. 4/15. Sir J.C. & S.

Army Form C. 2118.

WAR DIARY
or
INTELLIGENCE SUMMARY.
(Erase heading not required.)

Instructions regarding War Diaries and Intelligence Summaries are contained in F. S. Regs., Part II. and the Staff Manual respectively. Title pages will be prepared in manuscript.

Place	Date	Hour	Summary of Events and Information	Remarks and references to Appendices
ENNEMAIN	June 30th		REAR TROOPS. INSPECTION BY FIELD MARSHAL H.R.H. DUKE OF CONNAUGHT & STRATHEARN, K.P. K.T. K.C.B. G.V.O. K.C.I.E. &c &c. COLONEL-IN-CHIEF, of the regiment, of composite Squadron (comprising 1 Squn Greys, and 'O' Echelon Inniskilling Dns. Greys) 5.3 p.m., accompanied by	Photo.
				Photo.
				R Photo.
				R Photo.
				R Photo.
				R Photo.
			the Fourth Army Commander:- GENERAL SIR. H.S. RAWLINSON, BART, K.C.B. G.V.O. D.S.O. & EQUERRY. COMMANDER:- LIEUT-GENERAL SIR.C.T. Mc M. KAVANAGH, K.C.B. G.V.O. D.S.O. & EQUERRY. H.R.H. expressed his liveliest satisfaction at the smart appearance of the regiment, and the condition of the horses. He remarked that when opportunity offered he "wished to see the Inniskilling Dragoons" would uphold the known gain in the past. In taking	R Photo.
				R Photo.
				Photo.
			leave, he wished all ranks the best of luck in the war, and a speedy and victorious issue. The 150th Bn debouchee at 5.33 p.m. "	Photo.
"	"	30	REAR TROOPS. Nockia Kaura.	Photo.
HARGICOURT	"	30	FRENCH PARTY. Getting up report on Boshi troops.	Photo.

Richard Rosslin
LIEUTENANT, ADJUTANT
The Inniskilling Dragoons
30th June 1917

Serial No. 43

WAR DIARY

OF

THE INNISKILLING DRAGOONS
****

From

1st July 1917

to

31st July 1917.

::*:*:*:*:*:*:*

Army Form C. 2118.

INNISKILLING DRAGOONS

WAR DIARY
or
INTELLIGENCE SUMMARY.
(Erase heading not required.)

Instructions regarding War Diaries and Intelligence Summaries are contained in F.S. Regs., Part II. and the Staff Manual respectively. Title pages will be prepared in manuscript.

Place	Date	Hour	Summary of Events and Information	Remarks and references to Appendices
HARGICOURT	July 1st	1 am	Quiet day. No Casualties.	Ref.
"	2nd		COLOGNE FARM was raided by a party of 3 officers (Lt M.J.Duckgron, Lt U.S. Dunn and Lt W.De Kerrina) and 120 men. Raid successful. Result 11 prisoners and many Germans killed, also a lot of damage done. Casualties 1 officer Lt A.S. Dunn and 8 O.R. killed & 29 O.R. wounded. Attached operation orders of the 4th Div mounted B.de., and B.C. Sub-Sector. Also Special Order of the 4th Div mounted B.de. Retaliation started at 9am and went on more or less continuously all day.	Gto Junetin Attached
"	3rd	3.15am	Lt Penn Shilton took out a patrol to search No mans land for wounded men without result.	Gto
"	"	8.30am	Lt Adam Hodder took a patrol of 10 men to COLOGNE FARM and found the body of Lt Dunn and 8 O.R. 2 O.R. were killed and 4 wounded during the day.	Gto
"	4.		Quiet day. No Casualties. A certain amount of T.M.s were active on the front held by the Regiment. No casualties.	

2353 Wt. W2544/1454 700,000 5/15 D.D.&L. A.D.S.S./Forms/C.2118.

Army Form C. 2118.

WAR DIARY
or
INTELLIGENCE SUMMARY.

(Erase heading not required.)

INNISKILLING DRAGOONS

Hour, Date, Place.	Summary of Events and Information.	Remarks and references to Appendices
HARGICOURT July 5-	Intermittent shelling. No casualties.	JM
" 6-	Quiet day. No casualties.	JM
" 7-	Sector held by the regt. shelled by T.M. and 5.9 guns. Started about 8 am and continued most of the day. Casualties. 6 O.R. killed. 1 O.R. wounded.	JM
" 8-	Certain amount of shelling. Casualties 1 O.R. killed.	JM
" 9-	The reg. was relieved on the night of the 8-9- by the 23rd Bn of the Northumberland Fusiliers and returned to ENNEMAIN.	JM
2 cm.		

Army Form C. 2118.

WAR DIARY
or
INTELLIGENCE SUMMARY.
(Erase heading not required.)

Instructions regarding War Diaries and Intelligence Summaries are contained in F.S. Regs., Part II. and the Staff Manual respectively. Title pages will be prepared in manuscript.

Place	Date	Hour date	Summary of Events and Information	Remarks and references to Appendices
ENNEMAIN	July 10/12th		Halked Grazing: Squadron training	Hell?
—"—	13		—"—	Hell?
—"—	14th		—"—	Hell?
—"—	15		3 N.C.O's the D.C.M. 16 bridgers & Kennion awarded M.C. and	Hell?
—"—	16th		G.O.C. Brigade inspected Regiment in marching order	Hell?
—"—	17th/21st		Squadron training	Hell?
—"—	23rd/24		—"—	Hell?
—"—	25/26th		Divisional Horse Show. Regt: gained 3 firsts, 2 seconds, 1 third prize	Hell?
—"—	27		Squadron Training	Hell?
—"—	28th		Regimental Training	Hell?
—"—	29th		Sunday. Eight Syndicates joined from Base as reinforcements	Hell?
—"—	30th		Regimental Training	Hell?
—"—	31st		Squadron Training	Hell?

Hauldecoats Lt.
6th/Hdly Dragoons.

SECRET.   No. B.M. 149.   Copy No. 6

Reference 4th Cavalry Div. Map 1/2500.   28-6-17.

NOT TO BE TAKEN BEYOND SUBSECTOR HEADQUARTERS.

Operation for a date to be fixed later.

The following instructions are issued in supercession of those contained in Mhow Bde. Order No.11. of 24th inst., which should now be destroyed.

1. It is proposed to :-
   (a) Raid COLOGNE FARM and inflict as much loss as possible on the enemy.

   (b) Destroy any works and dug-outs found.

   (c) Carry off Machine Guns.

2. The troops to be employed are :-

   (a) 5 Officers and 123 Other Ranks Inniskilling Dragoons.

   (b) 1 R.E. Officer and - Sappers, 4th Field Squadron.

   (c) As much Artillery as can be placed at our disposal, including Heavy, Medium and Light Trench Mortars.

   (d) 20 Machine Guns, dispositions and targets given in Appendix A.

   (e) Bearer parties for casualties, included in (a) above.

3. The area to be raided and operated in by our troops will be restricted to :-

   S.E.Limit.- A line drawn from L.6.c.2.0. to a point L.6.c.65.40. in COLOGNE SUPPORT TRENCH.

   East Limit.- L.6.c.65.40. to L.6.c.5.8. in same trench.

   North Limit.- A line drawn from L.6.c.0.8. to L.6.c.5.8.

   All above bounds are inclusive to the raiding party.

   Artillery and Machine Gun Barrages have been calculated to enclose these limits, leaving a safe margin to the troops operating.

4. Assulting troops, distribution and objectives as in para 5, will, at Zero - 24 minutes on the night fixed for the raid be disposed as follows :-

   Right Platoon in splinter proof shelters about L.6.c.1.1.
   Left Platoon in the fire trench, about L.5.d.7.9.

   The garrison of the Quarry, with the exception of 1 Hotchkiss rifle and 6 men in the Russian Sap L.6.c.1.5. will have vacated the front line by Zero - 24 minutes and gone into their dugout and splinterproof trench.

   The trench garrison will occupy re-occupy the front line at Zero hour.

   The trench garrison of the trench in which the Left Platoon assemble will not vacate their position.

   The Right Platoon will leave their shelter at Zero - 1 minute, form up over the parapet, and start advancing to their objectives at Zero + 1 minute.
   The Artillery Rolling Barrage will start to move forward at Zero + 2 minutes.

The Artillery Enfilade Barrage will start to move forward at Zero + 3 minutes.

The Left Platoon will leave their trench at Zero - 1 minute and will be formed up in front of the parapet by Zero hour, when they will advance to their objectives.

Artillery Barrage timings the same as for the Right Platoon.

Heavy Trench Mortars open fire at Zero - 1 minute.

Medium Trench Mortars will fire on the wire from Zero - 4 minutes to Zero hour after which they will lengthen range.

Stokes Mortars open fire at Zero - 4 minutes and lengthen range at Zero + 3 minutes.

5. The Assaulting Troops will be divided into two parties to be known as the Right or DUNNE's Platoon, and the Left or KEMMIS' Platoon. The distribution and objectives of these two Platoons are as under:

RIGHT PLATOON.

1st Wave.   Platoon Leader.....Lieut DUNNE.
                              1 Runner.
                              1 Trumpeter.

    Right Blocking Party......1 Cpl. and 5 men, establish a bombing block in COLOGNE SUPPORT TRENCH at L.6.c.6.4.
    1 Bomber and 2 Carriers in party.

    Centre Blocking Party.....1 Cpl. and 2 men, establish a bombing block in COLOGNE SUPPORT TRENCH at L.6.c.5.5. (where road crosses trench).
    1 Bomber and 2 Carriers.

    Left Blocking Party.......1 Cpl and 3 men, establish a bombing block in COLOGNE SUPPORT TRENCH at L.6.c.65.65.
    1 Bomber and 2 Carriers.

    Forward Party.............1 Cpl. and 4 men, go to farm building just East of COLOGNE SUPPORT TRENCH.
    1 Bomber and 2 Carriers.

Total strength of 1st Wave Right Platoon :-
    1 Officer.
    4 Cpls.
    1 Trumpeter.
    15 men.

2nd Wave. ......1 Cpl and 4 men establish a bombing block in sunken road at T of COLOGNE TRENCH.
    1 Bomber, 2 Carriers, 2 Bayonet men.
    1 selected Pte. and 3 men work up COLOGNE TRENCH 40 yards from T of TRENCH.
    1 Bomber, 2 Carriers, 1 Bayonet man.
    1 Sergt. and 5 men go to hedge L.6.c.3.5.
    all Bayonet men.

Total strength of 2nd Wave Right Platoon.
    1 Sergt.
    1 Cpl.
    13 Men.

3rd Wave............1 Cpl. and 3 men work into the farm buildings
　　　　　　　　　　about L.6.c.4.5. from the South.
　　　　　　　　　　1 Bomber, 1 Carrier, 2 Bayonet men.
　　　　　　　　　　1 Sergt. and 4 men work into the farm buildings
　　　　　　　　　　about L.6.c.4.5. from the North.
　　　　　　　　　　1 Bomber, 2 Carriers, 2 Bayonet men.
　　　　　　　　　　1 Cpl. and 7 men work Northwards up Sunken Road
　　　　　　　　　　from T of TRENCH to junction with road running
　　　　　　　　　　S.E. by E. down which they then work, bombing
　　　　　　　　　　dugouts if found to exist. They then work through
　　　　　　　　　　the farm buildings from the East.
　　　　　　　　　　2 Bombers, 3 Carriers, 3 Bayonet men.

　　Total strength of 3rd Wave Right Platoon.:-
　　　　　　　　　　1 Sergt.
　　　　　　　　　　2 Cpls.
　　　　　　　　　　14 Men.

　　4 Stretcher bearers with 2 Regtl. Stretchers follow 3rd Wave.

　　Total Strength Right Platoon.:-
　　　　　　　　　　1 Officer.
　　　　　　　　　　2 Sergts.
　　　　　　　　　　7 Cpls.
　　　　　　　　　　1 Trumpeter.
　　　　　　　　　　42 Men.
　　　　　　　　　　4 Stretcher Bearers.

　　　　　　　　　　Left Platoon.

1st Wave......Left Platoon Leader...Lieut KEMMIS.
　　　　　　　　　　　　　　　　　1 Trumpeter.
　　　　　　　　　　　　　　　　　3 Runners.

　　　　　　　　　　1 Selected Pte. and 3 men block Sunken Road at
　　　　　　　　　　L.6.c.3.7.. All Rifle men; fire up Sunken Road
　　　　　　　　　　towards UNNAMED FARM.
　　　　　　　　　　1 Cpl. and 9 Men work up to most Northerly farm
　　　　　　　　　　buildings.
　　　　　　　　　　2 Bombers, 2 Carriers, 6 Bayonet men.

　　　　　　　　　　3 men for wire cutting precede 1st Wave.

　　Total strength 1st Wave, Left Platoon.
　　　　　　　　　　1 Officer.
　　　　　　　　　　1 Cpl.
　　　　　　　　　　1 Trumpeter.
　　　　　　　　　　19 Men.

2nd Wave......1 Sergt. and 10 Men work up to the two farm buildings
　　　　　　　　　　L.6.c.3.6. just North of "HEDGE". After clearing
　　　　　　　　　　buildings, clear up between these buildings and
　　　　　　　　　　COLOGNE TRENCH.
　　　　　　　　　　2 Bombers, 3 Carriers, 6 Bayonet men.

　　Total strength 2nd Wave, Left Platoon.
　　　　　　　　　　1 Sergt.
　　　　　　　　　　10 Men.

3rd Wave.......1 Cpl. and 6 men enter COLOGNE TRENCH where it
　　　　　　　　　　crosses North branch of road from COLOGNE FARMS to
　　　　　　　　　　Slag Heap and work up North to T Trench, 90 yards.
　　　　　　　　　　2 Bombers, 3 Carriers, 2 Rifle men.
　　　　　　　　　　1 Cpl. and 5 Men enter at same point and work back
　　　　　　　　　　down Sunken Road towards Slag Heap, and then from
　　　　　　　　　　junction work down Southern Arm to T of Trench,
　　　　　　　　　　L.6.c.4.3.
　　　　　　　　　　2 Bombers, 2 Carriers, 2 Bayonet men.
　　　　　　　　　　1 Sergt. and 7 Men enter COLOGNE TRENCH at same
　　　　　　　　　　point as above two parties and work along COLOGNE
　　　　　　　　　　TRENCH Southwards to Right Platoon Blocking Party
　　　　　　　　　　at T of TRENCH.
　　　　　　　　　　2 Bombers, 2 Carriers, 4 Bayonet Men.

In Rear of 3rd Wave.

All the R.E. except 1 Sapper who accompanies Right Platoon Leader.
2 Stretcher bearers with 2 Regimental Stretchers.

Total Strength 3rd Wave, Left Platoon.-
    1 Sergt.
    2 Cpls.
   18 Men.
    4 Stretcher Bearers.

The Raid Leader, Captain DUDGEON, follows in rear of 3rd Wave accompanied by a Signaller who runs out a telephone line from B.3. Advanced Hd. Qrs. Another line will be laid by a second signaller from B.3. Advanced Hd. Qrs. up Sunken Road to Capt. DUDGEON's H.Q. at Road Junction L.6.c.$\frac{1}{4}$.5$\frac{1}{2}$.
He has with him in addition 4 Runners and 4 men for cutting wire to prepare road for withdrawal.

    Total Strength of Left Platoon.

    1 Officer.
    2 Sergts.
    3 Cpls.
    1 Trumpeter.
  47 Men.
    4 Stretcher Bearers.

R.E.{

    With Raid Leader.

Raid Leader.
2 Signallers.
8 Men.

    At North West Corner of Slag Heap.

Lieut Winter Irving.
and 1 Man.

6. Co-operation on Flanks.

2nd Cavalry Division will simulate an attack on MALAKOFF Farm by Artillery and Machine Gun Fire.
Should the wind be favourable, smoke will be let off on the Right flank from about VILLERET.

7. Dress and Equipment.

The Khaki Serge will be worn.
All ranks taking part will wear a white band not less than four inches wide on each arm.
All badges and marks by which the enemy might obtain identifications will be removed. All identity discs, letters, pay books, etc., will be left behind.
1 P.H.G.Helmet in satchel will be carried by each man.

Rifles with fixed bayonets will be carried, magazines will be charged with 10 rounds, safety catches back. There will be no firing except by the covering parties.
Engineers will not carry rifles but will carry bayonets and bombs.
Each man taking part in the raid will carry 2 bombs in his pocket.
100 large Pattern Wire Cutters have been provided, the remaining men will carry wire cutters of the ordinary pattern.
A proportion of luminous watches has been provided.
A proportion of Knobkerries are being provided.

8. Communications. between Raid Leader and Platoons by Runner.
Between B.3. Subsector Adv. H.Q. and Raid Leader by Telephone and runner, two lines will be laid.
Between B.3. H.Q. and B.3. Adv. H.Q. by telephone and runner,

9. **Headquarters.** The Raid Leader's H.Q. will be at junction of roads leading from COLOGNE FARMS to Slag Heap.
O.C. B.3. Subsector will establish an Advanced H.Q. at L.5.d.3.9.
(4th house from East end of HARGICOURT on North side of road).

10. **Prisoners.** Will be handed over to a representative of the A.P.M. at North West corner of the Slag Heap.
In each of the Right and Left Platoons a small party will be detailed beforehand to deal with prisoners.
Officers, N.C.Os and Men must be kept seperate.

11. **R.E.** Arrangements are in charge of an officer 4th Field Squadron, who will accompany the Raid.
Bangalore Torpedoes, mobile charges and "P" Bombs will be carried.

12. **Withdrawal.** will be by time, bugle call and rocket signal, 30 minutes after Zero hour.
The signal for the withdrawal by the bugle will be the "Trot".
The signal for the withdrawal by Rocket Signal will be a group of 2 Red and 2 Green rockets fired from B.3. Adv. H.Q.
Sufficient rockets must be placed in position to ensure the above group being successfully sent up.
A man will be specially detailed by O.C. B.3. Subsector to attend to this.
A group of 3 Green Rockets will be fired from B.3. Adv. H.Q. on the order of O.C. B.3. Subsector when all are clear.
This will signify to the Artillery and others that the withdrawal is complete.

The main route for withdrawal, and which should be used, other things being equal, will be the Sunken Road running past the Slag Heap.

Alternative routes are those by which the Platoons enter COLOGNE FARMS.

Each Platoon will run out a tape from its jumping off place to where the wire in front of COLOGNE TRENCH is crossed. This tape will be pulled in on the completion of the withdrawal.

Both Platoons on withdrawing will make for B.3. Subsector H.Q. but in case there should be a hostile barrage on the Western exits of HARGICOURT at the time of the withdrawal, cellars have been cleared near advanced Subsector H.Q. These will be marked by Red Lamps on the night of the raid.

The position of the cellars will be reconnoitred by N.C.Os taking part in the raid previous to the night appointed.

A guide will be provided at Advanced Subsector H.Q. to point out the way to the cellars if necessary.

13. **Medical Arrangements.** An Advanced Regimental Aid Post will be established at L.5.c.8.6., in addition to the Aid Post at B.3. Subsector H.Q.
A.D.M.S. will provide two Regimental Stretchers to accompany each Platoon.
Also 4 Regimental Stretchers at North West corner of the Slag Heap.

14. **Code Words.** will be arranged and communicated to all ranks taking part in the raid.

15. **Synchronization of Watches** will be carried out just before leaving Subsector H.Q. from the watch of the Artillery Liaison Officer. This must be most carefully done.

ACKNOWLEDGE.

Copies to:-
No.1. 4th Cav. Div.
2. C.,R.H.A.
3. Engineer Officer accompanying Raid.
4. Major TERROT.
5. Raid Leader.
6. Right Platoon Leader.
7. Left Platoon Leader.
8. No.11. M.G. Squadron.
9. A.D.M.S.
10 - 13 Diary and File.

Captain.
Brigade Major.

Rifle Platoon Leader

4th DISMOUNTED BRIGADE.

SPECIAL ORDER.

The Corps Commander has telephoned conveying his hearty congratulations to Major TERROT, D.S.O., and the Officers and other ranks of the Inniskilling Dragoons and Royal Engineers who took part in the Raid.

He is very pleased indeed with the success achieved but regrets the list of casualties and sympathizes with the Regiment in their losses.

The Divisional Commander adds his own congratulations and sympathies to those of the Corps Commander.

I wish to thank all ranks who took part in the Raid for the very gallant manner in which they carried it through, it reflects the greatest credit on all concerned.

Neil Haig

Brigadier General.
Commanding 4th Dismounted Brigade.

2-7-17.

(4)

Orders for Raid night of 1/2 July 17

1. The wire is to be cut in front of Right Platoon and the parapet to be levelled by Zero -30

2. The sunken road is to be cleared and the Arch cut by Zero -30.

3. Trench garrison and Posts 2,3,4,5,+6 will either go into splinter proofs or withdrawn by Zero -30.

4. No Right Platoon to be in Quarry ready to go into splinter proofs by Zero -30

5. The wire will be cut between Post 8 and M.G. 22 by Zero -30

6. O.C. Harvard will clear Trench when Left Platoon occupies and will man Trench when Platoon goes over. He will also arrange for a Barrier officer who will be responsible for the wire cutting and the traffic control of the Trench.

7. Barrage of UNNAMED BARRAGE (4 is Indicated by Zero - 30 and will not lift until Zero + 1.

8. O.C. Mark and M/SS must arrange for knife rests to fill in the gaps

in the wire after the raid is over.

9. At each place where wire is cut one 3 One NCO (Inniskilling) will be stationed with a complete list of the raiding party. He will check parties coming in. 15 minutes after the signal for withdrawal they will take in the names to advanced Head Quarters

10. 2 runners detailed from HQ will proceed, one with Lieut Dudgeon and one with Lieut Dunne, to let CO know that all is ready at zero — 15

11. 3 Runners to be at advanced H.Q. to communicate with B3 H.Q.

12. 2 stretchers with four bearers to proceed with Lieut Winter Irving.

13. The 2 first aid posts to be well marked and all stretcher bearers to know where they are.

14. 6 men to go with Lieut W Irving to act as guides and assist M.P. with prisoners.

15. Rockets under the charge of Sgt Fawbrother and one man will be at advanced H.Q. The four tubes for firing them off will be fixed by 3pm

16. Advanced H.Q. must be clearly marked.
17. All men mentioned in Para's 9, 10, 11, 12, 14 and 15 will be furnished by Coys. and supports.
18. The remainder of Coys. and supports will man the BROWN LINE.
19. All watches will be synchronised at 11 pm at B3 H.Q. on the night of 1st July.
20. Zero hour 1 A.M. 2nd July 1917.

H Usher Lt. & Adjt
B3

CONFIDENTIAL

Serial No. 73.

WAR DIARY

of

INNISKILLING DRAGOONS.

from

1st. AUGUST 1917 to

31st. AUG.

*****

INNISKILLING DRAGOONS.

No. Confidential
Date. C/15/1

Army Form C. 2118

WAR DIARY
or
INTELLIGENCE SUMMARY.
(Erase heading not required.)

AUGUST 1917

Instructions regarding War Diaries and Intelligence Summaries are contained in F. S. Regs., Part II. and the Staff Manual respectively. Title pages will be prepared in manuscript.

Place	Date	Hour	Summary of Events and Information	Remarks and references to Appendices
ENNEMAIN	Aug 1st & 2nd		Regimental training.	A.1. PP
	3rd	1-5h	Training under Squadron arrangements.	A.1. PP
	" 4th	6h	Regimental training. Attack on village & woods.	A.1. PP
	" 4th & 5th		Squadron training.	A.1. PP
	"	eve	Staff Ride for all Officers.	A.1. PP
	"	23h-29h	Training under Sqdn arrangements.	A.1. PP
	"	30h	Staff Ride for all Officers.	A.1. PP
	"	31	Training under Squadron arrangements.	A.1. PP

Party of 23 N.C.Os. & Men proceeded to Eurekes as foresigners, & Staff

a) New Baths at Beauvois Gate.

3 Months proceeded on Equitation to 3rd, 4th & 5th Army Infantry Schls.

b) R.F.C. Head Qtrs.

M.L. Hodges H
5th Inniskilling Dragoons

Serial No. 73

CONFIDENTIAL

WAR DIARY

of the

INNISKILLING DRAGOONS.

for

S E P T E M B E R

1917

WAR DIARY
or
INTELLIGENCE SUMMARY.
(Erase heading not required.)

Army Form C. 2118

Place	Date	Hour	Summary of Events and Information	Remarks and references to Appendices
ENNEMAIN	Sept 1st – 3rd		Training under Squadron arrangements	Herö
"	4th		" " " " " " inspected all the horses in the Regiment	Herö
"	5th – 7th		Training under Squadron arrangements. The D.D.R. Cavalry Corps cav-corps Horseshow held on 2nd/3rd gained 2nd prize in light Equitation	Herö Herö
"	8th		Training under Squadron arrangements. 9 O.R. joined as reinforcements	Herö
"	9th		from Base depot Sunday	Herö Herö
"	10th – 15th		Training under Squadron arrangements	Herö Herö
"	16th		Sunday. The men 2 horses on detached duty with R.F.C. reported	Herö Herö
"	17th – 19th		Training under Squadron arrangements. The C.O. returned from leave on 19th	Herö Herö
"	20th		Respiration of medal ribbons by G.O.C. Bridge Division.	Herö Herö
"	21st		Training under Squadron arrangements.	Herö
"	22nd		" " " " " " The Innskilling Company	Herö
"	23rd		consisted of 5 Officers and 109 O.R. proceeded for duty in the trenches Saturday	Herö Herö

WAR DIARY
or
INTELLIGENCE SUMMARY.

Army Form C. 2118

Place	Date	Hour	Summary of Events and Information	Remarks and references to Appendices
ENGHIEN	Sept 26		Famous under Squadron arrangements	keep
—	27		Staff ride for all available Officers under the C.O.	keep
—	28-29		Training under Squadron arrangements	keep
—	30		Sunday	keep
			Signalling & bombing classes & instruction continued throughout the month	keep

H. de Pass
Inniskilling Dragoons

INNISKILLING DRAGOONS.

WAR DIARY.

1st October to
31st. October 1917.

73.

Army Form C. 2118.

WAR DIARY or INTELLIGENCE SUMMARY.

(Erase heading not required.)

6th Inniskilling Dragoons

Place	Date	Hour	Summary of Events and Information	Remarks and references to Appendices
EHNEMAIN	October			
	1st/10	2nd	Training under Bgde. arrangements. Hoff on Faiduup.	
	2nd	n.h.	Training under Squadron arrangements. Staff exercise all subalterns.	
	3rd/10	4	Training under Squadron arrangements.	
	5th/10	4	Regimental Parade. Squadron Training. Regt. Scheme.	
	8th	—	Squadron Training. Staff Ride.	
	9th/10	15 h	36. Horses transferred to 1st K.E.H. 15 recruits & 28 remounts strength on embarkation to MESOPOTAMIA.	
	13th/10			
	18th/10	15 h	Squadron training. 34. Riding Horses arrived from Base. Horse Lines to complete establd. 15/10/17.	
	16th	—	Marching order inspection. Lecture for Bgde. Squadron Training. Staff Ride for Officers.	
	17th	—	Regimental Parade. Regimental Scheme.	
	18th/10	20 h	Notn on completion of Horse Standing. Brigade ??	
	20th/9	20 h	Staff Ride for all Subalterns. Hoft on Horse Standing.	
	23rd	—	Stag Scheme. Hoft on Officers. 5 Officers Junior ?? from Aldershot.	
	25th	27th	Staff Ride for Officers. Hoft on Faiduup.	
	26th	—	Squadron Training. Hoft on Faiduup.	
	29th-30th			
	31st		Regimental Training. Scheme. Hoft on Faiduup.	

Strength at month. Signalling, Hotchkiss Gun Crashes, Erecting Horse Standing Hots 6 Lents.

H. McCaw.
Lieut.
Inniskilling Dragoons

WAR DIARY.
INNISKILLING DRAGOONS.

November 1st
to
November 30th 1917.

VOLUME.   No.

Army Form C. 2118.

WAR DIARY
or
INTELLIGENCE SUMMARY.

6th A. Snowshill Dragoons

(Erase heading not required.)

Instructions regarding War Diaries and Intelligence Summaries are contained in F.S. Regs., Part II. and the Staff Manual respectively. Title pages will be prepared in manuscript.

Place	Date	Hour	Summary of Events and Information	Remarks and references to Appendices
ETHMIN	1 Nov 1917		Annual was open arrangements. Work on Area Standings.	
	2		Regimental training.	
	3,4		Half day for all Sections.	
	4		Annual was open arrangements. Work on Area Standings.	
	5,6		Regimental training. Work on Area Standings.	B. Sqn a q. Ri p.a.o. Sqn Hrs.	
	7,8		Squadrons training.	
	10		Orders for all Squadrons. Work on Swastrip.	
	11,12	M.L	on to enl. were by Kent Squadron. Orders received from Bde Comdr. 'D' Sqn, orders east of Pat. Kavanagh.	
	13	8th	Regimental training. Work by Squadrons. Standing not p.a.o. Everything based so so.	
	14,	18th	One period to be twelve hours at one two notice, one report of scene arranged. Regimental HQ. Standing to one, hour notice.	
	19,20		Flying scouts to one, and aircraft to one, uncovered H.E. Fires set. 1½ loc to one later. B. Colors assumed not forward passing road. Then if not 9.20 am	
			B Colors furns bridle in Ethmin, to await orders from kmaid.	
FIND	21		Regiment started 15 of on hour either from kmaid.	

WAR DIARY
or
INTELLIGENCE SUMMARY.
(Erase heading not required.)

Army Form C. 2118.

Place	Date	Hour	Summary of Events and Information	Remarks and references to Appendices
Fins	24	12:40 P.M.	Regt. orders to return to ENNEMAIN. Orders recvd at 12:40 a.m. Left Fins 9:35 A.M.	yes
ENNEMAIN	24 - 25	—	Arrived ENNEMAIN. Orders 6 p.m. Regt. at once notified to move forward. Battles remained parked at waggon lines.	yes
Nr. VILLERS FAUCON	25	6:20 A.M.	Regt. moved to move into Arr. Forward concentration area N.W. of VILLERS FAUCON, arrived at 8:20 a.m. Regt. in readiness to move forward.	yes
VILLERS FAUCON	26	8 P.M.	Regt. ord. Forward to ENNEMAIN. arrived in camp about 11:30 p.m.	yes
ENNEMAIN	26	9:45 A.M.	Orders received that Div. will not move until 4-15. Regt. at four squad. to Templeux	yes
	27		Was standing in readiness, ready to go.	yes
	28		Men on Horse Lines.	yes
	29		Canada K "Scheminette" Passerieu in readiness for —	yes
	30	8:15 A.M.	Inniskilling Dragoons moved forward to forward rendezvous. CRUCIFIX - TEMPLEUX, Minute	yes
			8th Cav. Bde. J. L. Col E. Paterson DSO	
	30	10:25 A.M.	Regt. on the way to relieve infantry in line. Infantry ord. to retire immediate to Ennemain	yes
			attack orders ready for Mounted action.	
P. 20. d.	30	12:10 P.M.	Regt. moved on cavalry to cavalry Rendezvous point at P.20.d. 67.0. 4000.	yes J. C.
	30	2:30 P.M.	Regt. moved into Rdv. Sq. E.18 H 6 ST EMILB. arrived St Stephen	yes Lieut. Innishilling Dgns

WAR DIARY

of

INNISKILLING DRAGOONS

for

DECEMBER 1915.

VOL.   No.

Army Form C.2118

WAR DIARY
or
INTELLIGENCE SUMMARY.
(Erase heading not required.)

December 1917

Instructions regarding War Diaries and Intelligence Summaries are contained in F.S. Regs., Part II. and the Staff Manual respectively. Title pages will be prepared in manuscript.

Place	Date	Hour	Summary of Events and Information	Remarks and references to Appendices
VILLERS GUISLAIN Ridge	Dec 1		Arrived Astron vice attack situation (attacked recent) on VILLERS GUISLAIN RIDGE	nil
"	2		X 10 (eyd) N.E. of PIEZIERE Casualties 5 B.O. 10+ O.R. 187 Animals	nil
EMMENPIN	3+4	96	Exercise under squadron arrangements. Standing to at 1 hour notice to move.	nil
"	10	p.t	Reinforcements arrived from Base Depot. 125 O.R.s (69 remount not ex Base)	nil
"			Training under squadron arrangements. Rifasio of horse standings.	nil
"	15th	10h	Training under squadron arrangements. H 35 reinforcements joined from Base. New Riding troop	nil
"	16th	10h	marching order Parade. Orders for no last. joined itself	nil
"	18 1/6 018		Regt: ready to move at 1 hour notice from 4 a.m. to 8-30. saddles up.	nil
"			Dismounted Parade Order. 15 Riding troop joined from Base.	nil
"	28th	252	Training under squadron arrangements. 95 O.R. joined from Base Select Horses	nil
"	31st	8d	Training with squadron arrangements. Working party under Dismounted Services for	nil
			att'd at JEANCOURT. Working Party to BIHECOURT.	

Signed: Murphy Lt. As acting Adjutant, trumpet practice, signalling classes.

Summary of operations attached.
Roe, RfR.

Murphy Lt.
[signature]

	As soon as a suitable opportunity presents itself MHOW Brigade to move forward and seize and establish itself on the VILLERS Ridge about X.10., measures to be taken to watch the Right flank.
4.0.a.m.	Mhow Brigade Order No.22. issued on above.
5.30.a.m.	Brigade moved off to concentrate West of PEIZIERE. G.O.C. and B.M. proceeded to meet Divisional Commander at E.4.d.8.5.
6.45.a.m.	G.O.C. rejoined Bde. West of PEIZIERE. Brigade Report Centre established W.30.b.5.3. Situation and probable plan of action explained to Commanding Officers.
7.30.a.m.	Reports received from officers reconnoitring wire that there were exits by the PEIZIERE - VILLERS GUISLAN Road and by 14 willows road F.1.b.
8.10.a.m.	Reports received from Tank Liaison Officers that no Tanks arrived at rendezvous and that consequently Lucknow Bde. were unable to attack but were supporting Infantry in VAUCELETTE Fme.
8.15.a.m.	Order received from 4th Cav. Divn. "You are to endeavour to push forward towards your objective supported by the Artillery............"
8.20.a.m.	Commanding Officers arrived at Bde. H.Q. and situation explained. 2nd Lancers with 2 Machine Guns ordered to try and seize TARGELLE, QUAIL and PIGEON ravines. Inniskilling Dragoons and 4 Machine Guns to follow as soon as 2nd Lancers were seen approaching their objective and endeavour to seize and hold the VILLERS GUISLAN Ridge about X.10.
8.38.a.m.	Division informed the Brigade was moving forward at once, and a request made that 5th Cav. Divn. might co-operate and attack VILLERS GUISLAN. Artillery warned that Brigade was moving forward.
9.35.a.m.	2nd Lancers seen moving forward N.E. of the 14 willows. At the same moment the leading Squadron of the Inniskilling Dragoons moved off down the PEIZIERES - VILLERS GUISLAIN road closely followed by the more squadrons (One squadron had accompanied 2nd Lancers).
9.40.a.m.	Headquarters and 2 Squadrons Inniskilling Dragoons returned, having come under very heavy M.G.fire. No one returned of the leading squadron.
10.10.a.m.	Following report sent to 4th Cav. Divn. :- "2nd Lancers are believed to be in or about PIGEON Ravine, one Squadron Inniskillings is with them. I am now sending 2 squadrons C.I.H. in support of them and am following with remaining two squadrons via road running through X.26. - X.27. - X.22. 3 Machine Guns will also accompany me."
10.15.a.m.	2 Squadrons C.I.H. left their horses in EPEHY and proceeded forward dismounted, they could only reach X.27.central when they were held up by machine Gun fire.
10.20.a.m.	G.O.C. went to F.1.b.4.5. but nothing could be seen of the situation except led horses of the 2nd Lancers about X.27.b. 9.9. Brigade Report Centre then moved to Railway embankment near by.
10.50.a.m.	Following from 2nd Lancers received :- "2nd Lancers and Capt. MONCRIEFF's squadron in fortified sunken road X.22.c., also 4 Machine Guns. lately held by 1 Coy 418th Regt.

P.T.O.

SUMMARY OF OPERATIONS, MHOW CAVALRY BRIGADE,

November 30th to December 2nd 1917.

****

Nov. 30th.
10.35.a.m.   Brigade ordered to saddle up and concentrate at P.30.d.
              The Brigade were on their way to relieve the 72nd Infantry
              Brigade in the Centre Sector, 24th Divisional Front.
              Inniskillings returned to ENNEMAIN and packed saddles, ready
              for mounted action.   Lances and swords were sent up in
              wagons for 2nd Lancers and 38th C.I.Horse and issued later.

12.10.p.m.   Brigade, less 2nd Lancers, H.Q. and 8 guns 11th M.G.Sqdn.
              and advance parties from all units, in the trenches, con-
              centrated in P.30.d.

2.20.p.m.   Brigade moved off under orders to proceed to camp between
              LONGAVESNES and VILLERS-FAUCON.

3.10.p.m.   Orders received to proceed as fast as possible to camp
              S.W. of SAULCOURT E.14.b. (62.c.)

3.40.p.m.   Orders received to concentrate as quickly as possible in
              Square E.18. just North of St.EMILIE.

4.15.p.m.   G.O.C. and Brigade Major reported at 4th Cavalry Division
              H.Q. E.22.b.5.0., Brigade moved on to E.18.

6.0.p.m.   2nd Lancers and H.Q. & 8 Guns 11th M.G.Squadron joined the
              Brigade North of St.EMILIE.

6.45.p.m.   G.O.C. rejoined Brigade in E.18.

7.0.p.m.   Brigade Report Centre moved to E.24.c. Southern exit of
              St.EMILIE.

7.45.p.m.   Intimation received that 55th Division preparing reserve
              line through LEMPIRE - MALASSISE Fme. - X.26 - VAUCELETTE
              Fme.
              Mhow Cav. Brigade detailed to reinforce line in case of
              attack.
              Brigade Major proceeded to EPEHY to get in touch with 166th
              Infantry Bde. holding centre of line.   Returned 9.45.p.m.

9.5.p.m.   Order received to get in touch with 165th Infantry Bde. in
              St.EMILIE.

11.30.p.m.   Intimation received that an attack on LEMPIRE VAUCELETTE
              Line is considered likely early on morning of 1st.
              Mhow Cav. Bde. ordered to be ready to move on receipt of
              orders after 5.30.a.m.

Decr. 1st.
1.45.a.m.   Warning order received that Division, less Lucknow Bde. and
              'A' Echelon, will be in position West of PEIZIERE at 6.15.
              a.m..   Mounted Pack Sections to join Brigade at Rendezvous.
              All this to take place in event of Brigade not being required
              to reinforce LEMPIRE - VAUCELETTE Line at 5.30.a.m.

2.50.a.m.   4th Cavalry Division Order No.22. received.
              5th Cavalry Division, with Lucknow Bde. attached, to attack
              VILLERS GUISLAN and GAUCHE WOOD at 6.30.a.m.
              Tanks co-operating.
              4th Cavalry Division, less Lucknow Bde, to assemble West of
              PEIZIERE with object of taking advantage of the advance of
              the Tanks and seizing VILLERS GUISLAN Ridge (X.10. Sheet
              57.c.).

              Mhow Bde. allotted 1 troop 4th Field Squadron.
              Mhow Bde. to reconnoitre crossings through a line of our
              wire just E of PEIZIERE and to keep close liaison with the
              Tank attack.
                                                                P.T.O.

2.30.p.m.	G.O.C. Mhow Bde. informed O.C. 38th C.I.H. of the attack at 3.p.m. and directed that the two squadrons in advance at X.27.central should co-operate in this attack and would supported by 1 Sqdn. C.I.H. O.C. Inniskilling Dragoons was informed that in case of success of this attack his two squadrons would be required.
2.30.p.m.	Division informed of failure of attack in conjunction with Infantry and that total available force in hand of G.O.C. consisted of two weak squadrons Inniskilling Dragoons; 1 Sqdn. C.I.H. and 2 Machine Guns. Further that the enemy had been found to be extremely strong in machine guns and that with the small force available he felt he was unable to attack his original objectives with any hope of success.
2.30.p.m.	Message received from M.G.reinforcements that he was about X.27.central with the leading dismounted Sqdn. C.I.H.
3.0.p.m.	Message received from 2nd Lancers that their line ran X.28. central to X.22.c.9.4.. German strong points at X.22.c.5.9. and X.21.c.8.0., Left flank very much in air, attack developing from Left.
3.10.p.m.	165th Infantry Bde. were informed by G.O.C. 166th that 2 Sqdns Cavalry were in posts about X.27.central. That he was being relieved by 110th Infty. Bde. that night and would ask this Bde. to relieve those Cavalry Posts and throw out a string of posts to join up with troops, believed Cavalry, in KILDARE Post and near ADELPHI. He also informed 165th that Mhow Bde. were unable to communicate with Cavalry in KILDARE and ADELPHE. That G.O.C. Mhow approved his suggestion and wished 165th in inform troops in KILDARE and ADELPHI and tell them to send their horses back to EPEHY.
3.10.p.m.	Officer Commanding the two squadrons that co-operated in the Infantry attack at 1.p.m., was ordered to send back the M.G. reinforcement with him. And that he would remain in his present position until relieved by the Infantry in the evening.
3.25.p.m.	Following received from 2nd Lancers :- "Sqdn. of C.I.H. not arrived. AAA Some pressure on my Left flank and Left rear. AAA Total strength 2nd Lancers and T.F. about 200, position as before ". Sent off 3.10.p.m.
6.0.p.m.	Intimation received from 166th Infty Bde. that 165th were dealing with situation at KILDARE.
6.5.p.m.	Permission obtained from 166th Bde to withdraw three advanced sqdns of 38th C.I.H.
7.0.p.m.	In 3 Sqdns. C.I.H. rejoined remainder of regiment in Square E.6.d. (62.c).
8.40.p.m.	Orders received fro Mhow Bde. to be withdrawn from the line after handing over positions to the Infantry and then to bivouac in E.17. and be prepared to act as a reserve if required.
9.15.p.m.	Major KNOWLES D.S.O. 2nd Lancers reported at Bde. H.Q. that 2nd Lancers and 1 Sqdn. Inniskilling Dragoons had been relieved and had moved into Camp in E.6.d.
2nd Decr.	
1.0.a.m.	Intimation received of expected heavy Enemy attack on sector GONNELIEU - LA VACQUERIE. Troops warned to be on the alert.
6.0.a.m.	Brigade Report Centre established at ST EMILIE.
9.45.a.m.	Orders received to form Mhow Bde into a Dismounted Battn. to act as a Reserve to 4th Dismounted Bde. In the event of its being required, to proceed to Southern exit of EPEHY and thence to Railway cutting in X.25.a. - W.24.d

P.T.O.

(2) Herewith shoulder straps and papers of a prisoner, (sent to 4th Cav. Divn.)
(3) Enemy who retired from this position went North.
(4) Infantry in touch on our Right.
(5) Enemy shelling Little PRIEL Fme. which is believed empty."
Sent off 10.30.p.m.

11.0.a.m.   2nd Lancers asked if they were able to connect up with Infty, and hold out.
Informed that 1 Sqdn. C.I.H. dismounted was being sent to their support, and also that Inniskillings had had to withdraw.

11.15.a.m.   Division informed that 1 Sqdn. C.I.H. dismounted was being sent to assistance of 2nd Lancers; that it was impossible to get through mounted. That 166th Infty. Bde. were arranging to advance at 1.0.p.m. and that C.I.H. had been asked to inform 2nd Lancers of this and to tell them to hold out until then. That one troop C.I.H. was being sent mounted by a more southerly route to try and get in touch with the 2nd Lancers.

11.30.a.m.   G.O.C. Mhow Cav. Bde. conferred with G.O.C. 166th Infty. Bde. and arranged to lend him two dismounted squadrons C.I.H. to assist him in his attack on the MEATH - CATELET line at 1.p.m.

11.45.a.m.   Officers Commanding these two squadrons went to confer with O.C. 1/5 Kings Own.

11.55.a.m.   Following received from 2nd Lancers, :-

"Am connected with Infantry on Right about X.26.a.9.9. AAA Left flank about X.22.c.9.4. AAA Enemy M.G. 800 yds from left flank between us and you AAA Left flank in air and enemy attacking from left rear.

12.Noon.   Message received from G.O.C. 166th, which informed his Infty that the Cavalry would only assist him to get his objectives a and that he must arrange to take over the whole of his new frontage and release the Cavalry.

12.3.p.m.   Telephonic conversation with 4th Cav. Divn. informing them of arrangement to co-operate with the Infantry in their attack.

12.7.p.m.   Conversation confirmed.

12.45.p.m.   Message received from 2nd Lancers by lamp to effect that Colonel TURNER had been killed or wounded in advance, and that M.G. reinforcements were required.

12.50.p.m.   O.C. 11th M.G. Squadron informed and a reinforcement of Machine Gunners sent up.
They were unable to get through and remained with the Sqdn. C.I.H. who had been sent to reinforce 2nd Lancers.

1.0.p.m.   Message received from above sqdn. C.I.H. that they were held up and unable to advance, the enemy were coming down on their left and they were going to fall back, on the Infantry strong post if necessary.

2.0.p.m.   Verbal message received to effect that attack in conjunction with Infantry had failed with heavy loss and that the enemy were strongly entrenched and had many machine guns in position

2.15.p.m.   Order received from 4th Cav. Divn. giving enemy's apparent main line of resistance. Our Horse Artillery continuing to bombard RAPERIE till 3.p.m. At which hour Lucknow Bde. to attack RAPERIE from the West and Mhow Bde. to endeavour to obtain possession of some of their original objectives and RAPERIE from the South with the whole Brigade dismounted. One Battery East of EPEHY to come under orders of Mhow Bde. Sialkot Bde. to act as a mounted reserve and take advantage of any success obtained.

P.T.O

12.15.p.m.	Intimation received that 1st Cavalry Division would relieve 4th and 5th Cav. Divns. in the line that night.
11.10.p.m.	Orders received to move back to ATHIES area next morning.

3rd Dcr.

9.0.a.m.	Brigade moved off.
1.0.p.m.	Arrived in billets.

****

Report on the operations of "C" Squadron, Inniskilling Dragoons, on Decbr. 1st 1917.

This report may be divided into 3 headings:-
  (i)   The advance to the German wire and the occupation of the trench.
  (ii) The holding and defence of trench.
  (iii) The withdrawal after dark.

1. The Squadron advanced at a gallop on the left rear flank of the 2nd. Lancers from PEIZIERE to about K.22.c.central (sheet 57.c.1/40000), a distance of about 3 kilometres – the last half of which was over a fire-swept zone.

The mounted advance terminated at the German wire at obstacle distance from a fire trench held by the 415th Regiment, who left hurriedly on their wire being crossed. Here the Squadron dismounted for action, crossed the wire and gained the shelter of the trench just vacated by the enemy and already entered by the 2nd Lancers.

2. The trench occupied ran north and south, the direction of advance having been E.N.E. The Squadron held the northern end of this trench, which terminated in a sap-head commanded on three sides by a ridge under 100 yards distant; this ridge overlooked VILLERS-GUISLAIN to the north, and enfiladed the trench to the south.

To hold this, the post nearest the enemy, a post was pushed out on the ridge, and a machine gun: all the men and the M.G.Officer soon became casualties, the machine gun had to be withdrawn, and it was not possible after this to leave the sap-head. Owing to lack of space, this sap-head could only be held by 2 machine guns, 2 Hotchkiss guns, and a few men. The enemy soon crawled up and enveloped this flank from 3 sides.

Fortunately, several boxes of ammunition and bombs were found in the trench – formerly a British one, and the machine guns with a party filling belts, were able to check the repeated attempts of the enemy to crawl through the scrub and rush the sap-head.

Unsuccessful in this, the enemy bombed his way down a communication trench from the north-west leading into the main trench 50 yards south of the sap-head. A counter-bombing party was organized, bombs were fortunately at hand, also many German grenades which were experimented with and timed. This party was gallantly led by a Corporal, who killed the leading German; bombs were at the same time thrown with such good effect that one German was blown off his feet above the level of the parapet, and the remainder so hurriedly withdrew that they left the trench, came into the open under direct fire of the sap-head machine gun under which they were shot down. The enemy did not again attempt to advance down this communicating trench, but pressed the attack from the ridge. Had the enemy effected an entry into the sap-head, the whole length of the trench, untraversed, would have become untenable, and the five Squadrons would have been driven from it's shelter into the open. It was thanks to the machine guns, the magnificent way they were served, and the supply of ammunition found, that the position was held for 12 hours.

Reinforcement, communication and removal of casualties was rendered more difficult owing to the trench being filled with the horses (some wounded) of about 2 Squadrons 2nd Lancers and a few of our leading troop.

3. In order to carry out the withdrawal after dark, in agreement with Major Knowles, D.S.O., Commanding 2nd Lancers, this Squadron held the sap-head during the withdrawal of that Regiment. It was not found possible to withdraw under cover of the 2nd Lancers, owing to the necessity of their horses being led out in single file to the southern limit of the trench – necessitating one man to each horse. Very lights were fired frequently from the sap-head and successive covering positions taken up, until the wounded and horses were withdrawn, when the Squadron withdrew, arriving back at EPEHY at about 1 a.m.

M.T.G.

"C" Squadron's report - continued.

I have brought to the notice of the Officer Commanding Inniskilling Dns. the names of those who were conspicuous amongst all who showed such devotion to duty, and have rendered a separate report to the Officer Commanding No.11 Squadron, M.G.C. (Cav.).

                    Sd/   A.R.MCECRIEFF. Captain.
                    Commanding "C" Squadron,
                             The Inniskilling Dragoons.

4/12/17.

ACTION carried out by the INNISKILLING DRAGOONS on December 1st. 1917.

On the early morning of December 1st 1917, the Mhow brigade was brought from St. EMILE to a position of readiness N.E. of PEIZIERS.

The general order as given to Commanding Officers was that the 5th Cavalry Division and the LUCKNOW Brigade and 14 tanks were to attack GAUCHE wood and VILLERS GUISLAIN. If the operation proved successful, the 2nd Lancers were to move forward to seize and occupy TARGET RAVINE and there form a right defensive flank and cover the march of the Inniskillings on their attack on the VILLERS GUISLAIN ridge. The 5th Cavalry Division either did not attack or failed in the attack, and the enemy still held a line just N. of VAUCELLETTEFARM to BEET FACTORY, thence southwards towards TARGET RAVINE, their line being continued further westward.

About 9.15 a.m. the 2nd Lancers and "C" Squadron Inniskillings moved off through PEIZIERS and debouched from the S.E. edge, intending to cross through X.25, X.19, X.14 to their objective.

This movement failed however, owing to a large mass of the enemy on their left flank; they were diverted southwards and eventually the whole force attacked and occupied (a trench 100 yds S.E. of) TARGET RAVINE and the adjacent German trenches, which that they gallantly held against frequent counter-attacks until ordered to retire at dusk.

The remainder of the Inniskillings about 9.15 a.m. moved off from the N.E. edge of EAST PEIZIERE over the railway bridge at W.30.b.9.8. then along the road to X.19.c.4.4. when they took the sunken road southwards round our own infantry trenches and wire, into the valley leading to BEET FACTORY & VILLERS RIDGE.

Owing to "C" Squadron not having come down into the valley as originally planned, Captain Bridgewater, with "D" Squadron and maxims (these latter were originally ordered to go behind the second Squadron and should have gone behind "B" Squadron when "D" Squadron became advanced Squadron, but the fact was not noticed by C.O. in their advance) formed the advance guard and moved forward at the gallop as soon as the sunken road was cleared, and almost at once came under very heavy maxim fire from both flanks.

"A" & "B" Squadrons followed in line of troop columns and extended some six hundred yards in rear of the advanced Squadron, and they likewise came under heavy fire from both flanks after leaving the sunken road.

The advance guard Squadron in spite of very heavy losses continued their march as far as the BEET FACTORY, but at this time they were few in numbers, as they had to go through a heavy gun barrage from the direction of BEET FACTORY. On reaching BEET FACTORY a large mass of Germans rushed out from all sides and captured them.

On seeing the situation of the advanced Squadron, and the utter hopelessness of a further advance with any likelihood of success, C.O. ordered "A" & "B" Squadrons to retire on PEIZIERE.

Our losses in "D" and "C" Squadrons were heavy. Captain Bridgewater & Lieut. Miall are missing. Lieut. Campbell was seen taken prisoner. Lieuts. Carnegie and Birch-Reynardson were wounded. Lieuts. Fraser-Smith and Young had their horses shot under them. The casualties in the Regiment, including Maxim gunners, were:-

    Officers 6
 W.Os, N.C.Os & men 156
    Horses 187

Machine Gunners.
  Officers. ... 2
 N.C.Os and Men. ... 53
  Horses. ... 84

WAR DIARY
or
INTELLIGENCE SUMMARY.
(Erase heading not required.)

Army Form C. 2118.

4 D.I.N
M How Bty

Place	Date	Hour	Summary of Events and Information	Remarks and references to Appendices
Inconnue	11/1/18	to	Training under Squadron arrangements.	A.T.D
"	12/1/18	to	Presentation of ribbands of Medals awarded to 2 B.O. 1 W.O. & 7 O.Rs.	A.T.D
"	13/1/18	to	Training under Squadron arrangements. Reinforcements joined from Base 3 B.O.	A.T.D
"	16/1/18		" ; 5 animals	A.T.D
"	17/1/18		Training under Squadron arrangements. 14 R. Transferred to 26th D Machine Gun Sqdn. 17 O.Rs	A.T.D
"			to complete New to War Establishment; 9 O.Rs joined from Base	A.T.D
"	19/1/18	to	Exercise under Squadron arrangements.	A.T.D
"	22/1/18		6 Charges & 5 O.Rs joined from Base as reinforcements.	A.T.D
"	23/1/18	to	Training under Squadron arrangements.	A.T.D
"	31/1/18		"	

Strength for month — Working Parties of 9 B.O. & 200 O.Rs. finding A.T.D
for Shrush Nos at Bihecourt & Jeancourt A.T.D
1 Party & Co 95 O.Rs at Hiérville. A.T.D

J. Ridgeon Capt
Christhing Sqdn

WAR   DIARY

of

THE INNISKILLING DRAGOONS.

From: 1st February 1918

To: 28th. February 1918.

VOLUME.   No.

Army Form C. 2118.

WAR DIARY
or
INTELLIGENCE SUMMARY.
(Erase heading not required.)

INNISKILLING DRAGOONS.

Instructions regarding War Diaries and Intelligence Summaries are contained in F.S. Regs., Part II. and the Staff Manual respectively. Title pages will be prepared in manuscript.

Place	Date	Hour	Summary of Events and Information	Remarks and references to Appendices
	February 1918		Rear Troops.	
ENNEMAIN	1st		Training under Squadron arrangements.	
— " —	2nd		Regiment moved to new area, in squadrons. Lasting H.Q.r. 2/3rd MARCELCAVE	
MARCELCAVE	3rd		H.Q.rs w/2 Sqdn. moved at 7.30 a.m. to MOLLIENS VIDAME, next stop march	
MOLLIENS VIDAME 4th			H.Q.rs w/ 30 1st. moved at 11.30 a.m. to PERNAUNT. Billets. SELINCOURT, MERICOURT AREA.	
SELINCOURT	5th to 10th		Exercise under Squadron arrangements. 8 O.R joined from Base. Reinforcements	
— " —	11th to 25th		Exercise under Squadron arrangements. 4 O.R joined from Base. Reinforcements	
— " —	26th to 28th		Exercise under Squadron arrangements. Staff Ride to Battlefield	
— " —	28th		Regt. moved to new area. VAUCHELLE-les-DOMART, MOUFLERS, L'ETOILE, BRUCAMPS AREA and came under administration of Cavalry Corps. 5th Cav Division. New Orde. under orders to the EAST. Arrived new area from 28th inst.	

Kings trls. For the month moving party in forward party from MONTIGNY FARM. S.F. HARGICOURT.

K. Samuel Lieut-
O/Parisque Major Commanding Dragoons

Army Form C. 2118.

WAR DIARY
or
INTELLIGENCE SUMMARY.
(Erase heading not required.)

INNISKILLING DRAGOONS.

Place	Date	Hour	Summary of Events and Information	Remarks and references to Appendices
COTE WOOD	27/1/18		Trench Party, consisting of 11 Officers, 249 Other ranks, left billets for duty in the front line, arriving at support line at about 9.30pm 27th inst, moving next evening	ICL
THE EGG (HARGICOURT SECTOR; CAV. CORPS FRONT).	28/1/18		moved into front line trenches; relief completed by 11 p.m.	ICL
do.	29/1/18		Intermittent shelling on front line: quiet night. Hostile aeroplanes active during day and night.	ICL
do.	30/1/18		Intermittent shelling in our sector. Quiet night in front line. E.A. active over front and support line. Considerable bombing by enemy of back areas could be heard throughout night.	ICL
do.	31/1/18		Quiet day. Owing to heavy mist, few enemy T.M.S. on left sector during the night.	ICL
do.	1/2/18		Mist during morning towards mid-day. F. Artillery inactive. F.M.Guns active all day on 2 of our posts. Quiet night.	ICL
do.	2/2/18		Moved back into support line, relief being completed by 8.30 p.m. mainly during relief.	ICL

Army Form C. 2118.

WAR DIARY
or
INTELLIGENCE SUMMARY

(Erase heading not required.)

INNISKILLING DRAGOONS.

Instructions regarding War Diaries and Intelligence Summaries are contained in F. S. Regs., Part II. and the Staff Manual respectively. Title pages will be prepared in manuscript.

Place	Date	Hour	Summary of Events and Information	Remarks and references to Appendices
SUPPORT LINE (COTE WOOD)	3/2/18 to 8/2/18		Remained in support line: working parties found for front and support lines during day and night.	
THE EGG (HARGICOURT)	9/2/18		Moved into front line trenches; relief completed at 11.30pm MARTEN POST, VILLERET LANE and VILLERET lightly shelled throughout the day. Quiet night. Only 2 E.A. seen over enemy line all day.	
—do—	10/2/18		MARTEN POST and front line centre Sector shelled throughout the day. 5pm S.O.S. observed to be sent up by unit on our left. Our artillery replied immediately: units in front, support and reserve lines "stood to" until situation became normal: no enemy action following. Quiet night: enemy appeared extremely nervous, sending large number of VERY lights and combing his own wire throughout the night.	
—do—	11/2/18		Enemy artillery active on whole sector, probably owing to increase of visibility and fine weather.	

Army Form C. 2118.

WAR DIARY
or
INTELLIGENCE SUMMARY.
(Erase heading not required.)

INNISKILLING DRAGOONS.

Instructions regarding War Diaries and Intelligence Summaries are contained in F. S. Regs., Part II. and the Staff Manual respectively. Title pages will be prepared in manuscript.

Place	Date	Hour	Summary of Events and Information	Remarks and references to Appendices
THE EGG (HARGICOURT)	11/2/18	6.	E. Aeroplanes observed over his front line during day. Very quiet night. Enemy relief expected. Enemy took to support line, relief being completed by about 12.30 AM on 12th inst.	
COTE WOOD	12/2/18 to 15/2/18		Remained in support lines, furnishing daily and nightly working parties on front line and support lines. Went back to MONTIGNY FARM to be formed into a working party with exception of C.O. and Staff, who returned to billets in SELINCOURT, arriving by lorry at 6.10 am 16/2/18.	
			Total Casualties during tour in front and support lines :- One O.R. Killed (sniper) Two O.R. wounded.	

R. Sant 15 Pence Officer
Lieut J. Leigh-Jones
Inniskilling Dragoons

12.15.p.m.	Intimation received that 1st Cavalry Division would relieve 2nd & 5th Cav. Divns. in the line that night.
11.10.p.m.	Orders received to move back to ATHIES area next morning.

3rd Dcr.

9.0.a.m.	Brigade moved off.
1.0.p.m.	Arrived in billets.

****

1917-18
4TH CAVALRY DIVISION
MHOW CAVALRY BRIGADE

38TH (K.G.O.)
CENTRAL INDIA HORSE
JAN 1917 - MAR 1918

FROM 1 IND CAV DIV
Box 1176

TO EGYPT 4 CAV. DIV
10 CAV BDE

SERIAL NO. 115

Mhow

Confidential

War Diary

of

38TH (K.G.O.) CENTRAL INDIA HORSE.

FROM 1st JANUARY 1917 TO 31st JANUARY 1917

Army Form C. 2118.

WAR DIARY

or

INTELLIGENCE SUMMARY.

(Erase heading not required.)

Instructions regarding War Diaries and Intelligence Summaries are contained in F.S. Regs., Part II. and the Staff Manual respectively. Title pages will be prepared in manuscript.

Place	Date	Hour	Summary of Events and Information	Remarks and references to Appendices
NIBAS	2-1-17		Inspection of Band & Sqn. by the G.O.C. Brigade	A.D.R.
"	3-1-17		Regimental Inspection by the G.O.C. Division	A.D.R.
"	4-1-17		Arrival of 10 I.O. Ranks from the Indian Cav. adv. Base Rouen	A.D.R.
"	5-1-17		Departure of No. 2983 Kote Dafr. Boston Khan to Marseilles transferred to pension Establishment.	A.D.R.
"	10-1-17		Departure of Jemadar Nur Mohd Khan and 3177 Sowar Hazrat Shah to Ind. Cav. Adv. Base Rouen.	A.D.R.
"	11-1-17 11 A.m.		Departure of Mhow Pioneer Battalion consisting of 4 B.Os, 5 I.Os., 3 B.O.R.; 248 I.O.R. and 7 followers to VII Corps	A.D.R.
"	17-1-17		Departure of exchange party consisting of 1 I.O.R. to Marseilles	A.D.R.
"	23-1-17		Arrival of Resaldar Mohd Kamaluddin Khan No. 3177 Sowar Hazrat Khan Badah, and Cook Ferm a from Ind. Cav. Adv. Base Rouen	A.D.R.
"	26-1-17 10.30 A.m		Departure of 20 I.O. Ranks for a relief of C.I.H. Pioneer Company	A.D.R.
"	27-1-17 4 p.m		Arrival of 20 I.O. Ranks from C.I.H. Pioneer Company	A.D.R.

SACroke
Lt. Colonel
Commanding 38th C.I. Horse

CONFIDENTIAL Serial No. 115.

WAR DIARY

38th (K.G.O.) C.I. Horse

FOR

FEBRUARY 1917

Army Form C. 2118.

WAR DIARY
INTELLIGENCE SUMMARY.   38th C.I.Horse

(Erase heading not required.)

Instructions regarding War Diaries and Intelligence Summaries are contained in F.S. Regs., Part II. and the Staff Manual respectively. Title pages will be prepared in manuscript.

Place	Date	Hour	Summary of Events and Information	Remarks and references to Appendices
NIBAS	3-2-17	10 Am	21 9.O.R. left billets for 2nd Relief of C.9.H. Pioneer Coy.	aure
"	4-2-17	4-30pm	1 B.O. + 21 I.O.R. and 1 followers Rejoined the Regt. from C.I.H. Pioneer Coy.	aure
"	5-2-17	10 Am	Inspection of Explosive by the Divl. Comdr.	aure
"	8-2-17	-	Inspection of Transport by the G.O.C. Brigade	aure
"	13-2-17	-	3 B.Os., 3 I.O.s., 3 B.O.R. and 41 I.O.R. proceed to C.9.H. Pioneer Coy. on a 3rd Relief	aure
"	14-2-17	-	3 B.Os., 3 I.O.s., 3 B.O.R and 5 I.O.R. Rejoined the Regt. from C.I.H.Pioneer Coy.	aure
"	16-2-17	-	Lieut C.L. REID joined the Regt. from Ind. Cav. Adv. Base Rouen	aure
"	21-2-17	-	Tactical Scheme of Indian officers	aure
"	22-2-17	-	Lieut D.A. CAMERON and Lieut A.A. FILOSE joined the regiment from Indian Cav. Adv. Base Rouen and 1 I.O. Rank to Marseilles on pension	} aure
"	24-2-17	-	Tactical Exercise Indian officers	aure
"	25-2-17	-	1 I.O. Ranks and 1 follower joined the Regiment from Gen. Ind. Base Depot Marseilles	aure

A.J.Tone, Lieut Col
Comndg 38th (K.G.O.) C.I.Horse

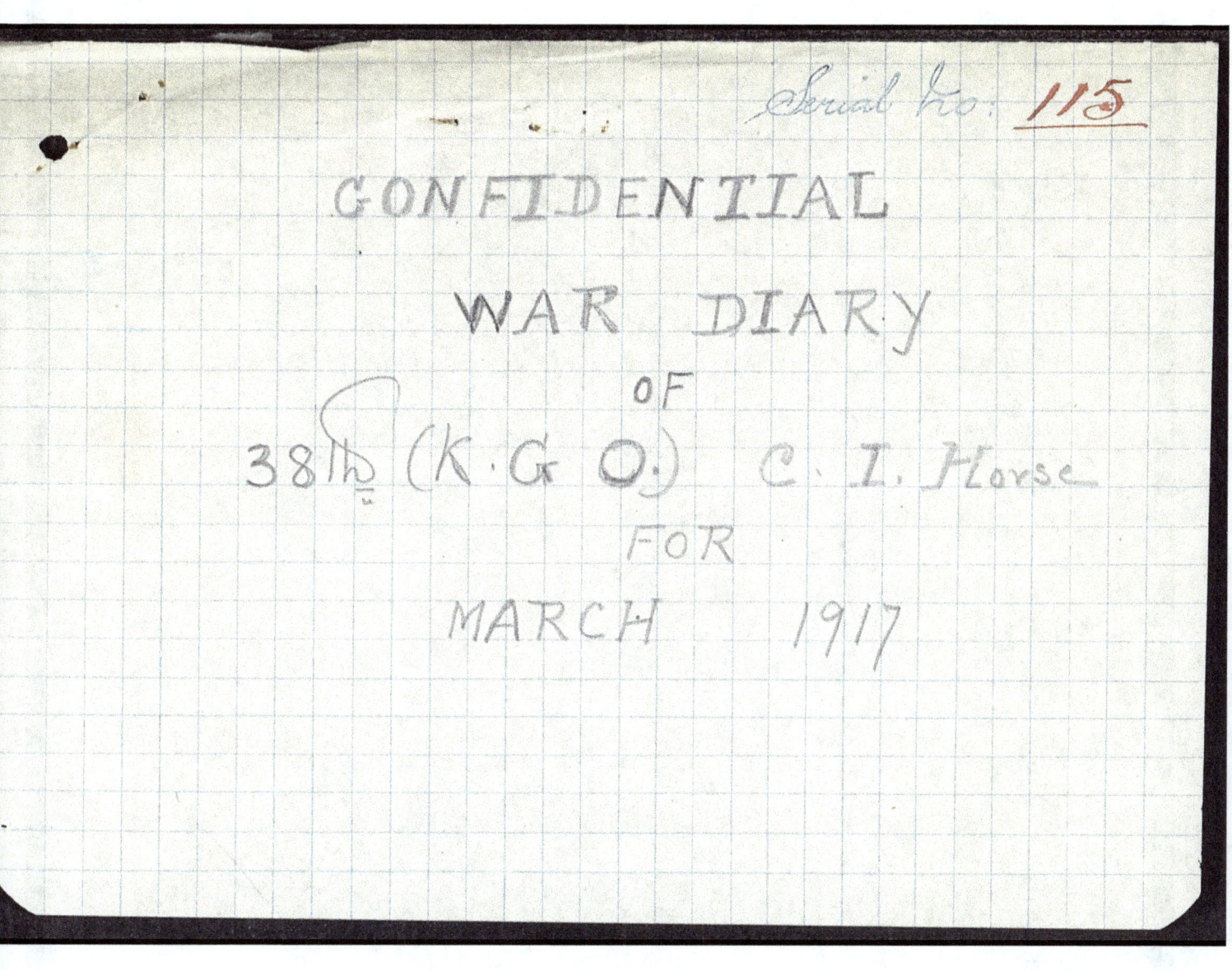

Serial No: 115

CONFIDENTIAL
WAR DIARY
OF
38th (K.G.O.) C.I. Horse
FOR
MARCH 1917

Army Form C. 2118

WAR DIARY
INTELLIGENCE SUMMARY.

of 38th C.I. Horse

(Erase heading not required.)

Instructions regarding War Diaries and Intelligence Summaries are contained in F.S. Regs., Part II. and the Staff Manual respectively. Title pages will be prepared in manuscript.

Place	Date	Hour	Summary of Events and Information	Remarks and references to Appendices
NIBAS	1-3-17		A Sqn. Inspection of arms by the Divl. Armourer and departure of Lt. Col. S. A. Cooke for India	Ans
"	2-3-17		B. Sqn. Inspection of arms by the Divl. armourer	Ans
"	3-3-17		C " " " " " " " "	Ans
"	4-3-17		D " " " " " " " "	Ans
"	5-3-17		H.Q. + A+B. Echelons " " " " " " " "	Ans
"	6-3-17		Commanding officer's scheme + Hotchkiss Gun Inspection	Ans
"	12-3-17		Signallers scheme with Aeroplane	Ans
"	13-3-17		Relief of C.I.H. Pioneer Coy; consisting of 2 B.Os + 2 B.O.R. and 38 Ind. O.R. and 1 follower left Billet 9-30 A.m.	Ans
"	14-3-17		Tactical Exercise of Indian officers and 1 B.O. 1 B.O.R. and 31 Ind. Other Ranks + 1 follower joined the Regt. from C.I.H. Pioneer Coy.	Ans
"	17-3-17		C.I.H. Pioneer Coy. consisting of 3 B.Os. 5 9.Os. 13 B.O.R. and 253 Ind. other Ranks and 6 followers joined the Regiment from VII Corps	Ans
"	19-3-17	11-30 A.m.	Regiment march to new billet at CAOURS + 29 37 J.O.R. joined the Regt from Rouen	Ans
CAOURS	20-3-17	10-30 A.m	Regiment march to new billet at BERTEAUCOURT	Ans
BERTEAUCOURT	21-3-17	"	Regiment march to new billet at AVELUY	Ans
AVELUY	24-3-17	-	Departure of Jem. Khan Mohd. Khan to Marseilles and No. 3040 Lance Daf. Faujan Singh to Rouen	Ans
" "	25-3-17	-	Arrival report of Lt. Col. J.R.C. Bell from Marseilles on the 25/3/17	Ans

OSJ Howard Lieut Col
Comdg 38th C.I. Horse

Serial No. 115.

CONFIDENTIAL
WAR DIARY
OF
38TH (K.G.O.) C.I. Horse

From 1st to 30th April 1917.

Army Form C. 2118.

38th C.I. Horse

WAR DIARY
or
INTELLIGENCE SUMMARY.
(Erase heading not required.)

Instructions regarding War Diaries and Intelligence Summaries are contained in F. S. Regs., Part II. and the Staff Manual respectively. Title pages will be prepared in manuscript.

Place	Date	Hour	Summary of Events and Information	Remarks and references to Appendices
AVELUY CAMP	3-4-17	7-30 Am	Regiment marched to camp between MIRAUMONT and IRLES	AsDs.
		10 to 17.1-30 pm	Regiment marched to a position of readiness in square B28, just S of MORY - (Brigade report centre near the MORY-FAVREUIL road) & returned to camp at 12 noon	
"	11/4/17	2-30 "	Regiment marched to square B28 just S of MORY at 2-30 Am. stayed there all day returning to camp at 5 p.m.	AsDs. AsDs.
"	13/4/17	9-45 Am	Regiment march to SARTON-AUTHIE area to billets at SARTON	AsDs.
SARTON	26-4-17	—	Inspection of B Squadron horses by the Corps Commander	AsDs.
"	30-4-17	—	Inspection of C Squadron by the G.O.C. Brigade.	AsDs.

Dancel Major

Commdg 38th (K.G.O.) C.I. Horse

Serial No. 115.

CONFIDENTIAL

WAR DIARY

38th (K.G.O.) C.I. Horse

FOR
MAY ~~1917~~ & June 1917.

Army Form C. 2118.

38th Central India Horse

WAR DIARY
or
INTELLIGENCE SUMMARY.
(Erase heading not required.)

Place	Date	Hour	Summary of Events and Information	Remarks and references to Appendices
SARTON	2-5-17		Regtl scheme with Aeroplane	A₁P₁
"	12.5.17		Inspection of signallers by the Divl. signalling officer	A₁P₁
"	15.5.17	9-30 am	Regiment march to MERICOURT	A₁P₁
MERICOURT	16.5.17	10 am	Regiment march to CAPPY	A₁P₁
CAPPY	17.5.17	9.20 am	Regiment march to ST. CHRIST	A₁P₁
ST. CHRIST	19.5.17	—	Dismounted men consisting of 2.B.O.S., 2 I.O.S. and 2.B.O.R. and 117 I.O.R. joined the Regiment, from Dismounted men 4th Cav. Division	A₁P₁
"	23.5/17	3 p.m.	C.I.H. Dismounted Regt. left the billets on 23.5/1917 for trenches near HARGICOURT. (Strength 10 B.O., 9 I.O., 10 B.O.R. 279 I.O.R. & 4 Followers)	A₁P₁

A.S. Pound Lieut. Col.
Comdg. 38th (K.G.O.) C.I.H.

Army Form C. 2118.

WAR DIARY
or
INTELLIGENCE SUMMARY.
(Erase heading not required.)

Place	Date	Hour	Summary of Events and Information	Remarks and references to Appendices
	23rd May	11-0 p.m.	C.I.H. Company relieved SOUTH STAFFORDSHIRE Reg.t in left half of left subsector of trenches E. of HARGICOURT.	A
	24th	11-20 p.m.	Lt. Dafadar Lal Khan took a fresh to the vicinity of NEW Trench and saw two figures.	A
	26th	10-0 p.m.	Wire round the end of BLOCK Trench.	A
	28th	4-0 p.m.	Daylight raid on German NEW Trench led by Lt. CAMERON attacked 2nd C.I.H. Party. Plan to obtain an identification, A.L.D. FATEH MOHD KHAN of A.Sqn. slightly wounded. Other men accompanying Lt. CAMERON No. 3192 S. IKHTAZUDIN KHAN of A Sqn, No. 3134 Sowar HABIB GUL KHAN of A Sqn, No. 2637 S. DOST MOHD KHAN and No. 3028 S. MOHD. SHARIF KHAN of C Sqn and 2 privates M.G.C. No. 3227 S. SHUJAWAL KHAN of C Sqn followed the party later with more bombs. Papers and articles of clothing and equipment were brought back. Lt. DURAND and Jemad. ? of the covering party and No. 2150 Zam. Doct. AHMAD YAR KHAN were slightly wounded. The raiding party was heavily fired at all the way out and back.	A
	29th	3-0 a.m.	No. 2568 S. HARNAM SINGH of A Sqn was wounded whilst sentry duty at the end of BLOCK TRENCH having attacked alone at himself by throwing bombs etc. a German patrol of ? men. Lt. CAMERON and A.L.D. ABDUL HAKIM KHAN 2/1st Cavalry A Sqn, 38th C.J. Horse returned up to the NEW	A

WAR DIARY or INTELLIGENCE SUMMARY

Army Form C. 2118.

Place	Date	Hour	Summary of Events and Information	Remarks and references to Appendices
	30th	10-30 p.m.	tried to ascertain whether it was held or not. They were bombed by the German Sentry about five yards from the trench and retired.	
			A Sqn in UNNAMED FARM trench were bombed by a party of Germans without result.	
			Wire successfully put out round UNNAMED FARM post. All day and very day, the we were relieved, intermittent fire from trench mortars on C Sqn front.	
	June 2nd	2.0 p.m.	UNNAMED FARM trench was heavily bombarded for three hours. Wounded: Ressaldar Major HAZURA SINGH, Ro 2390 Dafadar MEHR SINGH, Ro 2758 A.L.D. HAZARA SINGH, Ro 2467 A.L.D. BAT SINGH, Ro 3326 S. ANOKH SINGH, Ro 3135 S. HARNAM SINGH, Ro 3083 S. UDHAM SINGH, Ro 3378 S. MAKHAN SINGH, Ro 2885 S. SAUDAGAR SINGH. LT. PAGE took charge of the trench, evacuated the wounded, reduced the garrison of the trench and shortly after sent all the men except the telephonist forward to hold the far edge of the farm. He had no more casualties.	
		11-0 p.m.	UNNAMED FARM carried out under intermittent sniping. Ro 3138 S. INDER SINGH of B Sqn killed.	
	3rd	11-0 p.m.	C.I.H. Colony relieved by 29th Lancers Conforz N. J. [signature]	

CONFIDENTIAL
WAR DIARY
38th (K.G.O.) C.I Horse
FOR
JUNE 1917

Army Form C. 2118.

Instructions regarding War Diaries and Intelligence Summaries are contained in F.S. Regs., Part II. and the Staff Manual respectively. Title pages will be prepared in manuscript.

WAR DIARY
or
INTELLIGENCE SUMMARY.
(Erase heading not required.)

Place	Date	Hour	Summary of Events and Information	Remarks and references to Appendices
ST. CHRIST	4-6-17		Regiment march to HAMELET comp and C.I.H Dismounted Coy.	
HAMELET	5-6-17	1 p.m.	Reg'd the Billet at 4 a.m. on 4-6-17. C.I.H. Reinforcement coy. left the Regiment for Reinforcement consisting of 2 B.os, 2 J.os, 83 J.O. Rs. and of 2 followers	an/so an/so
"	6-6-17		2 B. os, 2 J.os, 2 B. O Rs. 3 J.O. Rs. transferred to Ind. Entrenching Batt'n	an/so
"	9-6-17		Inspection of horses by the Corps Commander	an/so
"	15-6-17	8·15 p.m.	M'try Batt'n consisting of 12 B. os, 9 J. os, 11 B.O. Rs, 275 J.O. Rs. and 10 followers left the Billet for J.H. Reinforcement. Coy. consisting of 2 B. os, 2 J. os, 2 B.O. R. 83 J.O. R. and 2 followers Rej'd the unit on the 15th June 1917 at 3 p.m.	an/so an/so
"	17-6-17	8·30 a.m.	Reg'. march to Back area nr't ENNEMAIN	an/so
ENNEMAIN	20-6-17	—	8 J.O. R. joined the Regt. from Ind. Entrenching Batt'n	an/so
"	27-6-17	—	2 J.O. R. joined the Regt. from Ind. Entrenching Batt'n	an/so
"	29-6-17	—	Lieut. R.A.M. Dur and 38th C.I.H. died in ~~~~~~~~~ from wounds received in action No. 5 C.C.S. at 2·30 p.m.	an/so

(Detailed Diary of C.H. Company's work in the line will follow)

O. Thoward Lt. Colonel
Comdg. 38th Central India Horse

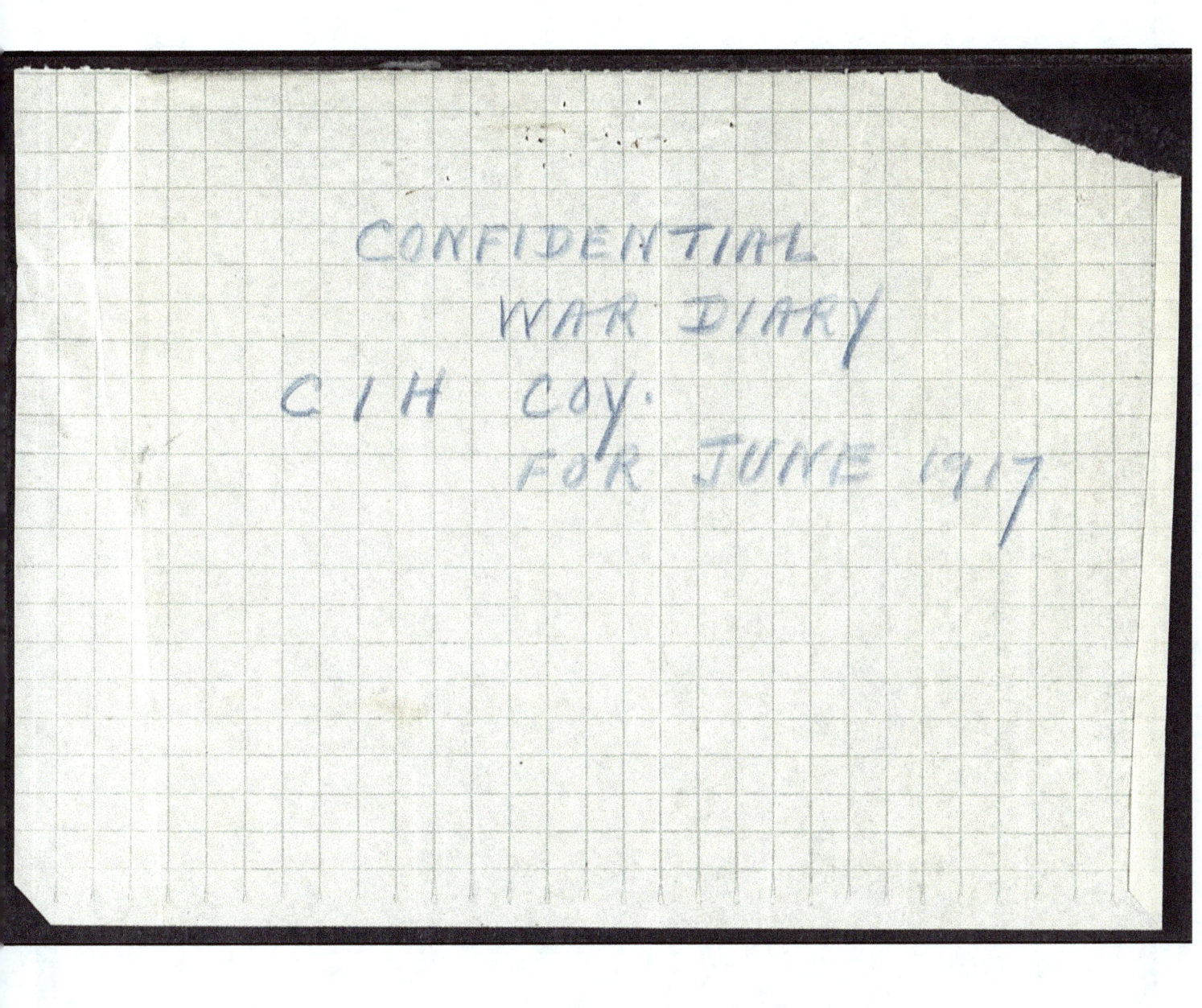

CONFIDENTIAL
WAR DIARY
C1H COY.
FOR JUNE 1917

Army Form C. 2118.

WAR DIARY
or
INTELLIGENCE SUMMARY.
(Erase heading not required.)

Instructions regarding War Diaries and Intelligence Summaries are contained in F. S. Regs., Part II. and the Staff Manual respectively. Title pages will be prepared in manuscript.

Place	Date	Hour	Summary of Events and Information	Remarks and references to Appendices
	16/6/16		Took over Trenches from 39th Lancers. Situation Normal. D+A 5 GRs in front line	
	17/6		Situation Normal. - No 2257 Sowar Surain Singh 4D Slightly wounded	
	18/6		Situation Normal	
	19/6		Situation Normal - No 2585 Sowar Kishan Singh D Slightly wounded.	
	20/6		Situation Normal - No 2932 Sowar Lal Singh D Evacuated sick.	
	21/6		Situation Normal - Slight enemy artillery activity during night - D+A 39th	
	22/6		Situation Normal	
	23/6		Situation Normal	
	24/6		Situation Normal	
	25/6		Situation Normal	
	26/6		Situation Normal. - No 2413 Sr. Kishen Singh Pbs. 39th C.I.H. killed by enemy sniper.	
	27/6		Situation Normal -	
	28/6		Carried out a raid on NEW TRENCH. - Two Patrols with Lt DURAND (wire cutting parties) Lt NILSON the last previously crept out to a place of embussing at the signal 8.00 their guns open into the enemy trench. 8 of the enemy are known to have	

Army Form C. 2118.

WAR DIARY
or
INTELLIGENCE SUMMARY.
(Erase heading not required.)

Instructions regarding War Diaries and Intelligence Summaries are contained in F.S. Regs. Part II. and the Staff Manual respectively. Title pages will be prepared in manuscript.

Place	Date	Hour	Summary of Events and Information	Remarks and references to Appendices
	28/6		Men killed by the raiding party. The party consisted Lt WILSONS of 4 men + Lt DURANDS of 10 men all of "B" Squadron. There are 4 casualties amongst our men + both Lt DURAND (since died of wounds) and Lt WILSON are wounded. Lt WILSON puts 12 men horses were only slightly wounded. All our party got back into our trenches by 11:50 p.m.	M
	29/6		Situation Normal.	M
	30/6		Situation Normal. Certain amount of enemy artillery activity during the afternoon.	M

W. Wrigley Capt.
O.C. Mess
30/6

CONFIDENTIAL Serial no: 115.

WAR DIARY

38th

(K.G.O.) C.I. Horse

FOR

JULY 1917

Army Form C. 2118.

WAR DIARY
or
INTELLIGENCE SUMMARY.
(Erase heading not required.)

Instructions regarding War Diaries and Intelligence Summaries are contained in F. S. Regs., Part II. and the Staff Manual respectively. Title pages will be prepared in manuscript.

Place	Date	Hour	Summary of Events and Information	Remarks and references to Appendices
ENNEMAIN	2-7-17	9 A.m.	The C.L.H. relief party consisting of 3 B.Os, 3 B.O'Rs and 14 J.O.Rs left the billet at 9 A.m. and the same number returned from trenches on 2-7-17	app
"	9-7-17		C.L.H. Company consisting of 9 B.Os, 9 J.Os, 11 B.O.R. and 259 J.O.Rs and followed Regt the Regiment from Trenches and 2 B.Os, 2 J.Os, 2 B.O.Rs and 18 J.O.Rs joined the Regiment from Ind. Entrenching Battalion Regimental Inspection by the G.O.C. Bde in marching order	app app
"	13-7-17		30 Remounts joined the Regiment from Remount Depot	app
"	15-7-17		Dismounted working party consisting of 2 B.Os, 1 J.O., 2 B.O.Rs and	app
"	23-7-17		58 J.O.Rs left the Regiment for attachment to 38 Division at VENDELLES and the inspection of horses by the J.G. of Cavalry in England in the lines at 10 Am	app
"	25-7-17 to 28-7-17		Inspection of arms by the Divisional Armourer Sergeant and Regimental Training	app
"	29-7-17		} Regimental Training	app
"	30-7-17			
"	31-7-17			

A.T. Powne, Lt Colonel
Cmdg. 3 Div C.L.H.

WAR DIARY
or
INTELLIGENCE SUMMARY

Army Form C. 2118

Place	Date	Summary of Events and Information	Remarks and references to Appendices
B3 Left Subsector East of HARGICOURT	2-7-17	Hostile artillery very active. 1 killed and 1 wounded, one of them died since.	A/Havildar Manohar Singh
	3-7-17	B and C Platoons relieved A and D in the line. Quiet day.	
	4-7-17	Intermittent and fairly heavy shelling of the fort. Two men wounded.	R.J. Hayes Major
	5-7-17	Hostile artillery active. 2 men killed and one wounded. Jem. Ishr Akbar Khan took out a patrol of three men. Ran up a very light near the German Sentry Box. He went ahead with A.L.D. Hajib Ali Khan leaving S/S. Hartel Khan & Shinga Khan in sentry box, and was nearly walked over by a German patrol of 16. A.L.D. Acchan Singh took out a patrol of 5 Duffadar Singh, Sowar Pal Singh, S. Isher Singh, S. Jessa Singh and Sowar Mannan Singh, with orders to go down disused trench towards COLOGNE FARMS, get out & go through the German wire, attack a German working and covering party detected there. The known night by A.L.D. Acchan Singh who got past the covering party alone and thought back one of the working party's rifles. From some way beyond the German wire, details of this initiative on the night of the 5-6 tomorrow the working party attacked him not there.	R.J. Hayes Major
	6-7-17	Continuous of quiet day.	
	7-7-17	A.L.D. Anju and J/Dar. Sowar Taimat Khan went out on a patrol to village — out a disused trench & Through long grass, and have since been reported missing. The Germans attempted small raids of VALLEY POST and part of INDIAN TRENCH but were repulsed by Hotchkiss and rifle fire and bombs. Lt. Penny and 1 wounded.	A/Havildar Manohar Singh R.J. Hayes Major 35th C.I.M.
B3	8-7-17	Relieved night of 8-7-17	

Serial No. 115.

CONFIDENTIAL
WAR DIARY
38th
(K.G.O.) C.I. HORSE
FOR
AUGUST 1917

Army Form C. 2118

WAR DIARY
or
INTELLIGENCE SUMMARY.
(Erase heading not required.)

Instructions regarding War Diaries and Intelligence Summaries are contained in F.S. Regs., Part II. and the Staff Manual respectively. Title pages will be prepared in manuscript.

Place	Date	Hour	Summary of Events and Information	Remarks and references to Appendices
ENNEMAIN	6-8-17	8-45 pm	Working party consisting of 2 B.Os., 3 I.Os., 2 B.ORs., 142 I.ORs. and 2 followers left the billet for Regt. from Ind. Cav. Adv. Remn.	also
"	7-8-17		2 Indian other Ranks joined the Regt. from Ind. Cav. Adv. Base Remn for training purposes	also
"	8-8-17		Indian other Ranks to be trained	also
"	12-8-17		Inspection of Horses by the A.D.V.S. in the Lines and 1 & 2 other Ranks proceeded to Rouen	also
"	19/8/17	9-45 am	The party consisting of 7 B.Os., 8 I.Os., 8 B.ORs., 94 Ind. other Ranks and 6 followers left the billet at 9.45 am to complete C.I.H. Corps. to Jaipur. Establishment 1 V.O., 2 I.ORs., and 2 followers joined the Regiment from Indian Cavalry Adv. Base Remn.	also
"	22/8/17		Capt. C.O.R. Panet and Lieut. E.J. Woodhouse relieved Capt. S.A. Cameron and Lt. J.C.N.A. Pinney	also
"	30-8-17			
"	31/8/17	5 pm	The following party of C.I.H. Amand C. Newton consisting of 2 I.Os., and 50 Ind. other Ranks left billet the billet at 5 pm.	also

Osborne Dr Colonel
Com of 38th C.I. Horse

2. IX. 17.

CONFIDENTIAL   Serial No. 115.

WAR DIARY

38th. (K. G. O.) Central India Horse

for

September ~~OCTOBER~~   1 9 1 7.

Army Form C. 2118.

WAR DIARY
or
INTELLIGENCE SUMMARY.
(Erase heading not required.)

Instructions regarding War Diaries and Intelligence Summaries are contained in F. S. Regs., Part II. and the Staff Manual respectively. Title pages will be prepared in manuscript.

Place	Date	Hour	Summary of Events and Information	Remarks and references to Appendices
ENNE MAIN	2-9-17		Lt. Col. A. S. Browne relieved Lt. Col. R. C. Bell in command of Mhow B.H.	A/S
"	3-9-17		Lt. Col. W.M.K. Page relieved Lt. Col. G. B. Waller	A/S
"	4-9-17	6 pm	Reliefs of B. and D. Platoons consisting of 4 I.O.S. and 52 Ind. other Ranks each left the billets at 6 p.m.	A/S
"	5-9-17		Capt. H.D.S. Keighley relieved Lt. Wilson in Inspection of all Regtl mares by the D.R. in the Lines	A/S
"	7-9-17	11 am	Risaldar Fazwan Khan and 5 Ind. other Ranks left billets for C.I.H. Coy.	A/S
"	9-9-17		Half limber and 2 draught Horses joined the Regt. from M.G. Squadron	A/S
"	10-9-17	10 am	30 Ind. other Ranks joined billets Chr. Notr Gate V.R. Royen	A/S
"	15-9-17	5/30 am	C.I.H. Coy. Consisting of 9 B.O.S., 9 I.O.S., 11 B.O.R. and 254 I.O.Rs. and 5 followers rejoined the Regt. from trenches.	A/S
"	16-9-17	–	1 I.O.S. and 67 Ind. other Ranks joined the Regiment from Indian Tenea Battn. and 2 British officer from Indian Car. Adv. Base Rowen	A/S
"	17-9-17		Regt rec'd Inspection by the G.O.C. Mhow Car. Bde. in marching order.	A/S
"	19-9-17	–	1 J.O. and 83 Ind. other Ranks transferred to Ind. Pioneer Battn.	A/S
"	20-9-17		Decoration Parade under the G.O.C. Denison	A/S
"	21-9-17	4:30 pm	C.I.H. Coy. Consisting of 8 B.O.S., 9 B.Os, 2 I.Os, 265 I.O.Rs and 7 followers left the Billets for relieving the Sialkot Car. Bde. at 4-30 p.m.	A/S

A.S. Browne, Lt. Col.
Comd'g 38th C.I. Horse

Army Form C. 2118.

WAR DIARY
or
INTELLIGENCE SUMMARY.
(Erase heading not required.)

Instructions regarding War Diaries and Intelligence Summaries are contained in F. S. Regs., Part II. and the Staff Manual respectively. Title pages will be prepared in manuscript.

Place	Date	Hour	Summary of Events and Information	Remarks and references to Appendices
	1 Sep	—	ORDINARY TRENCH WARFARE	CA
	Sat 2 "		GAS ALARM from FRENCH divin — NO CASUALTIES.	CA
	3 "		TRENCH WARFARE	CA
	4 "		Reconder Bostarkham wounded by shellfire by at SOMERVILLE WOOD	CA
	5 "		TRENCH WARFARE, Capt Keithley join No 3 Coy.	CA Return 3 own
	6 "		Capt DAUNT join C.H at No 1 as Secondin Command. A platoon + 1 left in support as No 3 Coy	CP
			Hostile Artillery more active	CA
	7 "		Ordinary Trench WARFARE	CA
	8 "		Major MACNABB takes over Command of CH on via Major Taunced	CA
	Sat 9 "		Ordinary Trench Warfare.	CA
	10 "		successfully wiring operations completed by Engineers at Toronto	CB
	11 "		ordinary Trench Warfare, some firing on DRAGOON POST.	CB
	12 "		ditto	CB
	13 "			
	14 "		Coy relieved by 36th Jacob's Horse at 11 p.m.	CA
			C O'B Daunt Capt C.H	

Army Form C. 2118.

WAR DIARY
or
INTELLIGENCE SUMMARY.
(Erase heading not required.)

Instructions regarding War Diaries and Intelligence Summaries are contained in F. S. Regs., Part II. and the Staff Manual respectively. Title pages will be prepared in manuscript.

Place	Date	Hour	Summary of Events and Information	Remarks and references to Appendices
NR. ASCENSION FARM	22/9/17	10 p.m.	C./I.A. Company took over trenches from 6th Cavalry	
"	23/9/17	5 a.m.	The German bombarded a portion of the line about ⅔ to ¾ of a mile long. An infantry attack followed which was completely prohibited by the M.G.s of the bombarded sector.	
"	24/9/17	10 a.m.	The bombarded sector. Friendly and hostile aircraft activity. Patrol under Lt Pinney reconnoitred LITTLE BILL, BIG BILL and ASCENSION WOOD which were reported unoccupied. Two loaded german rifles were brought back. They were found in the vicinity of LITTLE BILL and by the state they must have been out there for at least a week.	
"	"	12.30 p.m.	Lt Pelan reports his arrival having completed his honey moon satisfactorily.	
"	"	4 p.m.	Enemy Tour on returning from patrol with A Sqn and reports ASCENSION WOOD, LITTLE BILL and BIG BILL unoccupied. About 50 shells H.E. probably 42 fell near various posts chiefly No 4 and 5.	
"	25/9/17	"	Several 77 shells fell in vicinity of GRAHAM POST i.e. Coy. H.Q. of about 50 fired about 40 were duds.	
"	26/9/17	various to 7 p.m.	Intermittent shelling by enemy of targets over the ridge west of GRAHAM POST. About 10 shells probably 4.2 hours fell about 400 yds NW of GRAHAM POST. They did not explode in the usual way but were not duds. The position became mud.	2 Lt Cameron left Garden Garden attached 38th CM

(A592) W. W12659/M1293. 750,000. 1/17. D. D. & L., Ltd. Forms/C.2118.14.

Army Form C. 2118.

WAR DIARY
or
INTELLIGENCE SUMMARY.
(Erase heading not required.)

Instructions regarding War Diaries and Intelligence Summaries are contained in F. S. Regs., Part II. and the Staff Manual respectively. Title pages will be prepared in manuscript.

Place	Date	Hour	Summary of Events and Information	Remarks and references to Appendices
TRENCHES	26/8	10.45am	A general officer accompanied by another officer visited No 8 Post. Having shown his head and shoulders above the parapet for several minutes to view the country, he departed. He then proceeded to No 9 Post and did likewise. A few minutes after his departure, both the posts were shelled, 3 direct hits being obtained causing material damage but fortunately no casualties.	
NR ASCENSION FARM		11.30 am	Posts No 8 and 9 and GRAHAM were shelled roughly 60 H.E. probably 4.2. Artillery retaliation was applied for and shortly afterwards 6 rounds by our 18 prs. were fired. 3/7 Sergt Rkn Hoyt Tennalam Dgn Reg't both wounded by M.gun fire. Quiet day. Artillery activity and Aircraft below normal.	
	27/8	1 am	Artillery activity above normal. Posts 6, 8 and 9 were shelled at intervals during the day by 4.2 (H.E.) pozz'bly 5.9.	
	28/8	4 pm	4 of our Aeroplanes appeared over our lines. They attacked and drove away with their M. gun fire into the German trenches. They disappeared in a N direction when fired on by our Anti' aircraft guns, 2 Germans were seen walking from LITTLE BILL to GERMAN trenches.	
	29/8	6.30 pm	Capt. Jameson with patrol of D Sqn. reconnoitre LITTLE and BIG BILL also ASCENSION WOOD. When lying up for hostile patrols N.E. of BIG BILL his Covering patrols reported a party of Germans moving S. of our patrol	Sig German Copy

WAR DIARY or INTELLIGENCE SUMMARY

Army Form C. 2118.

Place	Date	Hour	Summary of Events and Information	Remarks and references to Appendices
Tincher	Sep 29/15		and other listening patrols reported bands of wire and reconnoitred none of N. Whittling to the N and N.E. A personal reconnaissance was made by patrol leader, but nothing was seen in either direction. The patrol then moved to LITTLE BILL and having reached it found it unoccupied, left a standing patrol of 1 N.C.O. and 5 men to stay there all day. Another standing patrol of 1. S.O. 10 men and 1 Hotchkiss rifle was left in ASCENSION WOOD and the patrol returned via. No 8 Post at 5-30 a.m.	Reconnaissance Reports
	29	6 am to 7 pm	LITTLE BILL was shelled by whizz bangs and trench mortars and was swept by M.G. fire at odd intervals during the day. PTLC BILL and ASCENSION WOOD were also shelled.	
		9 pm	Both standing patrols from LITTLE BILL and ASCENSION WOOD return having sustained no casualties, which was very fortunate in the case of S.P. in LITTLE BILL, the place being only 400 yds from GERMAN wire and no possible way of retreat and no dugouts or hole to lie in.	

Army Form C. 2118.

WAR DIARY
or
INTELLIGENCE SUMMARY.
(Erase heading not required.)

Place	Date	Hour	Summary of Events and Information	Remarks and references to Appendices
Trenches	29/6	9 p.m.	Patrol under Lt. Wilson with B.Sgn proceed from no 8 post to reconnoitre the enemy wire in front of LILY TRENCH and the junction of tracks in G.2.0. and G.26.6. The night was much too light to do this. Shortly in advance with Lt Wilson were spotted before they got to within 30 yards of the wire and were fired on by M.G. and rifle fire. The ground was very flat and afforded no cover from fire or view, the grass being very short. The party slowly crawled back & rejoined the remainder of the patrol when the whole party slowly retired crawling, being under heavy fire of M.G. and rifles. In men of 13 Sqn. were killed (S. Kisan Singh and S. Bhajan Singh and Harnam Singh) two wounded in the head two men of the British patrol of the 8th Bns, which accompanied our patrols, also had 2 men wounded - one seriously. S. Balop Singh behaved in a very gallant manner bringing in the two dead men to a place of comparative safety, they were lying in a very exposed position. The men under Lt Wilson behaved in a very	13th Cavalry Lapt

Army Form C. 2118

WAR DIARY
or
INTELLIGENCE SUMMARY.
(Erase heading not required.)

Instructions regarding War Diaries and Intelligence Summaries are contained in F. S. Regs., Part II. and the Staff Manual respectively. Title pages will be prepared in manuscript.

Place	Date	Hour	Summary of Events and Information	Remarks and references to Appendices
Trenches	29th		Returned in a very gallant way and the patrol returned to our lines bringing the dead and wounded with them at 3.30 a.m. on the 30th.	R.E. (Canteen Capt)
	30th		Three of our aeroplanes appeared over our lines pursued by Spads (Scouts)	
	30th 5.30 a.m.		Gas alarm was heard to the S. and gas rattles were rattled indicating presence of gas shells, but none were heard in vicinity of Graham's post (Coy HQ) and gas masks were not put on. Too the wind was blowing from the N. The gas alarm caught the Coy Commander at a very unfortunate moment! A cold ("Cyps") having him seized with sudden sense of duty stormed them for inspiration. They were very relieved when ordered to takes them off as most of them were on the verge of suffocation. The Remainder of Asgn (Kilts, guts) retreated recalled Tarko Weans Toast "20,000 Lagum under the Sea."	

Walcomeum Capt
for. Jones C. 1st H. Eng.
in how both

CONFIDENTIAL

WAR DIARY

OF THE 38TH. KING GEORGES OWN CENTRAL INDIA HORSE

FOR THE MONTH OF OCTOBER 1917.

Army Form C. 2118.

38th C.I. Horse

WAR DIARY
INTELLIGENCE SUMMARY.
(Erase heading not required.)

Instructions regarding War Diaries and Intelligence Summaries are contained in F.S. Regs., Part II. and the Staff Manual respectively. Title pages will be prepared in manuscript.

Place	Date	Hour	Summary of Events and Information	Remarks and references to Appendices
ENNEMAIN	1-10-17	6 A.M.	C.I.H. Company comprising of 8 B.O's., 9 I.O's., 9 B.O.R., 253 I.O.Rs. and 6 followers Regt. The Regt. and 13 I.O. and 2 Ind. other Ranks left the Regt. to ROUEN for duty with the Ind. Cav. Adv. Base Maj. Lewis and 2 I.O.R. left the Regt. to Rouen for duty with the Ind. Cav. Adv. Base and No 3836 Lance Dayadar Mothd. Akbar Khan to Marseilles under orders to Egypt for duty with Armoury Dunn and I Ind. other Ranks joined the Remote Regt. from Ind. Cav. Adv. Base Rouen.	
"	7-10-17		2nd Lieut. A.M. Well joined the Regiment for duty from Ind. Cav. Adv. Base Rouen	
"	11-10-17		1 Indian officer and 4 Ind. other Ranks joined the Regt. from Ind. Cav. Adv. Base Rouen	
"	13-10-17		2nd Lieuts. S.B. Good and A.M. Well left the Regt. under orders to India	
"	14-10-17		11 Indian other Ranks left the Regt. to Marseilles under orders to India on pensioned.	
"	15-10-17		Inspection of Regtl. signallers by the Divl. signalling officer	
"	18-10-17		2 Indian followers joined the Regt. from the Ind. Gnd. Base Depot Marseilles	
"	24-10-17		Capt. R. Westmacott, 2nd Lt. T.R. Marshall, Mr. Cox and B.R. Williams and 6 Ind. other Ranks joined the Regt. from Ind. Cav. Adv. Base Rouen	
"	26-10-17		3 Ind. other Ranks left the Regt. to Marseilles for duty with I.A.T.C.	

Argenieri Princetan
Captain
Adjutant 38th

M McColonel
Commanding 38th India Horse.

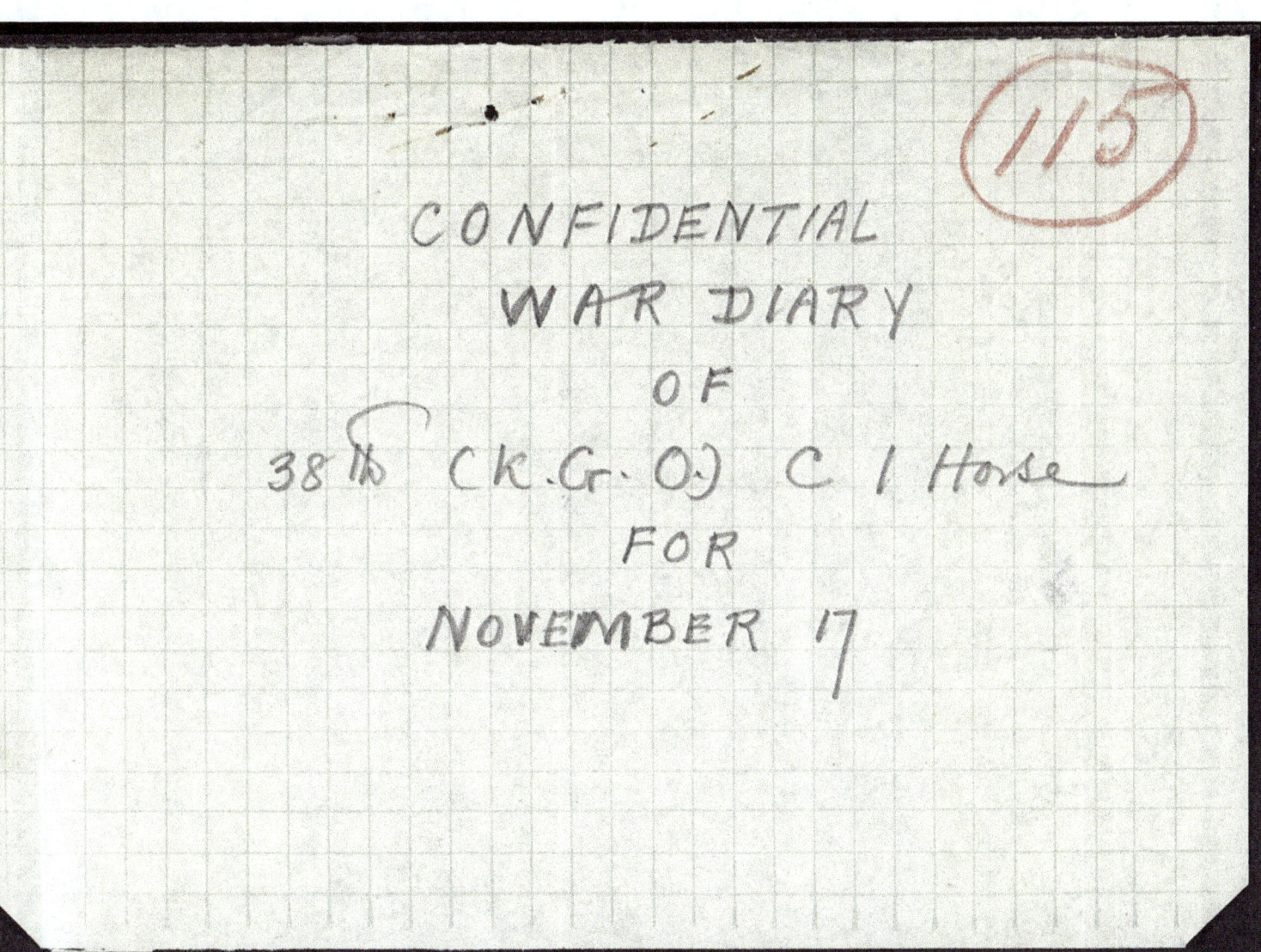

CONFIDENTIAL
WAR DIARY
OF
38th (K.G.O.) C I Horse
FOR
NOVEMBER 17

Army Form C. 2118.

WAR DIARY
INTELLIGENCE SUMMARY.
(Erase heading not required.)

38th C.I. Horse

Instructions regarding War Diaries and Intelligence Summaries are contained in F.S. Regs., Part II. and the Staff Manual respectively. Title pages will be prepared in manuscript.

Place	Date	Hour	Summary of Events and Information	Remarks and references to Appendices
ENNEMAIN	2.11/17		2 British officers, 15 Indian officers, Ranks and 6 followers joined the Regiment from Indian Cav. Advance Base Rouen	a.g.o.
"	10.11/17		1 B.O. and 3 Indian officers and 1 B.O.R. and 14 Indian other Ranks transferred to 4th Cavalry Pioneer Battn and 1 B.O. and 39 O.Rs joined the Regt. from Ind. Cav. Adv. Base Rouen.	a.g.o. a.g.o. a.g.o.
"	12.11/17		Marching order parade	a.g.o.
"	15.11/17		1 B.O. and 55 Indian other Ranks transferred to 4th Cav. Pioneer Battn	a.g.o.
"	17.11/17		Tactical Exercise	a.g.o.
"	18.11/17		Orders received that Regiment will be ready to move under short notice and 10 Indian other Ranks joined the Regiment from Indian Cav. Advance Base Rouen.	a.g.o.
"	21.11/17	3 A.m.	Regiment marched to FINS to operations and B Echelon left behind under Division at ATHIES.	a.g.o.
FINS	23.11/17	9 A.m.	Regiment returned back to ENNEMAIN and B Echelon rejoined the Regiment.	a.g.o.
ENNEMAIN	24.11/17		Regiment will be ready to move under one hour notice and 4th Cav. Pioneer Battn rejoined the Regiment and 5 Remounts joined the Regiment from Remount Camp.	a.g.o.
"	25.11.17		Regiment marched at 5:30 a.m. to a forward concentration area near VILLERS FAUCON. Regiment returned in the evening to ENNEMAIN	a.g.o.
"	30.11.17		1st & 4th Indian Dismounted Battalion started off at 8 a.m. for "B" Sector. Shortly after they had left, information arrived that enemy had broken our line, that 1st Dismounted Batta. had been stopped on its road, and that the Regiment was to form and any forced to join them as soon as possible. Moved off about 11:30 a.m. and joined 6th I.M. Group arm at ESTREES. Thence marched to and arrived at ST. EMILIE area of a forward position at about 6:30 p.m.	a.g.o.

A J Horne Lt. Col
Comdg 38th C I Horse

CONFIDENTIAL

WAR DIARY

38th. CENTRAL INDIA HORSE

FOR THE Month of DECEMBER 1917

WAR DIARY
or
INTELLIGENCE SUMMARY.
(Erase heading not required.)

Army Form C. 2118

Place	Date	Hour	Summary of Events and Information	Remarks and references to Appendices
ST. EMELIE	30-11-17	5 A.m.	Dismounted Company started for B. Sector (HARGICOURT). Party recalled and mounted and Brigade moved as Cavalry Brigade to ST. EMELIE, arriving there after dark. Stayed night in bivouac there.	AnDx
"	1-12-17	5.30 A.m.	Moved to PEIZIERES, arriving at 6 a.m., with the object of taking advantage of any opportunity occurring in the counter attack of 5th Cav. Division on VILLERS GUISLAIN. Eventually (A.C. +D. Squadrons made an unsuccessful dismounted attack on KILDARE TRENCH, E. of EPEHY. Casualties were 5 B.O.s 1 9.O., and 51 O.Rs. — All Squadrons were withdrawn after dark and Regt. remained just W. of EPEHY during the night.	BnDx
EPEHY	2-12-17	5 A.m.	Before dawn moved to original bivouac at ST. EMELIE stayed whole day and night there.	AnDx
ST. EMELIE	3-12-17	9 A.m.	Regiment marched back to huts at ENNEMAIN.	AnDx
ENNEMAIN	8-12-17		5 I.O.d. other Ranks joined the Regiment from Ind. Cav. Adv. Base Rouen. 1 B.O., 1 B.O.R. and 2 Ind. other Ranks and 4 horses left the Regt. for Cav. Corps Equitation Class CAYEUX and 1 B.O. 1 B.O.R. and 2 Ind. O.Rs. and 4 horses to Div. School DAOURS.	AnDx
"	9-12-17	6 p.m.	Regiment standing to at 1 hour notice till 6 p.m. 12-12-17	AnDx
"	11-12-17	-	2 (B.Os., 2 9. Os., 2 B.O.Rs. and 4 Ind. other Ranks and 10 horses left the Regiment for Div. School at DAOURS.	AnDx
"	12-12-17		Entrenching Battn. consisting of 1 9.O. and 25 Ind. Ranks and 1 follower left the Regt. for HERVILLOY at 9.45 A.m.	AnDx
"	14-12-17		13 Ind. other Ranks exchanged from Pioneer Battn. 11th Cav. Division and 16 Remounts joined the Regiment from Remount Depot.	AnDx
"	16-12-17		5 Ind. other Ranks left the Regiment to Marseilles for India under orders of D.H.Q.	AnDx
"	18-12-17	6 p.m.	Regiment standing to at 1 hour notice till 6 p.m. 21-12-17	AnDx
"	21-12-17		17 Ind. other Ranks joined the Regiment from Ind. Cav. Adv. Base Rouen.	AnDx

Army Form C. 2118.

WAR DIARY
or
INTELLIGENCE SUMMARY.

(Erase heading not required.)

Instructions regarding War Diaries and Intelligence Summaries are contained in F. S. Regs., Part II. and the Staff Manual respectively. Title pages will be prepared in manuscript.

Place	Date	Hour	Summary of Events and Information	Remarks and references to Appendices
ENNEMAIN	24-12-17	4.30 P.m	The Digging party Consisting of 2 B.Os., 2 J.Os. and 104 Ind. Other Ranks left the Regiment for JEANCOURT and rejd on the afternoon on 25th inst.	AAPo
"	25-12-17	3-45 P.m.	The Digging party Consisting of 2 B.Os., 2 J.Os. and 114 Ind. other Ranks left the Regt. for JEANCOURT and rejd on the forenoon 26th instant.	AAPo
"	29-12-17	12.45 P.m.	Digging party consisting of 2 B.Os., 2 J.Os. and 104 Ind. other Ranks left the Regt. for JEANCOURT in lorry and rejd on the forenoon 30th instant and J.O. and 5 Ind. other Ranks joined the Regiment from Ind. Cav. Adv. Base Remount Depot.	AAPo
"	30-12-17	"	Digging party consisting of 1 B.O., 2 J.Os., and 104 Ind. other Ranks left the Regiment for JEANCOURT in lorry and rejd on the forenoon 1-1-18.	AAPo

AGPoonl Lt-Col
Comdg 38th CIH & OC Horse

4 DIV
MHOW bde

CONFIDENTIAL

WAR DIARY

38th (K.G.O.) C.I. Horse

FOR

JANUARY 1918

Army Form C. 2118.

WAR DIARY
or
INTELLIGENCE SUMMARY.
(Erase heading not required.)

Instructions regarding War Diaries and Intelligence Summaries are contained in F.S. Regs, Part II. and the Staff Manual respectively. Title pages will be prepared in manuscript.

Place	Date	Hour	Summary of Events and Information	Remarks and references to Appendices
ENNEMAIN	1-1-18		Working party consisting of 1 B.O., 2 J.Os., 92 Ind. other Ranks left the Regt. for VANDELLES camp at 5·45 A.m. and rejd. on the same day.	
"	4-1-18		Working party consisting of 1 B.O., 3 J.Os. and 150 Ind. other Ranks left the Regt. for JEANCOURT at 7·30 A.m. and rejd on the same day at 9 p.m. And the students of Div. Sigl. School rejd on 4-1-18	
"	5-1-18		Working party consisting of 1 B.O., 3 J.Os. and 150 Ind. other Ranks left the Regiment for JEANCOURT at 1·30 p.m. And rejd on 1 A.m. 6-1-18 and 1 J.O. attd with C.R. 18 Div. Division Jouarville.	
"	6-1-18		Working party consisting of 1 B.O. and 1 J.O. and 2 B.Os. left the Regt. for HARVILLY at 7 A.m. and 50 J.Os. left the Regt. at 9·30 A.m. and students for Div. School Troops left the R.f.S.C.	
"	7-1-18		2 Ind. other Ranks joined the Regt. from Indian Pioneer Battalion and working party consisting of 1 B.O. 2 J.Os. and 150 J.Os. left the Regt for JEANCOURT at 7 A.m. and rejd on the same day at 8 p.m.	
"	8-1-18		Working party consisting of 1 B.O. 3 J.Os. 150 Ind. other Ranks left the Regt for BEHECOURT and rejd on the same day at 8 p.m.	
"	10-1-18		C.J.H. working party consisting of 1 B.O., 3 J.Os. and 150 J.Os. left the Regt. to JEANCOURT and rejd on the same day at 6 p.m. and 14 Ind. other Ranks joined the Regt. from Ind. Pioneer Battalion.	
"	11-1-18		C.P.H. working party consisting of 1 B.O. 3 J.Os. and 150 J.OR. left the Regt. to BEHICOURT and rejd on the same day at 9 p.m.	
"	12-1-18		Working party consisting of 1 J.O., 14 J.Os. joined the Regt. from Ind. Cav. Adv. Base Rouen.	
"	13-1-18		Working party consisting of 1 B.O. 2 J.Os. and 100 J.OR. left the Regt. for BEHICOURT and rejd on the same day at 8 p.m., and the corps Commander have presented the medals	
"	14-1-18		Working party consisting of 1 B.O. and 2 J.Os. and 100 J.Os. left the Regt. for square 62 C - VIIa. and rejd the Regt on the same day and 10 Ind. other Ranks joined the Regt. from Ind. Pioneer Battalion.	

Army Form C. 2118.

WAR DIARY
or
INTELLIGENCE SUMMARY.
(Erase heading not required.)

Instructions regarding War Diaries and Intelligence Summaries are contained in F.S. Regs., Part II. and the Staff Manual respectively. Title pages will be prepared in manuscript.

Place	Date	Hour	Summary of Events and Information	Remarks and references to Appendices
ENNEMAIN	16.1.18		Working party consisting of 1 B.O. 2 I.Os. and 100 Ind. other Ranks left the Regt. for BEHICOURT and reja on the same day at 7 p.m. and departure of Lieut. G.A. Keaburgh to India on first tenure under orders to India	over
"	17.1.18		Departure of Lt. Col. A.F. Browne on vacation commenced at the Regt.	over
"	19.1.18		Working party consisting of 2 I.Os. 3 9.Os. and 200 other Ranks left the Regt. for JEANCOURT and reja on the same day at 8 p.m.	
"	20.1.18		Working party consisting of 2 B.Os. - 3 9.Os. and 200 Ind. other Ranks left the Regt. for JEANCOURT and reja on the same day at 8 p.m. and left no 4 party consisting of 1 B.O. 19.O. and 30 Ind. O.Rs. and 2 B.O.Rs reja the Regt. from HARVILLY at 8 p.m.	over
"	21.1.18		Brigade Hotchkiss Gun Competition - And 19.O. and 5 Ind. other Ranks left the Regt. for Mersilles under orders to India	over
"	22.1.18		Working Party consisting of 1 B.O. 2 9.Os. and 100 I.Os. left the Regt. for BEHICOURT and reja on the same day at 8 p.m. and 17 Ind other Ranks left the Regt. for Ind. Reinfore Battalion.	over
"	23.1.18		Working Party consisting of 2 B.Os. 2 9.Os. and 200 Ind. other Ranks left the Regt. for JEANCOURT and rejd on the same day at 8 p.m.	over
"	25.1.18		Working Party consisting of 1 B.O. 2 9.Os. and 100 Ind. other Ranks left the Regt. for BEHICOURT and rejd. on the same day at 8 p.m. 3 B.Os. 2 9.Os. 3 B. O.Rs. and 600 Ind. other Ranks rejd. the Regt from Div School at DAOURS	over
"	27.1.18		C.9.H. Trench party consisting of 8 B.Os. 9 9.Os. 9 B.O.Rs and 232 I O.Rs and 6 followers left the Regt. at 2 p.m. in Mercry lorry	over
"	28.1.18		1 B.O. and 1 B.O.R. left the Regt. for a Small Arms Hotchkiss Gun Course	over
"	29.1.18		The 14 found an additional working party consisting of 1 B.O. and 13 O.Rs. left the Regt. for no. 14 working party at HARVILLY	over

A.S...
Captain
for Officer Commdg

CONFIDENTIAL 4 DIV
WAR DIARY
38th
(K.G.O.) C.I. Horse
FOR
February 1915

TO Bde Major
Mhow Cav Bde

Sender's Number: A/1
Day of Month: 28th
AAA

I forward herewith War Diary for the month February 1918

for O.C. 38/16 C.I Horse

Army Form C. 2118.

WAR DIARY
or
INTELLIGENCE SUMMARY.
(Erase heading not required.)

Instructions regarding War Diaries and Intelligence
Summaries are contained in F. S. Regs., Part II.
and the Staff Manual respectively. Title pages
will be prepared in manuscript.

Place	Date	Hour	Summary of Events and Information	Remarks and references to Appendices
Field	28/29 Jan	8 p.m.	C.I.H. took over left sector from 20th HUSSARS. Railway Trench - Sgot Col OSME FARM HARCOURT - divides line in our left. Marshalling Dyne on our right. Major MACNAB's Command of Regt.	
	29th	—	in NORMAL day	
	30th	—	Quite T.H. fire, otherwise quiet day	
	31st	—	CAPT. DAUNT returned. Lieut. WALTER as 2nd in command. One man S. FAKIRMAN killed on night 31/1st	
	Feb 1st	—	Quiet day - Some Casual Shelling. At 9.30 p.m. a patrol of 8 men went out under Lieut MARSHALL to reconnoitre our enemy Communication trench and wire.	
	2nd	—	C.I.H. party relieved in front line by 19th Lancers, and took up a position in COTE WOOD TRENCH in the support line.	
	3rd	—	Working parties in front line. Quiet day	
	4th	—	At 10.30 p.m. S.O.S. sent up from front line. C.I.H. manned alarm posts tw O.K. reported - when they returned to COTE WOOD TRENCH. Very heavy rapid rocket firing all through night of 4/5th.	
	5th	—	Working parties in front line	
	6th	—	ditto. Two men slightly wounded by Shrapnel when advance wire entanglements to front line at night	
	7th	—	ditto. Quiet day	

WAR DIARY
or
INTELLIGENCE SUMMARY.

(Erase heading not required.)

Army Form C. 2118.

Instructions regarding War Diaries and Intelligence Summaries are contained in F. S. Regs., Part II. and the Staff Manual respectively. Title pages will be prepared in manuscript.

Place	Date	Hour	Summary of Events and Information	Remarks and references to Appendices
ENNEMAIN	1-2-18	9-45am	1 J.O. and 4 followers left the Regiment for Marseilles, en route to India, as unfit further service in Europe and a billeting party left the Regiment for BAYONVILLERS	
BAYONVILLERS	2-2-18		Regiment march to Back area at BAYONVILLERS	
	3-2-18	7 A.m.	Regiment march to Back area at FRICAMPS	
FRICAMPS	4-2-18	9 A.m.	Regiment march back to FRICAMPS	
	15-2-18		C.M.S dismounted party consisting of 8 B.Os. 9 J.Os. 8 B.ORs. 123 J.ORs and 6 followers Bay Regt the Regiment from Trenches and 1 B.O. and 1 B.OR rejt the Regt from 5th Army small arm Hotchkiss Gun School.	
"	16-2-18		No 4 working party consisting of 1 B.O. 19.O. 1 B. ORs. and 35 J.ORs rejt the Regiment from HARMKY and 40 Ind. Other Ranks transferred to Ind. Cav Adv Base Rouen and a party consisting of 1 B.O. 1 B.ORs and 2 J.ORs and 4 Horses said Kit Regiment from Car Corps Equitation class.	
"	22-2-18		Regt inspection by the Corps Commander and an adv. party consisting of 2 B.Os. 3 J.Os. 101 Ind. Other Ranks and 3 followers left the Regiment for TARANTA and entrain from SATEUX. Pioneer Battalion consisting of 1 B.O. 13.O. 1 B. ORs and 94 J.ORs and 4 followers rejt the Regiment.	
"	23-2-18		A party consisting of 1 B.O. 19.O. and 10 Ind. Other Ranks left the Regt. for TARANTA and entraining from SATEUX Stn. and 3 Ind. other Ranks transferred to D.A.C Base at Marseilles	
"	24-2-18		A party consisting of 2 B.Os. 3 J.Os. 1 B. OR. + 25 J.ORs left the Regt for TARANTA and entraining from SATEUX Stn.	
"	26-2-18		7 Ind. other Ranks transferred to D.A.C Base at Marseilles	
"	28-2-18		A party consisting of 1 J.Os 83 Ind Other Ranks and 1 followers left the Regt for TARANTA and 1 B.O. and 1 ROR to 5th Army Corps Hd Qrs.	

R.L.M.L M-Lal
Commanding 38 L (Lugo) C.I. Horse.

WAR DIARY
or
INTELLIGENCE SUMMARY
(Erase heading not required.)

Army Form C. 2118.

Place	Date	Hour	Summary of Events and Information	Remarks and references to Appendices
	8.2.18	8.30pm	CIH relieved 19 Lancers in the same sector of the front line. Quiet night.	
	9.2.18	—	Quiet day, patrol went out at 6.30 pm. Ressaldar Kamal-ud-din Khan and 6 I.O.R. to reconnoitre enemy wire. I.O. accidentally wounded in the hand by a T.M. splinter. Some Rifle & M.G. fire at night.	
	10.2.18	—	Quiet day. At 5.10 p.m. Infantry moonlight stunt up I.O.T. Our group post under heavy barrage which lasted nearly. Quiet night. Patrol under Jem. MAL Singh (7.10 P.m.) went out at 9 pm reported all quiet.	
	11.2.18	—	NORMAL	
	12.2.18	—	NORMAL. About midnight what CANADIAN Raid was going on further south. The enemy put down a very heavy barrage behind our front line. Our support line — no casualties.	
	13.2.18	—	Quiet day. NORMAL	
	14.2.18	—	CIH relieved by North Staffs at 8 p.m. Party marches to TEMPLEUX then train to ROISEL.	
	15.2.18	—	CIH party returned to back billets near POIX by train and lorry	

C O'B Dawes Capt
CIH

Army Form C. 2118.

38 (6.G.O) Central
India Horse.

115

WAR DIARY
or
INTELLIGENCE SUMMARY.
(Erase heading not required.)

March 1918.

Instructions regarding War Diaries and Intelligence Summaries are contained in F.S. Regs., Part II. and the Staff Manual respectively. Title pages will be prepared in manuscript.

Place	Date	Hour	Summary of Events and Information	Remarks and references to Appendices
ERICAMPS	1/3/18	10 a.m.	Advance party consisting of 3 J.Os. 35 I.ORs. and 1 follower left the Regt. for oversea from SALEUX Ry. Station.	—
"	2/3/18	—	12 R.H.Os. Drivers transferred to D.A.C. Horse at Marseilles and 46 Riding horses 5 mules pack and 12 Draught mules hand over to 36 J. Horse and 12th M. Gun Sqn. and Jodhpore C.F.A.	—
"	4-3-18	—	1 Riding Horse and 12 B. mules hand over to Jodhpore Lancers	—
"	5-3-18	—	A party consisting of 7 N.C.Os. who are volunteered for transferred to D.A.C. left the regiment to Marseilles.	—
"	6-3-18	—	5 Pack mules and 10 Pack horses joined the Regiment from 2nd Deccan Horse and No 13 Machine Gun Squadron.	—
"	7-3-18	—	56 Remounts joined the Regiment from Remount depot and 5 Ind. other Ranks joined the Regiment from Mhow Cav. Brigade. 1 Ind. other Rank and 1 Br. other Rank and 3 Horses joined the Regiment from Signal Squadron 4th Cav. Division	—
"	12-3-18	—	One Ind. other Rank joined the Regiment from Inkermine Bay.	—
"	13-3-18	—	Departure of Joint H.Q. Pigot at the disposal of India office London.	—
"	15-3-18	—	Departure of Lt-Col. R.C. Bell, D.S.O. having been placed at the disposal of the India office London and Lt-Col. J. Goodie resumed Command of the Regiment.	—
"	20-3-18	—	B and D squadron of the 38 K.C.I Horse left the Regiment and billeted at CLARY - SAULCHOIX on the night 20/21st and entraining from SALEUX Sdg to Marseilles. (No. 34 Train)	—
"	21-3-18	—	The Regt. less B. and D. Squs. march to SALEUX Sdg. and entraining A and C Sqns in No. 35 Train and Regt Transport under Regtl H.Q. and motor trans Pole H.Q. and motor mob. vety. sec. in No 36 Train.	—

Army Form C. 2118.

WAR DIARY
or
INTELLIGENCE SUMMARY.
(Erase heading not required.)

Instructions regarding War Diaries and Intelligence Summaries are contained in F.S. Regs., Part II. and the Staff Manual respectively. Title pages will be prepared in manuscript.

Place	Date	Hour	Summary of Events and Information	Remarks and references to Appendices
MARSEILLES	24/3/18	midnight	The 1st train of B and D sqns. arrived at Marseilles at 12 the night of 23rd/24th and train of Regtl H.Q. and 2nd C. Sqn. arrived at Marseilles at 3 A.m. and 3rd train of Regtl transport and Adv HQ. arrived at Marseilles at 12 p.m. 24/3/18	
"	27/3/18		4 British other Ranks and left their units	
"	29/3/18		for advance Boat party consisting of 15 Ind. other Ranks left H.Q. Regiment in lorry to berth No. 14	
"	30/3/18		The following Embark at H.T. MENOMINEE on the 30th instant — Br. officers 3, Indian officers 4, B. o Rks 5, Ind. other Ranks 266 and 22 followers.	

James Fowler Lt Col.
Comdg. 38th CR (G.O.) C./Horse

4 - APR 1918

1917
4TH CAVALRY DIVISION
MHOW CAVALRY BRIGADE

SIGNAL TROOP
JAN-DEC 1917 — MAR 1918

SERIAL NO. 243.

Confidential

War Diary

of

SIGNAL TROOP, MHOW CAVALRY BRIGADE.

FROM 1st JANUARY 1917 ~~1916~~ TO 31st JANUARY 1917 ~~1916~~

Army Form C. 2118.

Signal Troop
7th Ind Cav Bde

WAR DIARY
or
INTELLIGENCE SUMMARY

(Erase heading not required.)

Instructions regarding War Diaries and Intelligence Summaries are contained in F. S. Regs., Part II. and the Staff Manual respectively. Title pages will be prepared in manuscript.

Place	Date	Hour	Summary of Events and Information	Remarks and references to Appendices
In the field	1/1/17 to 31/1/17		B ce routine work. (Signal classes daily)	MHRR
	4/1/17		2/Lt J LONGWORTH-DAMES 6th INNISKILLING DRAGOONS relieved by 2/Lt M H BIRCH-REYNARDSON 6 INNISKILLING DRAGOONS as B de signalling officer.	MHRR
	24/1/17		Signal Troop inspected by O.C. Signals 4th Cav. Div.	MHRR

M H Birch-Reynardson Lt
Inniskilling Dragoon
O.C. Signal Troop 7th Ind Cav Bde

Serial No 245.

CONFIDENTIAL.

WAR DIARY.

of

Signal Troop Mhow Cav Bde.

From 1-2-17   To 28-2-17

Army Form C. 2118.

Mhow Cavalry Bde
Signal Troop

WAR DIARY
or
INTELLIGENCE SUMMARY.
(Erase heading not required.)

Instructions regarding War Diaries and Intelligence Summaries are contained in F. S. Regs., Part II. and the Staff Manual respectively. Title pages will be prepared in manuscript.

Place	Date	Hour	Summary of Events and Information	Remarks and references to Appendices
Field	Feb 1st 1917 to Feb 28th 1917		Routine as usual.	

E. B. Wilkinson Capt
Cavalry Signal Troop
Mhow Cavalry Bde

Mhow Cavalry Bde
Army Form C. 2118
Signal Troop

WAR DIARY
or
INTELLIGENCE SUMMARY.

(Erase heading not required.)

Place	Date	Hour	Summary of Events and Information	Remarks and references to Appendices
Field	Feb 1st 1917 to Feb 28th 1917		Routine as usual.	

E. B. Wilson Capt.
Cavalry Signal Troop
Mhow Cavalry Bde

Serial No: 245.

CONFIDENTIAL

WAR DIARY

of

Signal Troop
Mhow Cavalry Brigade

from 1st March 1917 to 31st March 1917

SIGNAL TROOP
M I + W CAV BDE
Army Form C.2118.

WAR DIARY
or
INTELLIGENCE SUMMARY.

(Erase heading not required.)

Instructions regarding War Diaries and Intelligence Summaries are contained in F.S. Regs., Part II. and the Staff Manual respectively. Title pages will be prepared in manuscript.

Place	Date	Hour	Summary of Events and Information	Remarks and references to Appendices
Field	1.3.17 to 18.3.17		Routine in billets	Field Off.
	19.3.17		Marched to DRUCAT communication by D.R. to wire by telephone to Div. Off.	
	20.3.17		" " ST LEGERS-EN-PONTHIEU " " " " " "	
	21.3.17		" " AVELUY " " " " " "	
	22.3.17		2 L. Horses marched to camp at MIRAUMONT	
	28.3.17 to 31.3.17		At AVELUY	

eg Atkinson Cpl
O.C. Signal Troop
M I + W Cav Bde Role

Serial No. 249.

CONFIDENTIAL.

WAR DIARY OF

Signal Troop
Mhow Cavalry Brigade.

From 1-4-17. to 30-4-17.

Army Form C. 2118

Signal Troop –
Nthn Cav Bde. –

WAR DIARY
or
INTELLIGENCE SUMMARY.
(Erase heading not required.)

Instructions regarding War Diaries and Intelligence Summaries are contained in F. S. Regs., Part II. and the Staff Manual respectively. Title pages will be prepared in manuscript.

Place	Date	Hour	Summary of Events and Information	Remarks and references to Appendices
In the Field	1.4.17 to 2.4.17		AT AVELUY.	
	3.4.17		Marched to Camp 900 yards N of MIRAUMONT. DR to Units Telephone Commin with Div.	
	4.4.17 to 9.4.17		In Camp at MIRAUMONT. do	
	10.4.17		Marched to MORY & returned to Camp at MIRAUMONT idem – Office re-opened – DR to Units. Telephone Communication with Div.	
	11.4.17		Marched to MORY & returned to Camp at MIRAUMONT idem. Office re-opened DR to Units & Telephone Communication with Div.	
	12.4.17		In Camp at MIRAUMONT. DR to Units & Telephone Commn with Div.	
	13.4.17		Marched to SARTON. DR to Units Telephone Communication with Div	
	14.4.17 to 30.4.17		Routine in Billets at SARTON	

EJ Atkinson Capt.
O.C. Signal Troop.
Nthn Cav. Bde.

Serial No: 245

C O N F I D E N T I A L.

WAR DIARY.

of

Signal Troop
Mhow Cavalry Brigade

from 1st May 1917.   to 30th June 1917.

Army Form C. 2118

Signal Troop V.
Whose Cavalry Brigade

WAR DIARY
INTELLIGENCE SUMMARY.
(Erase heading not required.)

Instructions regarding War Diaries and Intelligence Summaries are contained in F.S. Regs., Part II. and the Staff Manual respectively. Title pages will be prepared in manuscript.

Summary of Events and Information 31st May '17

Place	Date	Hour	Summary of Events and Information	Remarks and references to Appendices
In the Field	13 May			O.C.
	14th May to 15 May		Billets. Training at SARTON closed.	
	16 "		Signal office at SARTON 9.35 am. Opened at MERICOURT 2.15pm Comm with Divn by DR only	
			Signal office at MERICOURT closed at 10.15 am Office opened at CAPPY 1pm - 9 other Ranks detached for duty with 5th Signal Tpn	
	17 "		Signal office at CAPPY closed at 8 am and opened at 2 Christ at 1 pm	
	18 " to 20 "		Routine at 2 Christ	
	21 -		1 Officer 15 OR + 1 Native attached to 4th Cavalry Divn Dismounted Bde including the 9 OR detached to 5th Signal Squadron on the 16th	
	22nd to 31st May -		Routine at 2 Christ	

E.J. Wilkins ? Capt ?
O.C. ? Signal Troop
Whose ?

CONFIDENTIAL.

WAR DIARY

of

Signal Troop
Mhow Cav Bde

from 1st June 1917.   to 30th June 1917.

CONFIDENTIAL.

WAR DIARY.

of

Signal Troop Meerut Cav Bde

4 DIV

from 1st June 1917.   to 30th June 1917.

Army Form C. 2118.

Signal troop
Mhow Cav Bde

WAR DIARY
or
INTELLIGENCE SUMMARY.
(Erase heading not required.)

Instructions regarding War Diaries and Intelligence Summaries are contained in F. S. Regs., Part II. and the Staff Manual respectively. Title pages will be prepared in manuscript.

Place	Date	Hour	Summary of Events and Information	Remarks and references to Appendices
St Ouost-B'os	1/6/17 – 3/6/17		Usual Bde Routine	appx
Hamelet	4/6/17 – 5/6/17		Bde moved to Hamelet & communications taken over from Lucknow Bde	
	6/6/17		Usual Bde Routine	
Authies	17/6/17		Bde moved to Ennemain but troop remained at Authies to work signal office at Authies. A sub office at Ennemain estd by telephone & F.F. same day.	
	18/6/17 – 20/6/17		Usual Bde Routine	
	21/6/17		New cable line laid to Ennemain	
	22/6/17 – 24/6/17		Usual Bde Routine	
	25/6/17 – 26/6/17		91 line laid to Ennemain	
	27/6/17		aeroplane scheme. One with Aldis lamp & ground strips panels refused	
Ennemain	28/6/17		troop moved to Ennemain. Authies office handed over to Sialkot Bde	
	29/6/17 – 30/6/17		Usual Bde Routine	

2/ Attwar Capt.
Ondg Signal Troop Mhow Bde

Serial No. **245**

of

Signal Troop
Mhow Cavalry Brigade

from 1st July 1917 to 31st July 1917

Army Form C. 2118.

Signal Troop
Nhow Cav Bde.

WAR DIARY

~~INTELLIGENCE~~ SUMMARY.
(Erase heading not required.)

Instructions regarding War Diaries and Intelligence Summaries are contained in F. S. Regs., Part II. and the Staff Manual respectively. Title pages will be prepared in manuscript.

Place	Date	Hour	Summary of Events and Information	Remarks and references to Appendices
In the Field	'17.			
	1st July to 10th July		In the line.	Appx
"	11th July to 31 July		Usual routine in billets at ENNÉMAIN.	Appx

A/Atkinson Captain.
OC. Signal Troop
Nhow Cav Bde.
31st July '17.

CONFIDENTIAL.   Serial No: 245.

War   Diary
   of
Signal Troop, Mhow Cavalry Bde

from 1-8-1917 to 31-8-1917

Army Form C. 2118.

WAR DIARY

Signal Troop V.
Mhow Cav Bde.

INTELLIGENCE SUMMARY
(Erase heading not required.)

Instructions regarding War Diaries and Intelligence Summaries are contained in F.S. Regs., Part II. and the Staff Manual respectively. Title pages will be prepared in manuscript.

Place	Date	Hour	Summary of Events and Information	Remarks and references to Appendices
	1917 August			
In the field	1st		Usual routine in billets at ENNEMAIN.	S/T
"	5th		do - 4 men detailed for duty in the line with 4th Dismounted Brigade.	S/T
"	6th, 7th		Brigade routine in billets	S/T
"	8th, 10th		do - Signallers Inmmuling Dragoons inspected and tested in Flags, Helios, Lamps by Capt ATKINSON.	S/T
"	11th, 18th		Brigade routine in billets.	S/T
"	19th		do - The 4 men detailed for duty with 4th Dismounted Brigade on the 5th instant returned to unit.	S/T
"	20th		Brigade routine in billets	S/T
"	21st		do - [5 men detailed for duty in the line with 4th Dismounted Brigade.	S/T
"	22nd, 24th		do	S/T
"	25th		do - [4 men proceeded to SIPOR to complete in Burmese Horse Shoes.	S/T
"	26th, 31st		do	S/T

E.J. Atkinson, Capt,
O.C. Signal troop V,
Mhow Cav Bde.

Serial No. 245.

WAR DIARY.

of the

1/How. Brigade Signal Troop

From 1st April '17 To 30th April 1917

Army Form C. 2118.

"WAR DIARY"
or
INTELLIGENCE SUMMARY. Mhow Cav Bde

Signal Troop

(Erase heading not required.)

Instructions regarding War Diaries and Intelligence Summaries are contained in F. S. Regs., Part II. and the Staff Manual respectively. Title pages will be prepared in manuscript.

Place	Date	Hour	Summary of Events and Information	Remarks and references to Appendices
In the field	1st Sept		Routine in billets Ennemain	Apps
"	2nd "			Apps
"	15 "		In the line	
"	15 "			
"	16 "		Routine in billets Ennemain	Apps
"	25 "			
"	30 "			

A.S. House Lt.
Comdg Signal Troop
Mhow Cav Bde
1st Cav Divn

30/9/1

T2134. Wt. W708—776. 500000. 4/15. Sir J. C. & S.

Confidential

WAR DIARY
of
Signal Troop
Mhow Cav Bde

from 1-10-17 to 31-10-17

Army Form C. 2118.

WAR DIARY

~~INTELLIGENCE~~ SUMMARY.

(Erase heading not required.)

Signal Troop.
Xth Cavalry Brigade.

Instructions regarding War Diaries and Intelligence Summaries are contained in F. S. Regs., Part II. and the Staff Manual respectively. Title pages will be prepared in manuscript.

Place	Date	Hour	Summary of Events and Information	Remarks and references to Appendices
In the Field	1917 1st Oct to 31st Oct		In billets at ENNEMAIN.	
	31st Oct 1917		G. Atkinson Capt. O.C. Signal Troop. Xth Cav. Bde.	

Confidential
WAR DIARY
of
Signal Troop
Mhow Cavalry Brigade

from 1-11-17 to 30-11-17

(245.)

Army Form C. 2118.

Signal book,
Mhow Cav Bde.

WAR DIARY

~~INTELLIGENCE SUMMARY~~
(Erase heading not required.)

Place	Date	Hour	Summary of Events and Information	Remarks and references to Appendices
In the field	1917 19th to 20th Novr		Usual routine in billets at ENNEMAIN.	
	21st Novr	3.45 a.m.	Marched to camp at FINS. Communication to units by foot orderly. Telephone communication with Division.	
	22nd Novr	—	In Camp at FINS.	
	23rd Novr	6 am 9.15	Returned to billets at ENNEMAIN. Office re-opened. Tel communication with Division + units.	
	24th Novr	—	In billets at ENNEMAIN.	
	25th Novr	6 am 5.45	Marched to camp at VILLERS FAUCON. Communication with Division + units by D.R. Returned to billets at ENNEMAIN arriving at 5 pm idem. Office re-opened. Tel communication with Division + units.	
	26th to 30th Novr		Usual routine in billets at ENNEMAIN.	

C O N F I D E N T I A L.

4 Div   WAR DIARY.
                   of
              Signal Troop
              Mhow Cav Bde

fro, 1-12-17.   to 31-12-17.

Army Form C. 2118.

Signal Troop,
mhow Cav Bde.

WAR DIARY
INTELLIGENCE SUMMARY

(Erase heading not required.)

Instructions regarding War Diaries and Intelligence Summaries are contained in F. S. Regs., Part II. and the Staff Manual respectively. Title pages will be prepared in manuscript.

Place	Date	Hour	Summary of Events and Information	Remarks and references to Appendices
In the field	1917. Dec 1st	Mid night	At ST-EMILIE.	Appx
		6.45am	Report Centre moved to W30.c.5.3 N.E. of PEIZIERE. Commn with Division + units by DR.	Appx
		10.20am	Report Centre moved to Railway embankment near St-Emilie. Commn with Division by Phone + DR. 2nd Lancers by visual other units by Despatch Rider. 1 Despatch rider +5 horses wounded	Appx
	Dec 2nd	6am	Report Centre moved to ST-EMILIE. Commn with Division by visual at 8am other units by DR.	Appx
	Dec 3rd	8am	Closed down at ST EMILIE. Brigade returned to Camp at ENNEMAIN.	Appx
		1pm	Arrived in billets. Commn established with Division by horse + phone. Telephonic Commn with units.	Appx
	Dec 4th to 31st		Usual routine in billets at ENNEMAIN.	Appx

Atkinson
Capt.
OC Signal Troop,
mhow Cav Bde.

"Confidential"

WAR DIARY.

4 DIV

M HOW. BDE SIGNAL TROOP

FOR
JANUARY 1918.

Army Form C.-2118.

WAR DIARY
or
INTELLIGENCE SUMMARY.
(Erase heading not required.)

Signal Troop,
Mhow Cav. Bde.

Place	Date	Hour	Summary of Events and Information	Remarks and references to Appendices
In the field	1918 Jan 1st to Jan 26th		Usual routine in billets at ENNEMAIN.	cgb
	Jan 27		Brigade routine in billets - 3 men detailed for duty with 4th Dismounted Division.	cgb
	Jan 28 to Jan 31st		In the line.	cgb

C Atkinson Capt,
OC Signal Troop,
Mhow Cav Bde.

CONFIDENTIAL.

WAR DIARY
of
Mhow Bde Signal Troop

From 1st February 1918. to 28th Bebruary 1918.

Army Form C. 2118.

Signal Troop.
1st Indian Cav Bde.

WAR DIARY
or
INTELLIGENCE SUMMARY.
(Erase heading not required.)

Place	Date	Hour	Summary of Events and Information	Remarks and references to Appendices
In the field	1918 Feby 1st to 10th		In the Line.	
	11th	9am	Returned to billets at COURCELLES. Comm with Division by horse. 2 Lancers & EQ Horse by phone.	
	12th to 28th		Usual routine in billets at COURCELLES.	

A W Carruthers 2/Lt.
O.C. Signal Troop,
1st Indian Cav Bde.

Instructions regarding War Diaries and Intelligence Summaries are contained in F. S. Regs., Part II. and the Staff Manual respectively. Title pages will be prepared in manuscript.

Army Form C. 2118.

WAR DIARY
or
INTELLIGENCE SUMMARY.
(Erase heading not required.)

March 1918

Instructions regarding War Diaries and Intelligence Summaries are contained in F. S. Regs., Part II. and the Staff Manual respectively. Title pages will be prepared in manuscript.

Place	Date	Hour	Summary of Events and Information	Remarks and references to Appendices
ST SAUFLIEU	1-3-18 / 6-3-18		Training and routine	
"	4-3-18	4 pm	Report centre closed. — 6 pm left billets for railhead. — 11.30 pm entrained for	
	8-3-18	2 am	Train left for MARSEILLES	
	9-3-18		On journey	
	10-3-18	4 pm	Arrived MARSEILLES. Report centre opened. Came to unit by D.R.	
MARSEILLES	11-3-18 / 14-3-18		Training and Routine	
	15-3-18		Report centre closed 9.30 am — marched to docks — embarked on H.M.T. KINGSTONIAN 4 pm.	
	16-3-18 / 17-3-18			
	18-3-18 / 19-3-18		Training and Routine on S.S.	
ALEXANDRIA	20-3-18	6 pm	Arrived ALEXANDRIA. Disembarked — Entrained for TEL-EL-KEBIR arrived 6.30 pm	
TEL EL KEBIR	20-3-18		Training and Routine — Came to unit by D.R.	
"	21-3-18	4 pm	Comm R. Sn. Col Dix (Abd) established.	

[signature]
Lieut
Cmdg Signal Troop
Imperial Svc. Bde

1917-18
4TH CAVALRY DIVISION
MHOW CAVALRY BRIGADE

11TH MACHINE GUN SQUADRON

JAN 1917 - MAR 1918

SERIAL NO. 32/

Confidential

War Diary

of

MACHINE GUN SQUADRON, MHOW CAVALRY BRIGADE.

FROM 1st JANUARY 1917 **TO** 31st JANUARY 1917 191

Army Form C. 2118.

WAR DIARY
or
INTELLIGENCE SUMMARY

Officer Machine Gun Squadron

(Erase heading not required.)

Place	Date	Hour	Summary of Events and Information	Remarks and references to Appendices
OFFEUX	31.12.18 to 31.1.19		Nil	

J C Heumpter Capt.
Cmdg M.G. Sqn.

SERIAL No 321.

CONFIDENTIAL.

WAR DIARY.

of

No 11. Squadron M.G. Corps (Cav)
(Lucknow Cavalry Brigade)

From 1-2-17   To 28-2-17

C.H. Pawling cpt
for O.C. 11th M.G. Sqdn

Army Form C. 2118.

WAR DIARY
INTELLIGENCE SUMMARY
(Erase heading not required.)

No. 11. Sqdn. M.G. Corps (Cavalry)

Place	Date	Hour	Summary of Events and Information	Remarks and references to Appendices
Offeux	1st to 4th 2/17		In billets.	
	5/2/17		Lt. A. W. Windham and Lt. L. F. & A. Kendall and 2nd Lt. J.S. Bradly and 2nd Lt. J.H. Walmesley, taken on strength, from M.G. Base Depot. Canvière.	CHP
	6th – 11th		In billets.	CHP
	12/2/17		2nd Lt. C.E. Gunther, taken on strength, from 4th M.G. Squadron	CHP
	13/2/17		Capt. C.H. Pawley taken on strength from 5th M.G. Squadron	CHP
	15/2/17		2nd Lt. R.R. Oakley and 2nd Lt. R.C. Hollis taken on strength, from M.G. Base	CHP
	28/2/17		2nd Lt. R.R. Oakley & J.H. Walmesley proceeded to Divisional School.	CHP
			Corgeau MR	CHP
	26/2/17		1 Corporal and 14 men with 7 L.G.S. waggons & trams & one riding horse proceed to join Lucknow Brigade.	CHP

C.H. Pawley Capt.
for O.C. 11th M.G. Squadron

WAR DIARY
of
No 11 MACHINE GUN SQDN
MACHINE GUN CORPS (CAV)
CONFIDENTIAL

Serial No. 321.

From 1st to 31st March 1917.

31/3/17

C.H. Paoli, Capt
Cmdg No 11 Sqdn. M.G Corps (Cav)

Army Form C. 2118.

WAR DIARY
INTELLIGENCE SUMMARY No. 11. Sqdn M.G. Corps (Cav)

(Erase heading not required.)

Instructions regarding War Diaries and Intelligence Summaries are contained in F. S. Regs., Part II. and the Staff Manual respectively. Title Pages will be prepared in manuscript.

Place	Date	Hour	Summary of Events and Information	Remarks and references to Appendices
OFFLUX	1.3.17 to 7.3.17		Billet Routine.	CHP
	7.3.17		Orders received to move to new billeting area	CHP
TRANLEY	8.3.17		Arrival in new billets at TRANLEY	CHP
"	9.3.17 to 18.3.17		Billet Routine	CHP
			Squadron moved to Le PLESSIER	CHP
LE PLESSIER	19.3.17		" " BERTEAUCOURT	CHP
BERTEAUCOURT	20.3.17		" " AVELUY.	
AVELUY	21.3.17		" " AVELUY.	CHP
AVELUY	21.3.17 to 31.3.17		Squadron in Bivouac at AVELUY.	CHP

C.H. Pantcroft, Intelligence Officer
11th M.G. Squadron

Confidential Serial No: **321**

War Diary No 11 Sqdn
M.G. Corps (Cav)

APRIL 1917

Field
30-4-17

J C Hemutrey Capt
Cmdg No 11 Sqdn. M.G.C.

WAR DIARY **INTELLIGENCE SUMMARY**

No. 11. Sqdn. M.G. Corps (Ca.)

ORIGINAL

Army Form C. 2118.

(Erase heading not required.)

Place	Date	Hour	Summary of Events and Information	Remarks and references to Appendices
AVELUY	April 1st		In bivouac at AVELUY. aufw.	
MIRAUMONT	2nd		Sqdn. moved into bivouac near MIRAUMONT – 1st section M.G. detailed daily for anti-aircraft work. aufw.	aufw.
	10th	1-30am	Sqdn. moved up near MORY – returned to camp in afternoon. aufw.	
	11th	2-30am	" " " " " " " "	
AUTHIE	13th		Sqdn. moved into billets at AUTHIE – Ordinary billet routine – special attention being paid to welfare of horses. aufw.	
THIEVRES	15th		Sqdn. changed billets to THIEVRES aufw.	
AMPLIER	25th		Sqdn. changed billets to AMPLIER. aufw.	
	26th		Horse inspection of 1 Sqdn and A&N Echelon by Corps Commander. aufw.	
	28th		1section M.G. (Composed of Officers 2, O.R. 77 Horses 9H and 2 L.G.S. waggons) moved into billets in AUTHIEUX aufw.	
	30th		Billet routine aufw.	

J.C. Humfrey Capt
Comdg 11th Sqdn

WAR DIARY FOR MAY 1917.
" " " June 1917.   Serial No. 321.

No 11. SQND. M.G. CORPS. (CAV.)

CONFIDENTIAL.

WAR DIARY.

Field.
May. 31st 1917.

R.R. Oakley 2 Lt.
Intelligence Officer.

WAR DIARY or INTELLIGENCE SUMMARY

Army Form C. 2118

No. 11 Sqn. M.G. Corps (Cavalry)

Instructions regarding War Diaries and Intelligence Summaries are contained in F.S. Regs., Part II. and the Staff Manual respectively. Title pages will be prepared in manuscript.

(Erase heading not required.)

Place	Date	Hour	Summary of Events and Information	Remarks and references to Appendices
Amplier	May 1st		Ordinary billet Routine	
	2nd		"	
	3rd		"	
	4th		"	
	5th		"	
	6th		"	
	7th		"	
	8th		"	
	9th		"	
	10th		"	
	11th		"	
	12th		Weather fine generally; some showers	
	13th		Received orders to be ready to move to area S.E.	
HEILLY	14th	6.30am	Received detail orders. Turn forward to area MERICOURT – HEILLY – RIBEMONT	R.R.O.
		6.30pm	Orders received to move forward. Moved off 6.45 p.m. Formed bivouac and awaited orders	R.R.O.
HEILLY	15th	10 AM	Marched out and moved forward to BRAY. Arriving 1.30pm. Area BRAY – CAPPY	R.R.O.
BRAY	15th	6 PM	Orders received to move forward to area BRIE – ST CHRIST. Rain during evening	R.R.O.
BRAY	16th	8 AM	Marched out and moved forward to BRIE. Bivouaced in U3.b with units. HQ at U3.b. 2.7.	R.R.O.
BRIE U3.b. 62.c 1.40.000	16th 12.4 am		Moved to two M.G.s – Anti aircraft defence and carried out Camp Routine. Weather Dull	R.R.O.
U3.b. 62c 40.000	17th		In bivouac – ordinary Camp Routine	R.R.O.
Brie S of BRIE	18th 19th		" Weather fine	
	20th		In bivouac. Reconnaissance by Capt. Humphrey to forward travel line with view to taking over from 174 Coy. M.G. Corps	R.R.O.
	21st	12.45 p.m	Orders received (MHow. Cav. Bde. Operation Order No.5 d/21-5-17) Containing orders for taking over from and relief of 174 Inf Bde O.Co. arrangements in F.S. Instructions and R.Signals. Evening Wet	R.R.O.
	22nd	4 P.M.	Proceeded forward in motor lorries. Contrary to M.How Cav Bde. Operation Order No.5 d/21-5-17 ROISEL, Shortly (K Officer 6 - O.R. 119 arrived. L.D. Horses. 18 Charger. 2 Vehicles 3" (Iron) and 1 cook and 12 O.R. 7.30 PM moved left of ROISEL in T.P.T Lorries Relief of 174 Inf Coy took column through ROUEX & TEMPLEUX – le – GUERARD – Thence forward to Front line system. Bar. L.22.0.7.6 62 cNE.6 14.6. 4.7. 62c NE. M.E.	R.R.O.

WAR DIARY
or
INTELLIGENCE SUMMARY.
(Erase heading not required.)

Army Form C. 2118

Instructions regarding War Diaries and Intelligence Summaries are contained in F. S. Regs., Part II. and the Staff Manual respectively. Title pages will be prepared in manuscript.

Place	Date	Hour	Summary of Events and Information	Remarks and references to Appendices
L.10.a.6.6. 62°.N.E. 1:20000 H.Q. No.11 Sqn. M.G. Corps Coded M.Q.	23	2 a.m.	Relief was completed by 2 a.m., passing of 23rd inst. without enemy interruption. (Relief returns to that of the 19th: M.G. Coy. Only and word the Inf. Bdg. that we are not relieved till night of 23/24 (sharp). Night fine and moderately dark. Morning report: situation as normal.	R.R.O.
	23	6 a.m.	In and about QUARRY. Gun positions in L.4.C. Slight shelling.	
	23	4 P.M.	Day passed normally. Orders received to one relief of 176th Inf. Bde. by M.G. and Sialkot Detachments Regt. by normal fire only.	R.R.O.
	23	10 P.M.	Relief commenced of 176th Bat. by Sialkot Dismounted Bde. Coyd. by Machine Guns of 10.11.15 Squ. M.G. Corps (Eds.) Relief was completed by 2 a.m. when all ex. report clear.	
L.10.a.6.6. 62°.N.E. 1:20000 H.Q. No.11 Sqn. M.G. Corps Coded M.Q.	24	4 a.m.	Reports received shows that night passed quiet - generally. Normal M.F. fire was opened on MALAKOFF FARM at 3.15 a.m. with a view of disturbing enemy reliefs. Night fine and moderately dark.	R.R.O.
	24	10.30 P.M.	Fire was opened at 10.30 P.M. on MALAKOFF FARM L. 2 M.G.S. in response to S.O.S. signal, which was eventually proved to have been sent up by the enemy. Shelling of our position was normal.	
L.10.a.6.6. 62°.N.E. 1:20000 H.Q. No.11 Sqn. M.G. Corps Coded :- M.Q.	25	10 A.M.	Situation remains normal through the day. Weather very hot.	R.R.O.
	25	10.40 P.M.	Aeroplane, nationality unknown, flew over our positions from N. to GRAND PRIEL WOOD and dropped a green flare at about 10.40 P.M.	
L.10.a.6.6. 62°.N.E. 1:20000 H.Q. No.11 Sqn. M.G. Corps Coded M.Q.	26	4 a.m.	Situation remains normal. Some 5.2 Shells on and around our position in North Shulter Road L.4.C.f.2 62° N.E. between 9 a.m. and 10 a.m. Nothing further of importance occurred.	R.R.O.
	26	4 P.M.	Fire was normal both sides during the night. Night undoubtedly dark and cloudy.	
L.10.a.6.6. 62°.N.E. 1:20000 H.Q. No.11 Sqn.Bn M.G. Corps	27	4 A.M.	Situation normal - Night generally quiet on Sub. Sect. Front. Considerable Artillery activity to Northward.	R.R.O.
	27	4 P.M.	Situation quiet. Shelling Nil. Weather fine and dry.	
L.10.a.6.6. 62°.N.E. 1/20000 M.G. Corps Coded MUSE M.X	28	4 a.m.	Night passed quiet generally. 12 H.E. Shell thrown in Cross Road W. of HARGICOURT between 10.30 and 11 P.M. At about 3.30 a.m. a short burst of T.M. fire was opened in Sub. Sect. front. Inf. fire Nil both sides. Night moderately dark and cloudy.	R.R.O.
	28	4 P.M.	Situation Normal. Wind N.E. Zero.	

T/134. Wt. W708-776. 500,000. 4/15. Sir J. C. & S.

Army Form C. 2118

WAR DIARY
or
INTELLIGENCE SUMMARY
(Erase heading not required.)

Instructions regarding War Diaries and Intelligence Summaries are contained in F. S. Regs., Part II. and the Staff Manual respectively. Title pages will be prepared in manuscript.

Place	Date	Hour	Summary of Events and Information	Remarks and references to Appendices
L.10.a.6.6. 62°C.N.E.1000 H.Q. No.11 Coy. M.G. Corps Codes MUSE	28th	11 P.M.	At about 5.30 p.m. 2 men of MUSE raided a sniping post had been demolished by a T.M. Battery. Two Germans reported killed and one wounded & wounded six. At about 6.20 p.m. another raid on same point was carried out under Lieut CAMERON 38th C.I.H. Party returned with letters and Newspapers but no enemy discovered dead. Raid un-witnessed by MUSE - investigating.	R.R.O.
L.10.a.6.6. 62°C.N.E.1000 H.Q. No.11 Coy. M.G. Corps MUSE	29th	4 a.m. 4 p.m.	Remainder of night reported quiet. At 2 a.m. 13 H.E. Shells were thrown on Cross Roads N. of HARGICOURT. Weather dully. Night dark and cloudy. Situation Normal. At about 6.30 p.m. 3 H.E. Shell fell within 50x of H.Q. No.11 Sqn. in QUARRY. 2.10. Shelling of enemy of X Rds W. of HARGICOURT was kept up all night. Weather dry. Night moonlight cloudy at intervals.	R.R.O.
L.10.a.6.6. 62°C.N.E.1000 H.Q. No.11 Sqn. M.G. Corps MUSE	30th	7 a.m. 4 p.m.	At 3 a.m. Enemy bombarded M.G. Emplacement in Switch Trench & S.E. 7 m. objective & SUGAR FACTORY with Rifle Grenades and L.T. MORTARS – this bombardment lasted till 4 a.m. No damage was done. 33 projectiles were thrown on this position during the bombardment. Situation unchanged. Weather fine.	R.R.O.
L.10.a.6.6. 62°C.N.E.1000 H.Q. No.11 Sqn. M.G. Corps MUSE	31st	4 a.m. 4 p.m.	Situation reported unchanged. Quiet night except slight Night Cloudy. Situation Normal. Considerable hostile artillery activity around an position on N.SUNKEN ROAD from 8 a.m. to 4 p.m. Enemy probably ranging on X roads W. of HARGICOURT.	R.R.O.

J.C. Humfrey Capt
Comdg 11th Coy M.G.C.

Confidential

WAR DIARY

JUNE 1917

No 11 Sqdn M.G. Corps (Cavalry)

A.W.J.Lyndham Lt.
Cmdg No 11 Sqdn M.G. Corps (Cav)

field
30-6-17

WAR DIARY
INTELLIGENCE SUMMARY
No 11 Sqdn. M.G.C.
JUNE 1917

Army Form C. 2118

Place	Date	Hour	Summary of Events and Information	Remarks and references to Appendices
Map Ref 62dSW June L.16.a.6.6.	1st/2nd		No Cos disposed in line HARGICOURT Sector. With Head Quarters in Quarry L.10.a.6.8. Situation normal.	
"	2-3		No 11 Sqn relieved by No 12 Sqn M.G. Corps (Cav) relief commenced 10 p.m. No enemy activity by N. night situation on completion; 11 P.M. raining, marching was completed by 12 midnight. No 11 Sqn marching, arriving at 2.20 a.m. 3.6.17 less one Section which proceeded to Haversley for MG duty.	99
HAMELET	3rd	June	In Camp at HAMELET or Subsection machine Guns on MG duty at HERVILLY (2nd Wellesley)	
"	4"	"	Ordering Camp Routine.	99
"	14"	"	"	9
"	14"	"	Received orders Car Bde. Order No 9 of /14.6.17 Ordering relief for Sqdn in B Section No 11 Sqdn to relieve No 10 Sqdn Ar.G. Corps Cav. Brig. M.G. 14/15th June 1917. No 11 Sqdn left Camp HAMELET at 9.30 p.m. 14.6.17 and took over via HERVILLY (picking up on route the Subsection of Guns whilst took over on MG duty at that place) and HESSECOURT and L.14 unde L.10 c.2.7 62 c.NW. Relief commenced at 10.30 p.m. and was completed	99
COTE WOOD L.10c.7.2	15"	4/1 A.M. 15.6.17 without any interruption.		

WAR DIARY — Sheet II

INTELLIGENCE SUMMARY

(Erase heading not required.)

Army Form C. 2118

Instructions regarding War Diaries and Intelligence Summaries are contained in F.S. Regs., Part II. and the Staff Manual respectively. Title pages will be prepared in manuscript.

Place	Date	Hour	Summary of Events and Information	Remarks and references to Appendices
COTE WOOD	14	—	5 guns were at disposal of O.C. B/I Sub-sector and 1 gun at this H.Q. in BROSSE WOOD under 2 Lt. HOLLIS and OAKLEY. 4 guns parked in GRAND PRIEL WOOD under remaining.	
	15		The remaining 7 guns with 2 guns belonging to 12th Sqdn formed Inn Garrison of A.G. in B.2 Sub-sector with H.Q. in COTE WOOD and Gun positions in VILLARET village and BROWN line as shown on attached sketch. Situation Normal.	29/A 28/
	16		Disposition of guns remain as above. Situation remained normal over the period from 16 to 28th.	
		12.30am	On the night of the 28/29 two guns Nos 607 under 2 Lt Hollis were pushed forward into the advanced positions and put up a barrage from Mallison End of Cat. Alley Trench F.19.39.9. to F.14.C.44 co-operating with artillery and a Lewis which supplied the Tree pine southern end. 7000 rounds were fired. The patrol reported that the Tree was occupied & seeing who were to same immediately the barrage began. That the enemy was occupied; but it was impossible to tell whether any enemy were killed.	
	2.20		A mining of 22 inch Hotch T.M. Fires caused slight casualties (2 O.R. wounded) at No. 9 Post.	29/ 28/
	3.30am		No M.G. casualties occurred during period. Slight Natural gun position destroyed.	29/

J. C. Humphrey Capt
Acting O.C.

T2131. Wt. W708-776. 50000. 4/15. Sir J.C. & S.

Appendix I
to
War Diary. June 1917
No 11 Sqdn. M.G. Corps (Cav)
30-6-17

Gun positions are shown in center of circles as under :-
    Ordinary Positions
    Reserve   "
    Alternative "

German trenches marked ~~~~
    "   wire   "   xxxxx

Part of BELLENGLISE   1:20,000   2nd Edition Sheet IV

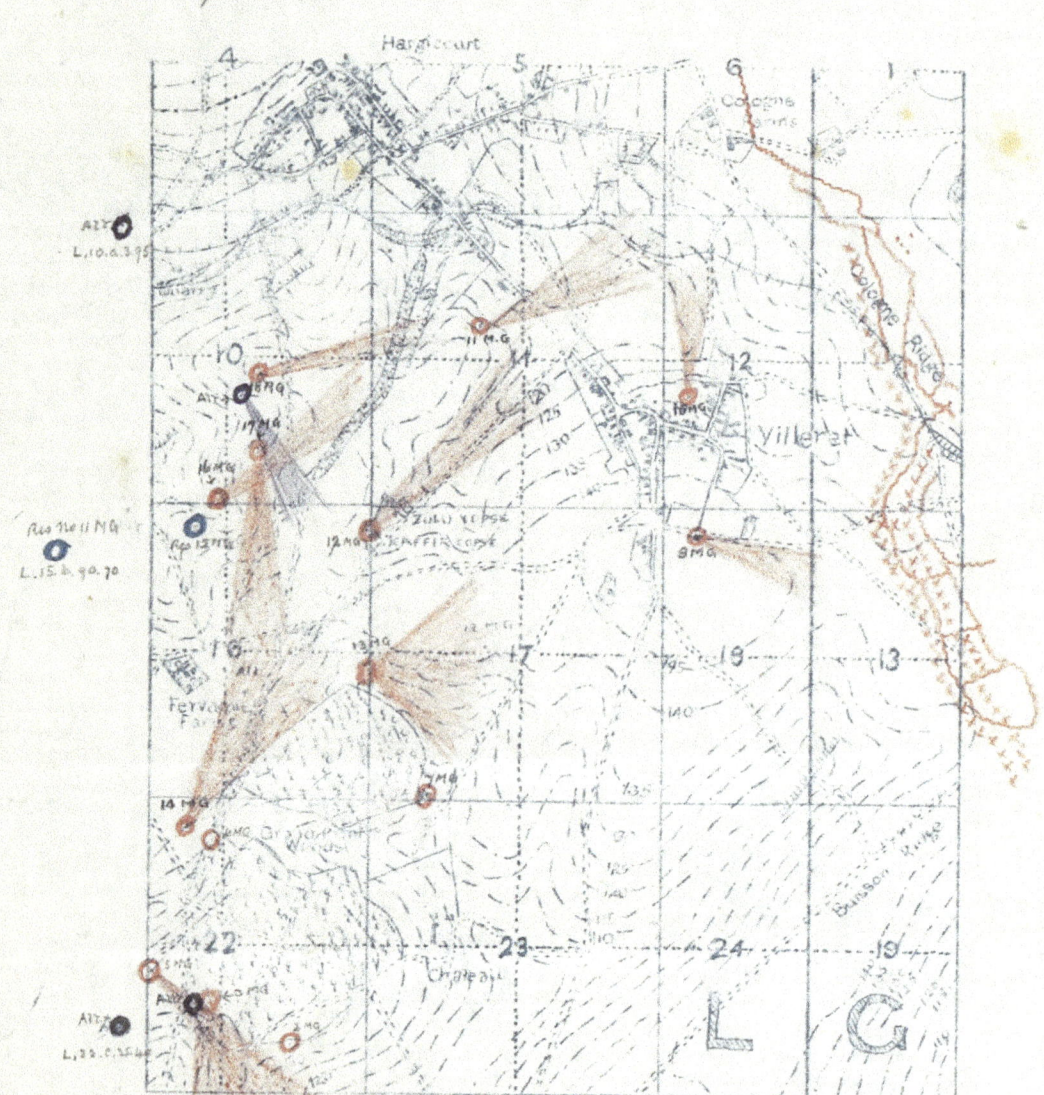

J.B.

Serial No. 321.

War Diary

Confidential

July 1917

No 11 Sqdn. M.G. Corps (Cav)

J.C. Humfrey. Capt
Cmdg No 11 Sqdn M.G Corps
(Cav)

Field
2-8-17

Army Form C. 2118.

WAR DIARY
or
INTELLIGENCE SUMMARY.
(Erase heading not required.)

Instructions regarding War Diaries and Intelligence Summaries are contained in F. S. Regs., Part II. and the Staff Manual respectively. Title pages will be prepared in manuscript.

Place	Date	Hour	Summary of Events and Information	Remarks and references to Appendices
Hq. 101st Bde	July 1st		In the line S. of HARGICOURT. 4 guns left H.q. w/ (O.te wood), in B.2 subsector	July
10ee S2 B 2 C.N.E.		5 a.m.	B 1 subsector with detached H Q at BROSSE WOOD.	
		1 p.m.	Raid on COLOGNE FARM. Artillery + M.G. Barrage opened at 1 p.m. The sum of 11 M.G.'S were used; 9,500 rounds per gun being fired.	July
	2		Situation Normal.	
	3			
	4			
	5			
	6			
	7th		Raid on enemy positions in front of D 1 subsector. Four guns from BROSSE WOOD were used to support the raid. Fire opened at 11:15 p.m. + was maintained for 25 minutes on given objectives. 3,500 rounds per gun were fired.	July
	8th	10.30 pm	Relief of the seven guns in B 2 subsector by 101st M.G. Coy. Begun.	July
		1.15 pm	Relief completed, and the Squadron less 5 guns in BROSSE WOOD marches back to camp near ENNEMAIN.	

T2134. Wt. W708-776. 50C000. 4/15. Sir J. C. & S.

Army Form C. 2118.

WAR DIARY
or
INTELLIGENCE SUMMARY.
(Erase heading not required.)

Place	Date	Hour	Summary of Events and Information	Remarks and references to Appendices
ENNEMAIN	9th	5.15 am	The Sqdn (less 5 guns in BRUSSE WOOD) arrived at ENNE MAIN. MG	
	10th	1 pm	5 Guns in BRUSSE WOOD were relieved by guns of 102nd MG Coy. MG	
	10th	5.30 am	arrived in Camp at ENNE MAIN.	
	11th		From July 11th to 31st. The Sqdn was in camp at ENNEMAIN during which time ordinary camp routine was carried out.	

MG

J C Hunter Capt
A/Adjt XI MG Sqn

No 11 Sqdn: Machine Gun Corps (Cav)

Serial No: 321.

WAR DIARY

AUGUST 1917

CONFIDENTIAL

The Field
1/9/17

JC Humfrey.
Cmdg No 11 Sqdn: M G Corps (Cav)

Army Form C. 2118.

WAR DIARY
or
INTELLIGENCE SUMMARY

(Erase heading not required.)

Instructions regarding War Diaries and Intelligence Summaries are contained in F. S. Regs., Part II. and the Staff Manual respectively. Title Pages will be prepared in manuscript.

Place	Date	Hour	Summary of Events and Information	Remarks and references to Appendices
ENNEMAIN	Aug 1st to 10th		Squadron training and billet routine	J.C.H.
EPEHY SECTOR	10th		The Squadron moved up to 35th Div. One Section of guns moved into the line NORTH of LEMPIRE	J.C.H.
	11th & 12th		The remaining two Sections went into camp near VILLERS FAUCON. The one gun in tion Sections moved into the line. One Section near YAK POST 2049 N.E LEMPIRE. One Section to SART FARM.	J.C.H. J.C.H.
	13th to 17th		The Squadron was in camp near VILLERS FAUCON where dismounted training was carried on.	J.C.H.
	17th	8pm	The Squadron moved into the line, one Section at SART FARM one Section near YAK POST. Three guns to GRAFTON POST near LITTLE PRIEL FARM one gun in EAGLE QUARRY.	J.C.H. J.C.H. J.C.H.
	18th	4 AM	AT dawn the 35th Division attacked THE KNOLL and GUILLEMONT FARM. The Machine guns at GRAFTON POST put up a LEFT Flank Barrage. The YAK POST Section & one firing in THE KNOLL and there put up a creeping barrage and finally stood on MAQUINCOURT TRENCH	J.C.H. J.C.H. J.C.H. J.C.H.

WAR DIARY or INTELLIGENCE SUMMARY

Army Form C. 2118.

(Erase heading not required.)

Place	Date	Hour	Summary of Events and Information	Remarks and references to Appendices
EPEHY SECTOR	Aug 18th		The SART FARM section put up a standing barrage in MAQUINCOURT VALLEY	JCH
	19th	4.30AM	The enemy made a counter attack but were driven back by artillery and machine gun fire	JCH
	20th	2PM	Between made a second counter attack but were again driven back by Artillery and machine gun fire	JCH
	22nd	4AM	The enemy made a third counter attack but were again repulsed	JCH
HARGICOURT SECTOR	23rd	1AM	The Squadron was relieved and moved to TEMPLEUX QUARRIES in 34th Division Area	JCH
	23rd	1pm	The Squadron dug emplacements on road L17D SOUTH of VILLERET	JCH
	24th	4.30AM		
	24th	7pm	The Squadron dug emplacements road L17D	JCH
	25	4.30AM		
	25	7pm	The Squadron improved the position in road L17D	JCH
	26	4.30AM	The 3rd Division made an attack on MAXAMIFF & COLOGNE FARMS. The Squadron Supplied flank from the right flank with a creeping barrage	JCH

2449 Wt. W14957/Mg0 750,000 1/16 J.B.C. & A. Forms/C.2118/12.

Army Form C. 2118.

WAR DIARY
or
INTELLIGENCE SUMMARY
(Erase heading not required.)

Instructions regarding War Diaries and Intelligence Summaries are contained in F.S. Regs., Part II. and the Staff Manual respectively. Title Pages will be prepared in manuscript.

Place	Date	Hour	Summary of Events and Information	Remarks and references to Appendices
HARCOURT SECTOR	27th	3 A.M.	The Division made a further attack on COLOGNE RIDGE	JCH
			The Squadron put up a right flank barrage	JCH
		9 P.M.	The enemy counter attacks followed shown driven back by machine gun barrage	JCH
	29th	4.30 A.M.	The enemy counter attacks h.p. were repulsed	JCH
	night 30th		The Squadron gradually withdrew to a new position near ZULU COPSE in L.11.D	JCH
	31st	5 A.M.	The enemy made a determined counter attack which was beaten back after hand to hand fighting	JCH

J.C. Hunter, Capt.
Comdg. XVth M.G. Sqn.

WAR DIARY

CONFIDENTIAL

No 4 Sqdn M.G. Corps (Cavalry)

SEPTEMBER 1917

The Field

J C Humfrey. Capt
Cmdg. No 4 Sqdn M.G. Corps (Cav)

Army Form C. 2118.

WAR DIARY
INTELLIGENCE SUMMARY
(Erase heading not required.)

Instructions regarding War Diaries and Intelligence Summaries are contained in F. S. Regs., Part II. and the Staff Manual respectively. Title Pages will be prepared in manuscript.

Place	Date	Hour	Summary of Events and Information	Remarks and references to Appendices
HARICOURT SECTOR	Sept 19		In front & East of RAFFIN COPSE with all guns laid on S.O.S. line. Barrage	JCH
	8 PM		The squadron relieves 103rd M.G. Coy in "A" Sector	JCH
	Sept 19	12 mn	Nine guns of the squadron cooperated with an infantry attack on GROVE PRIEL WOOD	JCH
			The firing on BUISSON GALLAINE FARM and trench below NORTH was maintained for ½ hour when the guns were withdrawn	JCH
	Sept 21 to 24/21		The squadron remains in the sector but no moves of any importance occurred	JCH
	Sept 24		The squadron were relieved by 2nd M.G. Coy.	JCH

JC Hann for Capt
Comdg 21st M.G. Sqdn

2449 Wt. W14957/M90 750,000 1/16 J.B.C. & A. Forms/C.2118/12.

CONFIDENTIAL. (321)

WAR - DIARY
OF
No 11 SQUADRON
MACHINE GUN CORPS (CAVALRY)

OCTOBER 1917.

Army Form C. 2118

WAR DIARY
or
INTELLIGENCE SUMMARY

No 11. Squadron MG Corps (Cav)

(Erase heading not required.)

Instructions regarding War Diaries and Intelligence Summaries are contained in F. S. Regs., Part II. and the Staff Manual respectively. Title pages will be prepared in manuscript.

Place	Date	Hour	Summary of Events and Information	Remarks and references to Appendices

CONFIDENTIAL (321.)

WAR DIARY

No 11 Sqdn M.G. Corps (Cav)

NOVEMBER
1917

Field
5-12-17

Capt
Cmdg 11th M.G. Sqdn
Mhow Cav Bde

Army Form C. 2118.

No 11. Squadron. M.G. Corps (Cav)

WAR DIARY
or
INTELLIGENCE SUMMARY
(Erase heading not required.)

Instructions regarding War Diaries and Intelligence Summaries are contained in F. S. Regs., Part II. and the Staff Manual respectively. Title Pages will be prepared in manuscript.

Place	Date	Hour	Summary of Events and Information	Remarks and references to Appendices
Amiens	Nov 1st – 17th		From Nov 1st – 17th the squadron was employed in building stables and billets. Scheme of squadron Training was also carried out.	
	Nov 18th		The squadron remained in a state of readiness to move.	
		9.30 pm	The squadron were ordered to be saddled up & ready to move at 6.45 next day	
	Nov 19th		Squadron stood by to	
Demuin Hut	Nov 19	3.0 am	The squadron marched to Demuin wood near Fins. They arrived at 10 am.	
	Nov 22	9.55	Squadron returned to Attrées. They arrived at 2 pm.	
62.c. Fins Attrées	Nov 25	6.am	Squadron moved to forward area at 62.c. E14 & 25 & returned to Attrées at 5 pm.	
	Nov 30	7.30 am	Four officers + 74 O.Rs proceed to forward area to take over part of the Cav. (Villerette schaslor)	
		11.am	Remainder ordered to forward area. Marched off camp at 1 pm. + reached St Émilie at 6 pm. The French party joined them here at 7 pm	

for O.C. No 11. M.G. (Cav)

<u>CONFIDENTIAL</u>

<u>No 11 Squadron Machine Gun Corps (Cav)</u>

<u>WAR DIARY</u>

<u>DECEMBER</u>

<u>1917</u>

<u>The Field</u>
<u>31-12-17</u>

J C Humfrey. Capt
Cmdg No 11 Sqdn M.G.C (Cav)

WAR DIARY or INTELLIGENCE SUMMARY.

Army Form C. 2118

Place	Date	Hour	Summary of Events and Information	Remarks and references to Appendices
Mt Equihen	Dec 1 1917	5 am	Brigade moved to PEIZIERES.	
			2nd Lancers & No 1 subaltern 11th MG Squadron were ordered to sally out and seize Targelle RAVINE and the ridge S.E. of VILLERS-GUISLAIN. They came under machine gun fire and seized a sunken road in rear. One Squadron dismounted, & no 1 subaltern followed the retirement & occupied a sunken road in X22 central. Two squadrons of the 20 LANCERS held on all day & came back that night. They were shelled & constantly attacked during the day. Nos 2 & 5 subsections followed D squadron of the Inniskillings who went down a ravine to the left of that channel and the 2nd LANCERS went. Two Squadrons & the 2 MG's obsection suffered very heavy casualties from MG fire & were eventually cut-off. The Squadron moved to St EMILIE.	Appx.
			Casualties. killed 2 OR. missing 10ff 43 OR. wounded 10ff. 14 OR.	Appx.
E 12 d 65	Dec 2		Horses 97.	
			officers missing Lt J H WALMSLEY	
			" wounded Lt R R OAKLEY	
ATHIES	Dec 3		Squadron moved to camp in ATHIES.	Appx.
	Dec 4 to Dec 8		Stables & ordinary Squadron Routine.	Appx.

Army Form C. 2118

WAR DIARY
or
INTELLIGENCE SUMMARY.
(Erase heading not required.)

Instructions regarding War Diaries and Intelligence Summaries are contained in F. S. Regs., Part II. and the Staff Manual respectively. Title pages will be prepared in manuscript.

Place	Date	Hour	Summary of Events and Information	Remarks and references to Appendices
ATHIES	Dec 9	7 A.M.	Squadron stood to, sentries up 4.15 a.m.	nil
"	10	7 AM	" " " "	nil
"	11	"	" " " "	nil
"	12	"	" " " "	nil
"	13-15		Squadron stood to, one Rooms notice	nil
			The following NCOs & men were awarded the Military Medal.	
			No 59365 Pte LANE. W.L.	
			No 40067 L/Cpl Greenwood. S.	
			" 57069 Cpl EA HARPER.	
			No 5.092 Pte FW BARRATT.	
ATHIES	Dec 16-17		The Squadron carried out ordinary routine	nil
"	Dec 18-20		The Squadron stood to from 7 PM till 8.30 PM	nil
			2/Lt R.C. HOLLIS & L/Cpl 20 OAKLEY were awarded the Military Cross.	
	Dec. 21-22			nil
	Dec 23-25		Squadron stood to from 7 AM - 8.30. On Dec 29 a digging party was sent up to the line.	nil
	26		digging party proceeded at 8.45 PM.	nil
	27-28		Digging party	nil
	29-31		" "	nil

M Gray Capt.

T./131. Wt. W768—776. 500000. 4/15. Sir J. C. & S.

CONFIDENTIAL.

WAR DIARY

4 DIV
MHOW Bde OF

No 11 SQUADRON M.G.C.(CAV)

FOR

JANUARY 1918

Lt Younghusband for Capt.
Cmdg. No 11 Squadron M.G.C.

WAR DIARY or INTELLIGENCE SUMMARY

Army Form C. 2118.

(Erase heading not required.)

Place	Date	Hour	Summary of Events and Information	Remarks and references to Appendices
ATHIES	Jan 1st		Ordinary Billet Routine	Easy
"	2nd		Capt McGray and 28 O.R. proceeded to VERMAND with 8 guns relieving 8 guns Easy	
			1st DM Divn on Barrage Lines	
"	9th		Capt McGray and 27 O.R. returned from VERMAND with 8 guns being relieved by Easy	
			2 Dismtd Divn	
"	14th		Lt A.W.G. Windham and 29 O.R. with 8 guns proceed to VERMAND relieving Easy	
			8 guns of 2nd Dismtd Divn on Barrage Lines	
"	19th		Lt F.A. Burton & 11 O.R. proceeded to HERVILLY to be attached to 258th	
			Tunnelling Company for Dugout construction	
"	23rd		Capt McGray and 40 O.R. relieved Lt A.W.G. Windham and 29 O.R. on duty Easy	
			with Barrage Battery at VERMAND	
"	25th		Lt F.A. Burton and 11 O.R. return from duty with 258th Tunnelling Coy at Easy	
			HERVILLY	
"	27th		Capt J.C. Humfrey as D.M.G.O. 3 Officers and 105 O.R. with 8 guns relieved	
			8 guns of 2nd Dismounted Divn in VILLERET Sector, with Sqdn H.Q. at	
			COTE WOOD L.16.a.8.5. 62c.	

Army Form C. 2118.

WAR DIARY
or
INTELLIGENCE SUMMARY.
(Erase heading not required.)

Place	Date	Hour	Summary of Events and Information	Remarks and references to Appendices
ATHIES	Jan 31st		Capt Humfrey D.M.G.O. 4th Div with 3 Officers 65 O.R. with 8 guns in line in VILLERET Sector. With horses and details of sqdn and transport in camp at ATHIES.	Esyoure humfrey Lt

CONFIDENTIAL.

WAR * DIARY

OF

11TH MACHINE GUN SQUADRON

FOR

FEBRUARY, 1918.

11th Machine Gun Sqdn

WAR DIARY
INTELLIGENCE SUMMARY. JCH

January 1918.

Army Form C. 2118.

321

Place	Date	Hour	Summary of Events and Information	Remarks and references to Appendices
ATHIES	1st		In Camp at ATHIES JCH	
	3rd		1 Officer + 28 O.R. proceeded to VERMAND area to dig M.G. of emplacements JCH	
	9th		1 Officer + 28 O.R. returned from VERMAND JCH	
	11th		1 Officer + 25 O.R. proceeded to VERMAND JCH	
	19th		1 Officer + 11 O.R. proceeded to HERVILLY to learn handling JCH	
	23rd		1 Officer + 40 O.R. proceeded VERMAND to relieve party JCH	
	25th		1 Officer + 111 O.R. returned from HERVILLY JCH	
	27th		4 Officers + 65 O.R. with 89 guns proceeded to VILLERET SECTOR to relieve 2nd Gd. Cavalry Brigade MG Squadron JCH	
			In line	
	31st		Remainder of Squadron in Camp at ATHIES JCH	

Army Form C. 2118.

WAR DIARY
or
INTELLIGENCE SUMMARY.

(Erase heading not required.)

11th M.G. Sqdn.
February 1918
Volume

Place	Date	Hour	Summary of Events and Information	Remarks and references to Appendices
VILLERET SECTOR	17th		Eight guns were in the line. Five guns at CAUTION DUGOUT. Three guns at SHEPHERDS COPSE. One gun at VILLERET JCH	
ATHIES	23rd		The Sqdn less 8 guns moved to WIENCOURT JCH	
WARFUSÉE	3rd(?)pt		The Sqdn less 8 guns moved to BOUZIES JCH	
			The Sqdn less 8 guns moved to ST AUBIN JCH	
BOUZIES				
VILLERET SECTOR	night 14/15		The eight guns in the line were relieved by 72" M.G. Coy. returning at VIDEL railway ST AUBIN at 9.30pm 15th JCH	
AUBIN	26		The Sqdn moved forward to DOMMARTIN JCH	
DOMMARTIN	27		The Sqdn moved forward to HARBONNIER JCH	
HARBONNIER	28		The Sqdn moved forward to Camp near the apex of 1st Canadian Divn in JCH	

J.C. Humphrey Capt
Cmd 11th M.G. Sqdn

CONFIDENTIAL

WAR DIARY

OF

No 11 SQUADRON   M.G.C. (CAV)

attached to 32 Division

FOR

MARCH 1918

Field
31/3/18

E.W. Younghusband Lieut,
Cmdg. No 11 Squadron M.G.C.C.

WAR DIARY or INTELLIGENCE SUMMARY.

Army Form C. 2118.

(Erase heading not required.)

Instructions regarding War Diaries and Intelligence Summaries are contained in F. S. Regs., Part II. and the Staff Manual respectively. Title pages will be prepared in manuscript.

Place	Date	Hour	Summary of Events and Information	Remarks and references to Appendices
BRUSLE	1st		The Squadron stated as follows — Rear part and H Q at BRUSLE about 5 kilometres EAST	
			of PERONNE. Forward part consisting of 2 officers 4th O.R. with 8 M.G's were concerned	
			about the ground behind A.A. dump at ROISEL, also in readiness to take up	
			battle positions in case of attack at TEMPLEUX QUARRIES.	Ruy.
BRUSLE	13th 10th		One officer and routine Ruy.	
"	10th		Forward party rejoined Ruy.	
"	11th 12th 13th		Ordinary camp routine Ruy.	
			Squadron moved at 12 noon to BRAE area. HQ at U.S.B.3.7. (Sheet 62 e. Ruy)	
			16 O.R. 32 L.D. horses, 16 L.G.S wagons attached for move to rear area Ruy.	
			Lt. P.W. Younghusband assumed command of Squadron on Colt. J.C. Murphy	
			being transferred to 6th M.G. Squadron Ruy.	
BRAE	14th	11 AM	Squadron moved to VAIRE-SUR-CORBIE Ruy.	
VAIRE-CORBIE	15	8.30 AM	Squadron moved to VERS. Ruy.	
VERS	16	8 AM	Squadron moved to FRANCIERS via S. & 4 kilometres of railway transport at at	
			EAUCOURT-SUR-SOMME Ruy.	
FRANCIERS	17th		Ordinary billet routine Ruy.	

Army Form C. 2118.

WAR DIARY
or
INTELLIGENCE SUMMARY.
(Erase heading not required.)

Instructions regarding War Diaries and Intelligence Summaries are contained in F. S. Regs., Part II. and the Staff Manual respectively. Title pages will be prepared in manuscript.

Place	Date	Hour	Summary of Events and Information	Remarks and references to Appendices
FRANCIERS	16th	11 AM	B squadron moved to L'ETOILE and 96 I.G.S. Wagons attached with personnel and horses moved to A.M.T. depot ABBEVILLE. Busy.	
L'ETOILE	18th & 19th		Ordinary billet routine. Busy	
"	21st		10 horses sent to Canadian Cav. Bde. Busy.	
"	22nd		Ordinary billet routine. Busy.	
"	23rd	4.30 am	Lt. W.H.E. Weil and 25 O.R. entrained go horses for MARSEILLES. Busy	
"	24th		Transport less 1 G.S. wagon under Lt. F.A. Butler proceeded to forward area. Busy	
"	25th		Four officers and 95 O.R. & 12 M.G.s under command of Lt. E.W. YOUNGHUSBAND moved to horse to BELLACOURT arriving at B.p.m. Busy	
BELLACOURT	26th		Squadron transport arrived at 9.20 pm. Rear party at L'ETOILE moved to LONG. Busy	
"	27th	4 pm	Forward party moved to HUMBERCAMP arriving at 11.30 pm.	
HUMBERCAMP	28th	2 am	Forward party moved as under – 5 officers, 97 O.R. & 12 guns under Lt. E.W. Younghusband to QUESNOY FARM to take up positions for defence of "battle line".	
			The transport bivouacked in field at Y 4 BIENVILLERS (Sht Lens 11).	

Army Form C. 2118.

WAR DIARY
or
INTELLIGENCE SUMMARY.
(Erase heading not required.)

Instructions regarding War Diaries and Intelligence Summaries are contained in F. S. Regs., Part II. and the Staff Manual respectively. Title pages will be prepared in manuscript.

Place	Date	Hour	Summary of Events and Information	Remarks and references to Appendices
VERSHEY FARM 28			Disposal of guns as follows – 2 guns at F.14.6.2.8. (shut 57.D.) 2 guns at F.13.a.7.8. – 4 guns at THICKSET BRUSHWOOD HEDGE at F.13.d. – 2 guns h set twit at F.14.a. and 2 guns h red Read at F.25.a. 2104. H.Q. at F.13.b.6.4. (Shut 57.D.) Day	
	29th		Situation on the whole was quiet – our targets were engaged 2104.	
TUESNY FM 30th			Situation unchanged. 2104.	
" " 31st			Some Stogun fortenio were subjected to considerable shelling – otherwise situation unchanged. 2104.	
			Field. 1-4-18. EisYoung Husband Lt. O.C. XI. M. & S. Squadron	

1917-18
4TH CAVALRY DIVISION
MHOW CAVALRY BRIGADE

MOBILE VETY SECTION
JAN 1917 — FEB 1918

SERIAL NO. 201.

Confidential

War Diary

of

MOBILE VETERINARY SECTION, MHOW CAVALRY BRIGADE.

FROM 1st JANUARY 1917. ~~1916~~ TO 31st JANUARY 1917. ~~1916~~

Army Form C. 2118.

WAR DIARY
INTELLIGENCE SUMMARY

(Erase heading not required.)

Place	Date	Hour	Summary of Events and Information	Remarks and references to Appendices
BELLOY Sur Mer	Jan 15.1.17		Took over Vety Charge of JODHPUR LANCERS at VALINES.	
"	16.1.17		Inspected section - visited Machine Gun Squadron at OFFEUX	9/VtB
"	17.1.17		Inspected progress with Horse Dip. Routine work as usual.	9/VtB
"	18.1.17		Admitted four sick horses, visited Jodhpur Lancers at Valines, also Machine Gun Squadron	9/VtB
"	19.1.17		Admitted one sick horse, evacuated nine to ABBEVILLE, inspected Dip at No 5 Veterinary Hospital, & took notes & minute details reference Dipping Mange.	9/VtB
"	20.1.17		Visited Machine Gun Squadron & inspected for contagious diseases & shoeing	9/VtB
"	21.1.17		Admitted one sick horse, inspected horses (one cast) by DADR of Aux. Horse Transport.	9/VtB
"	22.1.17		Visited Jodhpur Lancers at VALINES. Inspected all suspicious Mange Cases.	9/VtB
"	23.1.17		Showed up horses for casting to D.A.D.R. at OFFEUX, inspected sick horses Machine Guns.	9/VtB
"	24.1.17		Visited Machine Gun Squad. suspected for contagious diseases & shoeing.	9/VtB
"	25.1.17		Visited sick horses Auxiliary Horse Transport.	9/VtB
"	26.1.17		Inspected sick horses of Jodhpur Lancers, Divis. Ammn. Column, Reserve Park	9/VtB
"	27.1.17		Evacuated twenty horses cast by D.A.D.R. sent to No. 22 Vety Hospital ABBEVILLE	9/VtB
"	28.1.17		Routine work as usual	9/VtB
"	29.1.17		Admitted one sick horse, visited Jodhpur Lancers at Valines	9/VtB
"	30.1.17		Visited sick horses of Inniskillens Aux. Horse Transport, Div. Ammn. Col. & Reserve Park	9/VtB
"	31.1.17		Handed over Vet Infirmary Charge of Jodhpur Lancers to Capt Bordway.	9/VtB

Army Form C. 2118.

WAR DIARY
or
INTELLIGENCE SUMMARY

(Erase heading not required.)

MHOW BRIGADE

Place	Date	Hour	Summary of Events and Information	Remarks and references to Appendices
BELLOY-Sur-MER	1-1-17		Routine work as usual.	Q.M.B.
"	2-1-17		Visited 38" R.I.H. at NIBAS & OCHANCOURT. Inspected sick animals	Q.M.B.
"	3-1-17		Admitted three sick horses. Visited Machine Gun Squadron at OFFEUX	Q.M.B.
"	4-1-17		Visited sick animals. Auxiliary Horse Transport.	Q.M.B.
"	5-1-17		Evacuated seven horses by road to No 22 Veterinary Hospital ABBEVILLE. Lt Hoagland on leave.	Q.M.B.
	6-1-17		Routine work as usual. Visited Section on taking over temporary command.	
	7-1-17		Admitted one sick horse and paid men of Section	
	8-1-17		Admitted one sick horse. Visited 38"6.I.H. OCHANCOURT & inspected sick horses.	
	9-1-17		Admitted two sick horses. Visited sick horses at FRIVILLE. Lt Contignor's Horses a Shoeing.	
	10-1-17		Visited sick horses Machine Gun Sqn. at OFFEUX.	
	11-1-17		Visited Aux Horse Transport, and inspected sick horses	
	12-1-17		Evacuated 4 sick horses by road to No 22 Veterinary Hosp. AB BEVILLE. Capt Williams took over charge of 38 "C.I. Horse.	
	13-1-17		Admitted 2 sick horses.	
	14-1-17		Visited sick horses belonging to Machine Gun Sqn. for Contignor Reserve at OFFEUX	

SERIAL No 201.

C O N F I D E N T I A L.

W A R   D I A R Y.

of

Mobile Veterinary Section
Mhow Cavalry Brigade

From 1-2-17   To 28-2-17

Army Form C. 2118.

WAR DIARY
or
INTELLIGENCE SUMMARY
(Erase heading not required.)

Geoffrey W. Rennel Lt. AVC

Instructions regarding War Diaries and Intelligence Summaries are contained in F. S. Regs., Part II. and the Staff Manual respectively. Title Pages will be prepared in manuscript.

MOBILE VETERINARY SECTION 2-17 ☆ MHOW BRIGADE

Place	Date	Hour	Summary of Events and Information	Remarks and references to Appendices
BELLOY	1-2-17		Visited sick horses Aux. Horse Transport.	9MB
"	2-2-17		Two sick horses admitted to section - routine work as usual - Evacuated two horses to ABBEVILLE	9MB
"	3-2-17		One sick horse admitted, visited machine gun squads at Offeux.	9MB
"	4-2-17		One sick horse admitted, destroyed one belonging to Div. Ammunition Column at Fressenville	9MB
"	5-2-17		Handed over units to B.V.O who had returned from leave -	9MB
"	6-2-17		Routine work as usual	9MB
"	7-2-17		Routine work as usual	9MB
"	8-2-17		Visited sick horses Aux Horse Transport.	9MB
"	9-2-17		Marching order parade & Section & rifle inspection -	9MB
"	10-2-17		Visited Triville to arrange billets for men & horses.	9MB
"	11-2-17		Routine work as usual.	9MB
"	12-2-17		Inspected Mhow Brigade Headquarters Transport for shoeing -	9MB
"	13-2-17		Inspected Aux Horse Transport for contagious diseases & shoeing -	9MB
"	14-2-17		Moved section to new billet in Triville -	9MB
TRIVILLE	15-2-17		Routine work, & arranged additional accommodation for men & horses.	9MB
"	16-2-17		Routine work.	9MB

Army Form C. 2118.

WAR DIARY
or
INTELLIGENCE SUMMARY

(Erase heading not required.)

Geoffrey H Bennell Lt AVC

Place	Date	Hour	Summary of Events and Information	Remarks and references to Appendices
TRIVILLE	17.2.17		Visited Machine Gun Squadron at Offeux - inspected shoeing -	GWB
"	18-2-17		Routine work as usual -	GWB
"	19-2-17		Routine work as usual -	GWB
"	20-2-17		Inspected Sick horses Aux Horse Transport.	GWB
"	21-2-17		Visited sick horses Machine Gun Squad⁵	GWB
"	22-2-17		Routine work - Admitted one sick horse.	GWB
"	23-2-17		Inspected Aux Horse Transport for contagious disease.	GWB
"	24-2-17		Visited Machine Gun Squad⁵ Sick horses -	GWB
"	25-2-17		Inspected progress of DIP with A.D.V.S.	GWB
"	26-2-17		Routine work as usual -	GWB
"	27-2-17		Rehearsal with 3 other Sections from 5ᵗʰ Cav Divⁿ for regulation of traffic into Dip. Inspection of section drills afterwards by A.D.V.S. - Admitted one sick horse -	GWB
"	28.3.17		Clerical work for End of month -	GWB

Serial No. 201.

CONFIDENTIAL

WAR DIARY.

of

Mobile Veterinary Section
MHOW Cavalry Brigade.

from 1st March 1917 to 31st March 1917

Army Form C. 2118.

WAR DIARY
or
INTELLIGENCE SUMMARY
(Erase heading not required.)

Instructions regarding War Diaries and Intelligence Summaries are contained in F. S. Regs., Part II. and the Staff Manual respectively. Title Pages will be prepared in manuscript.

Jeffrey H Renner
O.C. 4th Vety. Sec. 4th Indian Cav. Bde

Place	Date	Hour	Summary of Events and Information	Remarks and references to Appendices
FRIVILLE	1.3.17		Visited Divn. Horse Transport sick horses.	9/4/B.
"	2.3.17		Routine work as usual.	9/4/B.
"	3.3.17		Inspected Machine Gun Squadron sick horses & one section for shoeing.	9/4/B.
"	4.3.17		Arranged for starting of Horse Dip. Pipes for water burst in the evening.	9/4/B.
"	5.3.17		Inspected sick horses for Reserve Park.	9/4/B.
"	6.3.17		Visited Divn. Horse Transport sick horses. Admitted one sick horse. Inspected Reserve Park H.D. horses with ADVS.	9/4/B.
"	7.3.17		Inspected Machine Gun Squadron sick horses.	9/4/B.
"	8.3.17		Routine work as usual.	9/4/B.
"	9.3.17		Inspected sick horses Reserve Park.	9/4/B.
"	10.3.17		Inspected Heavy Draught Horses Divn. Horse Transport.	9/4/B.
"	11.3.17		Admitted six sick horses + evacuated five to No. 22 Veterinary Hospital ABBEVILLE.	9/4/B.
"	12.3.17		Inspected sick horses Reserve Park.	9/4/B.
"	13.3.17		Routine work as usual.	9/4/B.
"	14.3.17		Inspected sick horses Machine Gun Squadron + one section for shoeing.	9/4/B.
"	15.3.17		Attended one horse left by 36th Jacobs Horse at Frivillers.	9/4/B.
"	16.3.17		Inspected sick horses Reserve Park.	9/4/B.
"	17.3.17		Received orders to move next day. All preparations complete to depart horses Tuesday.	9/4/B.
"	18.3.17		Notified. Received orders midnight to move next day.	9/4/B.
"	19.3.17		Left one sick horse at Marie ESCARBOTIN belonging to M.G.S. marched by road to DRUCAT.	9/4/B.

Army Form C. 2118.

WAR DIARY
or
INTELLIGENCE SUMMARY
(Erase heading not required.)

Instructions regarding War Diaries and Intelligence Summaries are contained in F. S. Regs., Part II. and the Staff Manual respectively. Title Pages will be prepared in manuscript.

Place	Date	Hour	Summary of Events and Information	Remarks and references to Appendices
DRUCAT	20.3.17		Admitted 2 sick horses and evacuated 2 by road to No 22 Vet' Hospital ABBEVILLE. Marched from DRUCAT to ST LEGER	9/tB.
ST LEGER.	21.3.17		Admitted one sick horse. And marched to AVELUY.	9/tB.
AVELUY.	22.3.17		Inspected horses in Section & visited all units.	9/tB.
"	23.3.17		Admitted 18 sick horses in section. inspected units.	9/tB.
"	24.3.17		Admitted 2 sick horses and evacuated 16 from ALBERT to No 7 Vet' Hosp. FORGES-les-EAUX	9/tB.
"	25.3.17		Admitted 1 sick horse from 122 H.B. R.F.A. & evacuated 6 from AVELUY to No.7 Vet' Hospital	9/tB.
"	26.3.17		Admitted 3 sick horses.	9/tB.
"	27.3.17		Admitted 10 sick horses. Routine work as usual	9/tB.
"	28.3.17		Admitted 4 sick horses. Evacuated 16 by road from AVELUY to No.7 Vet' Hospital.	9/tB.
"	29.3.17		Received orders to proceed to IRLES. order cancelled later.	9/tB.
"	30.3.17		Inspected horses of all units.	9/tB.
"	31.3.17		Routine work.	9/tB.

GH Rennel Lave

O.C. Mobile Veterinary Section
Anhars. Cav. Brigade

31.3.17

Serial No. 201.

CONFIDENTIAL

WAR DIARY OF

Mobile Veterinary Section
Mhow Cavalry Brigade

From 1 - 4 - 17.   to   30 - 4 - 17.

Army Form C. 2118.

WAR DIARY
or
INTELLIGENCE SUMMARY
(Erase heading not required.)

4 Div
J.H.Bennett Lane
O.C. Mobile Veterinary Section

Place	Date	Hour	Summary of Events and Information	Remarks and references to Appendices
AVELUY	1.4.17		Routine work.	9MVS
"	2.4.17		Routine work.	9MVS
"	3.4.17		Admitted one sick horse to Section. Brigade moved to MIRAMONT	9MVS
MIRAMONT	4.4.17		Visited Machine Gun Squadron. Inspected all horses.	9MVS
"	5.4.17		Admitted one sick horse to Section. Visited 38th C.I.H. and inspected all horses.	9MVS
"	6.4.17		Admitted five sick horses to Section. And evacuated six horses.	9MVS
"	7.4.17		Admitted seven sick horses. Visited Machine Gun Squadron	9MVS
"	8.4.17		Admitted fourteen sick horses to Section. Visited 38th C.I.H.	9MVS
"	9.4.17		Evacuated sixteen sick horses. Routine work as usual.	9MVS
"	10.4.17		Admitted five & handed over thirteen to Lucknow Mob. Vet. Section. Brigade moved to MORY. 1:30 A.M. returned to same day to MIRAMONT and evacuated twenty two horses on our return.	9MVS
"	11.4.17	2:45 A.M.	Brigade moved to MORY 2:45 A.M. returned to evening. Admitting one sick horse.	9MVS
"	12.4.17		Admitted eleven sick horses to Section. Routine work.	9MVS
"	13.4.17	10 A.M.	Brigade moved to SARTON 10 A.M. left sergeant and five men in charge of twenty one sick horses at MIRAMONT	9MVS
SARTON.	14.4.17		Those horses handed over to 62nd Divisional Mob. Vet. Section. Sergeant and three men arrived in the evening from MIRAMONT. Two men left behind with sick horses for evacuation.	9MVS
"	15.4.17		Admitted twenty two sick horses to Section.	9MVS
"	16.4.17		Admitted three sick horses.	9MVS
"	17.4.17		Admitted four sick horses.	9MVS

Army Form C. 2118.

WAR DIARY
or
INTELLIGENCE SUMMARY

(Erase heading not required.)

Instructions regarding War Diaries and Intelligence Summaries are contained in F. S. Regs., Part II. and the Staff Manual respectively. Title Pages will be prepared in manuscript.

Place	Date	Hour	Summary of Events and Information	Remarks and references to Appendices
SARTON	18.4.17		Admitted six sick horses and evacuated thirty one.	QMB.
"	19.4.17		Visited Machine Gun Squadron at THIEVRES.	QMB.
"	20.4.17		Visited 3g4 C.I.H. at SARTON.	QMB.
"	21.4.17		Routine work as usual.	QMB.
"	22.4.17		Visited Machine Gun Squadron sick horses.	QMB.
"	23.4.17		Admitted thirty two sick horses and evacuated Saturday.	QMB.
"	24.4.17		Visited 3gt C.I.H. inspected all horses.	QMB.
"	25.4.17		Admitted one sick horse to Section. Routine work.	QMB.
"	26.4.17		Admitted three sick horses, inspected shoeing of No Section Machine Gun Squad?	QMB.
"	27.4.17		Admitted seven sick horses to Section. Routine work as usual. DDVS 5th Army visited Section. Visited 3gt C.I.H.	QMB.
"	28.4.17		Admitted six sick horses.	QMB.
"	29.4.17		Visited one horse sick to Section. Visited machine gun Squadron.	QMB.
"	30.4.17		Admitted four sick horses. Routine work as usual.	QMB.

J.H.Bennett Lieut.
O.C. Mobile Veterinary Section
Wilson Can. Bde.—

Serial No. 201.

CONFIDENTIAL.

WAR DIARY.

of

Mobile Veterinary Section
Mhow Cavalry Brigade

from 1st May 1917.   to 30th June 1917.

Army Form C. 2118.

WAR DIARY
or
INTELLIGENCE SUMMARY

Mobile Veterinary Section
Mhow Cavalry Brigade

(Erase heading not required.)

Instructions regarding War Diaries and Intelligence Summaries are contained in F. S. Regs., Part II. and the Staff Manual respectively. Title Pages will be prepared in manuscript.

Place	Date	Hour	Summary of Events and Information	Remarks and references to Appendices
SARCEN	1.5.17		Routine work as usual.	Qr/S
	2.5.17		Admitted 8 horses to section. Visited 2nd Lancers.	Qr/S
	3.5.17		Visited sick horses Mhow. Q.Sgt inspected shoes.	Qr/S
	4.5.17		Admitted 13 sick horses to section.	Qr/S
	5.5.17		Routine work as usual.	Qr/S
	6.5.17		Visited 38th C.I.H. sick horses.	Qr/S
	7.5.17		Evacuated 21 sick horses by rail to Abbeville.	Qr/S
	8.5.17		Admitted 8 sick horses to section. Routine work as usual.	Qr/S
	9.5.17		Admitted 11 sick horses. Evacuated 18 to Abbeville.	Qr/S
	10.5.17		Admitted 5 sick horses to section. Visited 34th C.I.H.	Qr/S
	11.5.17		Admitted 3 sick horses to section. Routine work as usual.	Qr/S
	12.5.17		Routine work as usual.	Qr/S
	13.5.17		Routine work as usual.	Qr/S
	14.5.17		Evacuated 12 sick horses. Brigade marched to MERICOURT.	Qr/S
MERICOURT	15.5.17		Brigade moved to CAPPY.	Qr/S
CAPPY	16.5.17		Brigade moved to St CHRIST.	Qr/S
St CHRIST	17.5.17		Routine work as usual.	Qr/S
	18.5.17		Admitted 3 sick horses to section.	Qr/S

J.K. Dempsey
Lieut.
O.C. M.V.S. Mhow Bde.

Army Form C. 2118.

WAR DIARY
or
INTELLIGENCE SUMMARY

(Erase heading not required.)

Instructions regarding War Diaries and Intelligence Summaries are contained in F. S. Regs., Part II. and the Staff Manual respectively. Title Pages will be prepared in manuscript.

Place	Date	Hour	Summary of Events and Information	Remarks and references to Appendices
ST CHRIST	18.5.17		Admitted 3 sick horses. Routine	App
"	19.5.17		Admitted 12 Sick horses to Sick Route work as usual	App
"	20.5.17		Routine work as usual	App
"	21.5.17		Visited 38 C.I.H. Sick horses	App
"	22.5.17		Admitted 4 sick horses and evacuated 16 to ABBEVILLE	App
"	23.5.17		Rainy. not a view?	App
"	24.5.17		Admitted seven sick horses Rect?	2 + 13
"	25.5.17		Routine work examined	App
"	26.5.17		Visited Machine Gun Squad?	2 u 13
B	27.5.17		Visited 18 C.I.H. Sick horses	2 u 13
"	28.5.17		Routine work as usual.	App
"	29.5.17		Visited 38 C.I.H. suspected one spadra meutagine disease Fibres	2 u 13
"	30.5.17		Visited 10 Grewal? Sick horses	App
"	31.5.17		Routine work as usual	App

J.H Bennet Kive
O.C M.V.S Indian BL

CONFIDENTIAL.

WAR DIARY.

of

*Mobile Vety Section
Mhow Cavalry Bde*

from 1st June 1917.   to 30th June 1917.

WAR DIARY or INTELLIGENCE SUMMARY

Army Form C. 2118.

Mobile Vety Section Mhow Bde

Place	Date	Hour	Summary of Events and Information	Remarks and references to Appendices
ST CHRIST	1.6.17		Routine work as usual. Admitted 4 sick horses.	JMB
	2.6.17		Evacuated ten sick horses by rail to Forges les EAUX	JMB
	3.6.17		Visited sick horses 38th C.I.H	JMB
	4.6.17		Bde moved to HAMELET.	JMB
	5.6.17		Routine work as usual. Visited Machine Gun Squad=	JMB
	6.6.17		Admitted two sick horses to Section	JMB
	7.6.17		Admitted one sick horse to Section, routine work as usual.	JMB
	8.6.17		Admitted eight sick horses, visited General Kennedy's horse and sick horses 38th C.I.H	JMB
	9.6.17		Evacuated eight sick horses by rail.	JMB
	10.6.17		Admitted three sick horses. Visited Machine Gun Squad=	JMB
	11.6.17		Admitted nine sick horses. Was sent myself to 36. C.C.S with rheumatic fever. Capt Barton looking after the Section.	JMB
	12.6.17		Admitted one sick horse. Evacuated fourteen by rail to FORGES les EAUX.	JMB
	13.6.17		Admitted two sick horses. Routine work as usual.	JMB
	14.6.17		Routine work.	JMB
	15.6.17		Admitted four sick horses to section.	JMB
	16.6.17		Evacuated eight sick horses and twenty six horses cast by D.D.R	JMB
	17.6.17		Returned from hospital to duty. Bde moved to ENNEMAIN.	JMB

Army Form C. 2118.

WAR DIARY
or
INTELLIGENCE SUMMARY
(Erase heading not required.)

Instructions regarding War Diaries and Intelligence Summaries are contained in F. S. Regs., Part II. and the Staff Manual respectively. Title Pages will be prepared in manuscript.

Place	Date	Hour	Summary of Events and Information	Remarks and references to Appendices
ENNEMAIN	18.6.17		Pasture work as usual. One horse admitted	9hrs
	19.6.17		Admitted three horses to section.	2hrs
	20.6.17		Visited Machine Gun Squad's Sick lines	8hrs
	21.6.17		Routine work as usual. K.R. inspection.	9hrs
	22.6.17		Admitted four sick horses. Section visited 35th C.F.H.	9hrs
	23.6.17		Admitted one sick horse. Evacuated eight sick to Forge les Eaux	9hrs
	24.6.17		Visited Sialkot Cavalry Field Ambulance & inspected remounts	9hrs
	25.6.17		Routine work as usual	9hrs
	26.6.17		Admitted 3 sick horses to section	9hrs
	27.6.17		Admitted 2 sick horses to section. Visited 2 R. Horse Machine Gun Squad	9hrs
	28.6.17		Routine work	9hrs
	29.6.17		Admitted 3 sick horses. Pasture work	9hrs
	30.6.17		Admitted nine sick horses to Forges-les-Eaux. Inspected sick horses of 35th C.F.H.	9hrs

J.H. Rennell
Lieut.
OC

MOBILE VETERINARY SECTION
30.6.17
MHOW BRIGADE

CONFIDENTIAL.   Serial No. 201

WAR   DIARY

OF

Mobile Veterinary Section
Mhow Cavalry Brigade

from 1st July 1917 to 31st July 1917

Army Form C. 2118.

WAR DIARY
or
INTELLIGENCE SUMMARY

(Erase heading not required.)

Instructions regarding War Diaries and Intelligence Summaries are contained in F. S. Regs., Part II. and the Staff Manual respectively. Title Pages will be prepared in manuscript.

Place	Date	Hour	Summary of Events and Information	Remarks and references to Appendices
ENNEMAIN	1.7.17		Admitted one sick horse to Section. Routine work as usual	9/AB.
	2.7.17		Admitted four sick horses. Visited Machine Gun Squadron.	9/AB.
	3.7.17		Evacuated five sick horses from PERONNE CHAPELETTE to Troyes by EAUX	9/AB.
	4.7.17		Admitted one sick horse. Inspected shoeing in Machine Gun Squads	9/AB.
	5.7.17		Visited sick horses 38th C.I.H	9/AB
	6.7.17		Routine work as usual	9/AB
	7.7.17		Visited sick horses 38th C.I.H & M.G.S.	9/AB
	8.7.17		Kit inspection. Little to do. Routine work as usual	9/AB
	9.7.17		Admitted two sick horses to Section. Visited Machine Gun Squads	9/AB.
	10.7.17		Visited 38th C.I.H Sick horses, inspected musquad? for contagious diseases	9/AB.
	11.7.17		Routine work as usual	9/AB
	12.7.17		Routine work. Inspection. Admitted three sick horses.	9/AB.
	13.7.17		Admitted six sick horses to Section. Visited Machine Gun Squads	9/AB
	14.7.17		Evacuated ten sick animals to FORGES les EAUX	9/AB
	15.7.17		Routine work as usual	9/AB.
	16.7.17		Inspected the Section Machine Gun Squad? for contagious diseases + sheer?	9/AB.
	17.7.17		Visited sick horses 38th C.I.H Admitted ten sick horses to Section.	9/AB.
	18.7.17		Routine work as usual	9/AB.
	19.7.17		Admitted ten sick horses to Section	9/AB.
	20.7.17		Visited sick horses Machine Gun Squad?	9/AB

Army Form C. 2118.

WAR DIARY or INTELLIGENCE SUMMARY

(Erase heading not required.)

Instructions regarding War Diaries and Intelligence Summaries are contained in F.S. Regs., Part II. and the Staff Manual respectively. Title Pages will be prepared in manuscript.

Place	Date	Hour	Summary of Events and Information	Remarks and references to Appendices
ENNEMAIN	21.7.17		Evacuated eighteen sick horses from PERONNE to FORGES Les EAUX.	9 MR 3
	22.7.17		Rifle & Sword inspection in Section. Routine work	9 MR 3
	23.7.17		Admitted one sick horse to Section. Routine work	7 MR 3
	24.7.17		Routine work as usual	9 MR 3
	25.7.17		Routine work as usual	9 MR 3
	26.7.17		Admitted two sick horses. Visited 28th C.I.H. Routine work as usual	9 MR 3
	27.7.17		Visited Machine Gun Squad's sick horses.	8 MR 3
	28.7.17		Visited C.I.H. & inspected one squad for contagious diseases & horses	9 MR 3
	29.7.17		Routine work as usual	9 MR 3
	30.7.17		Visited Machine Gun Squad's sick horses.	9 MR 3
	31.7.17		Routine work as usual	9 MR 3

J.H. Bennet Lieut
No. Mobile Veterinary Section
MHOW BRIGADE
31.7.17

CONFIDENTIAL.

Serial No: 201.

War Diary

of

Mobile Veterinary Section
Mhow Cavalry Bde.

from 1- Aug 1917 to 31 Aug 1917

Army Form C. 2118.

WAR DIARY
or
INTELLIGENCE SUMMARY

(Erase heading not required.)

[Signed] J. Rennel Captain
O.C. M.V.S. Indian Cav. [Corps]

Instructions regarding War Diaries and Intelligence Summaries are contained in F.S. Regs., Part II. and the Staff Manual respectively. Title Pages will be prepared in manuscript.

Place	Date	Hour	Summary of Events and Information	Remarks and references to Appendices
ENNEMAINE	1.8.17		Routine work as usual.	9MB.
"	2.8.17		Admitted one horse to section.	9MB.
"	3.8.17		Visited 38th C.I.H. sick horses	9MB.
"	4.8.17		Evacuated four sick horses by rail from PERONNE CHAPELLETTE	9MB.
"	5.8.17		Admitted 3 sick horses to section. Visited Machine Gun Squadron.	9MB.
"	6.8.17		Visited 38th C.I.H. sick horses. Admitted two sick horses to section	9MB.
"	7.8.17		Routine work as usual.	9MB.
"	8.8.17		Inspected 38th headquarter horses for shoes	9MB.
"	9.8.17		Admitted one sick horse to section.	7MB.
"	10.8.17		Routine work as usual	9MB.
"	11.8.17		Evacuated 5 sick horses to FORGES-les-EAUX.	9MB.
"	12.8.17		Visited No.11 M.G.S. & inspected for contagious diseases etc.	9MB.
"	13.8.17		Routine work as usual.	9MB.
"	14.8.17		Routine work as usual.	7MB.
"	15.8.17		A.D.V.S. inspected this section. Routine work as usual.	7MB.
"	16.8.17		Admitted one sick horse to section	7MB.
"	17.8.17		Admitted three sick horses to section.	7MB.
"	18.8.17		Evacuated five sick horses to FORGES-les-EAUX from PERONNE la CHAPELLETTE	9MB.

Army Form C. 2118.

WAR DIARY
or
INTELLIGENCE SUMMARY

(Erase heading not required.)

Instructions regarding War Diaries and Intelligence Summaries are contained in F. S. Regs., Part II. and the Staff Manual respectively. Title Pages will be prepared in manuscript.

Place	Date	Hour	Summary of Events and Information	Remarks and references to Appendices
ENNEMAINE	19.8.17		Routine work as usual.	9/MB
"	20.8.17		Admitted 3 sick horses to section.	7/MB
"	21.8.17		Admitted 3 sick horses to section. Inspected sick horses 38th C.I.H.	9/MB
"	22.8.17		Visited No 11 Machine Gun Squadron.	7/MB
"	23.8.17		Admitted 8 sick horses to section. Routine work as usual.	9/MB
"	24.8.17		Routine work as usual.	7/MB
"	25.8.17		Evacuated eleven sick horses by rail to FORGES les EAUX.	9/MB
"	26.8.17		Routine work as usual.	9/MB
"	27.8.17		Visited 38th C.I.H. Sick horses.	9/MB
"	28.8.17		Routine work, two horses admitted for evacuation.	Ch. B
"	29.8.17		Visited 2 squadrons R.E's	Ch. B
"	30.8.17		Visited Dunstables & C.I.H. Routine work	Ch. B
"	31.8.17		Visited Machine Gun Squadron & inspected horses for shoeing.	Ch. B
"	1.9.17		Evacuated to Forges les Eaux 14 Sick Horses	Ch. B

Cn. Barker Capt. MC

Serial No. 201.

W A R   D I A R Y.

of the

Mobile Veterinary Section
MHOW CAVALRY BDE

From 1-9-17 To 30-9-17

Army Form C. 2118.

WAR DIARY
or
INTELLIGENCE SUMMARY

(Erase heading not required.)

Instructions regarding War Diaries and Intelligence Summaries are contained in F. S. Regs., Part II. and the Staff Manual respectively. Title Pages will be prepared in manuscript.

Place	Date	Hour	Summary of Events and Information	Remarks and references to Appendices
ENNEMAIN	1.9.17		Evacuated 4 Horses to 8o? Vet. Hospital from LA CHAPELLETTE	
"	2.9.17		Routine work as usual.	
"	3.9.17		Visited C.I.H. sick Horses	
"	4.9.17		Routine work as usual.	
"	5.9.17		Admitted sick Horse from M.G.S.	
"	6.9.17		Visited 8o.11 Machine Gun Squadron	
"	7.9.17		Routine work as usual.	
"	8.9.17		Sent Horse Contusion Shoulder to Butcher. Sold for 180 Frs.	
"	9.9.17		Routine work as usual.	
"	10.9.17		Visited 38th C.I.H. sick Horses	
"	11.9.17		Admitted Two sick Horses to Section	
"	12.9.17		Routine work as usual. Admitted two sick Horses to the Section	
"	13.9.17		Visited 8o.11 Machine Gun Squadron sick Horses.	
"	14.9.17		Routine work as usual.	
"	15.9.17		Evacuated 8 y. I. sick Horses to FORGES-LES-EAUX from LA-CHAPELLETTE	
"	16.9.17		Routine work as usual.	
"	17.9.17		Visited 38th C.I.H. sick Horses.	
"	18.9.17		Routine work as usual.	
"	19.9.17		Routine work as usual	
"	20.9.17		Visited 8o.11 Machine Gun Squadron	

Army Form C. 2118.

WAR DIARY
or
INTELLIGENCE SUMMARY

(Erase heading not required.)

Instructions regarding War Diaries and Intelligence Summaries are contained in F. S. Regs., Part II. and the Staff Manual respectively. Title Pages will be prepared in manuscript.

Place	Date	Hour	Summary of Events and Information	Remarks and references to Appendices
ENNEMAIN	21.9.17		Routine work as usual. Admitted 20 sick Horses to Section	AV/B
"	22.9.17		Evacuated 29 sick horses to FORGES-LES-EAUX. from LA-CHAPELLETTE.	AV/B
"	23.9.17		Routine work as usual	AV/B
"	24.9.17		Visited 38th C.I.16 sick Horses	AV/B
"	25.9.17		Routine work as usual	AV/B
"	25.9.17		Visited 8o11 Machine Gun Squadron Admitted one sick Horse to Section	AV/B
"	26.9.17		Routine work as usual	AV/B
"	27.9.17		Routine work as usual. D.D.V.S. Inspected the Section	AV/B
"	28.9.17		Admitted 4 sick Horses to the Section. Evacuated two sick Horses to FORGES-LES-EAUX from LA-CHAPELLETTE	AV/B
"	30.9.17		Routine work as usual.	AV/B

J.W. Kennedy
Capt R.C.

[Stamp: MOBILE VETERINARY SECTION MHOW BRIGADE 4.10.17]

(201)

Confidential

WAR DIARY
of
Mobile Veterinary Section
Mhow Cavalry Brigade

from 1-10-17 to 31-10-17

WAR DIARY

INTELLIGENCE SUMMARY

Army Form C. 2118.

Mobile Veterinary Section "Box"
(Mhow Car Box)

(Erase heading not required.)

Instructions regarding War Diaries and Intelligence Summaries are contained in F. S. Regs., Part II. and the Staff Manual respectively. Title Pages will be prepared in manuscript.

Place	Date	Hour	Summary of Events and Information	Remarks and references to Appendices
ENNEMAIN	1.10.17		Visited 38th C.I.H. Sick Horses.	
"	2.10.17		Routine work as usual.	
"	3.10.17		Visited 8/11 Machine Gun Squadron	
"	4.10.17		Admitted 4 Sick Horses	
"	5.10.17		Routine work as usual	
"	6.10.17		Evacuated 4 Sick Horses to No.7 Vet. Hospital FORGES-LES-EAUX.	
"	7.10.17		Routine work as usual.	
"	8.10.17		Admitted 5 Sick Horses.	
"	9.10.17		Visited 38th C.I.H. Sick Horses. Admitted two Sick Horses.	
"	10.10.17		Routine work as usual.	
"	11.10.17		Routine work as usual	
"	12.10.17		Visited 8/11 Machine Gun Squadron.	
"	13.10.17		Evacuated Eight Sick Horses to No.7 Vet. Hospital FORGES-LES-EAUX.	
"	14.10.17		Routine work as usual	
"	15.10.17		Routine work as usual.	
"	16.10.17		Visited 38th C.I.H. Sick Horses.	
"	17.10.17		Routine work as usual.	
"	18.10.17		Visited 8/11 Machine Gun	
"	19.10.17		Routine work as usual.	

Army Form C. 2118.

WAR DIARY
INTELLIGENCE SUMMARY
(Erase heading not required.)

Instructions regarding War Diaries and Intelligence Summaries are contained in F. S. Regs., Part II. and the Staff Manual respectively. Title Pages will be prepared in manuscript.

Place	Date	Hour	Summary of Events and Information	Remarks and references to Appendices
ENNEMAIN	20.10.17		Routine work as usual.	9MB
"	21.10.17		Routine work as usual.	9MB
"	22.10.17		Visited 35th C.I.H. sick Horses	9MB
"	23.10.17		Routine work as usual.	9MB
"	24.10.17		Admitted 3 sick Horses	9MB
"	25.10.17		Routine work as usual. Admitted 2 sick Horses	9MB
"	26.10.17		Admitted 4 sick Horses	9MB
"	27.10.17		Evacuated 7 sick Horses to No 7 Vet. Hospital FORGES-LES-EAUX	9MB
"	28.10.17		Routine work as usual	9MB
"	29.10.17		Visited 35th C.I.H. sick Horses	9MB
"	30.10.17		Admitted 2 sick Horses	9MB
"	31.10.17		Admitted 1 sick Horse.	9MB

J.H.Dennel
Capt. A.V.C.
Mobile Vety Section
Mhow Bde

Confidential

WAR DIARY

of

Mobile Veterinary Section
Mhow Cav Bde

from 1-11-17 to 30-11-17

(201)

Army Form C. 2118.

WAR DIARY
or
INTELLIGENCE SUMMARY

Mobile Veterinary Section
MHOW Brigade.

(Erase heading not required.)

Instructions regarding War Diaries and Intelligence Summaries are contained in F. S. Regs., Part II. and the Staff Manual respectively. Title Pages will be prepared in manuscript.

Place	Date	Hour	Summary of Events and Information	Remarks and references to Appendices
ENNEMAIN	1.11.17		Attended A.V.S's Office with Imperial Account. Killed C.I.H 4 reported in Horse died.	App.A
"	2.11.17		Admitted 3 Sick Horses.	App.B
"	3.11.17		Evacuated 5 Sick Horses.	App.B
"	4.11.17		Routine work as usual.	App.B
"	5.11.17		Inspected Horses for Casting by S.V.R. 2nd Lancers. Killed Sick Horses C.I.H. Admitted Sick Horses.	App.B
"	6.11.17		Inspected 6th Dragoons Horses for Casting. Admitted one Sick Horse.	App.B
"	7.11.17		Sold two Horses to Butcher at Ham for Food. Admitted one Sick Horse.	App.B
"	8.11.17		Attended A.V.S's Office.	App.B
"	9.11.17		Visited C.I.H Sick Horses. Admitted 3 Sick Horses.	App.B
"	10.11.17		Visited B.H.Q. Sick Horses.	App.B
"	11.11.17		Routine work as usual.	App.B
"	12.11.17		Attended 3 Sick Horses. Admitted 2 Sick Horses.	App.B
"	13.11.17		Visited "A" Battery Sick Horses. Admitted 5 Sick Horses.	App.B
"	14.11.17		Visited C.I.H. Sick Horses.	App.B
"	15.11.17		Visited A.V.S's Office. Destroyed Horse from "A" Battery. Tick Tick.	App.B
"	16.11.17		Visited C.I.H. Sick Horses	App.B
"	17.11.17		Routine work as usual	App.B
"	18.11.17		Routine work as usual	App.B
"	19.11.17		Admitted 2 Sick Horses.	App.B
"	20.11.17		Admitted 5 Sick Horses.	App.B
"	21.11.17		Head of the 2nd to INS. Evacuated 9 Sick Horses	App.B
"	22.11.17		Routine Work as usual.	App.B
"	23.11.17		Returned to ENNEMAIN.	App.B

J.H. Bennell Capt AVC

Army Form C. 2118.

WAR DIARY
or
INTELLIGENCE SUMMARY

(Erase heading not required.)

Mobile Veterinary Section
MHOW Brigade

Instructions regarding War Diaries and Intelligence Summaries are contained in F.S. Regs., Part II. and the Staff Manual respectively. Title Pages will be prepared in manuscript.

Place	Date	Hour	Summary of Events and Information	Remarks and references to Appendices
ENNEMAIN	24.11.17		Admitted one Sick Horse.	9 WB
"	25.11.17		Hwd up to VILLERS FAUCON & relieved. Evacuated 1 Horse to SAALKOT Mobile.	9 WB
"	26.11.17		Admitted 9 Sick Horses.	9 WB
"	27.11.17		Evacuated 6 Sick Horses. Wired C.V.H. Sick Horses.	9 WB
"	28.11.17		Admitted 2 Sick Horses. ADVS visited Section	9 WB
"	29.11.17		Visited A.D.V.S. Office. Admitted 2 Sick Horses.	9 WB
"	30.11.17		General work as usual.	9 WB

J.H. Newell
Capt AVC

CONFIDENTIAL.

WAR DIARY.

of
Mobile Veterinary Section
Mhow Cavalry Brigade

From, 1-12-17.   to 31-12-17.

Army Form C. 2118.

WAR DIARY
or
INTELLIGENCE SUMMARY.

(Erase heading not required.)

Mobile Vety. Sect.
Mhow Bde.

No. 201.

Instructions regarding War Diaries and Intelligence Summaries are contained in F. S. Regs., Part II. and the Staff Manual respectively. Title pages will be prepared in manuscript.

Place	Date	Hour	Summary of Events and Information	Remarks and references to Appendices
St Emile	1.12.17		OC & ten men proceeded to Ebuly Village arriving at 8.15am. Collected wounded horses and sent them back to remainder of Section at St Emile	Col. B
"	2.12.17		Evacuated 95 Wounded animals to 55th DIV Mobile Vety Sect.	Col. B
Esnemain	3.12.17		Moved back to Esnemain with Brigade at 9am. Passing through Rozel. Enemy Aeroplanes bombed the column. No casualties.	Col. B
"	4.12.17		10 sick animals evacuated	Col. B
"	5.12.17		8 sick animals evacuated	Col. B
"	6.12.17		9 sick animals admitted	Col. B
"	7.12.17		17 sick animals evacuated	Col. B
"	8.12.17		5 sick animals admitted. OC visited sick lines Bde HQ	Col. B
"	9.12.17		1 sick animal admitted. ADVS visited section. OC evacuated sick.	Col. B
"	10.12.17		Horses of 6th Innis. Dragoons	Col. B
"	11.12.17		6 sick animals admitted	Col. B
"	12.12.17		1 sick animal admitted. 11 sick animals evacuated	Col. B
"	13.12.17		11 sick animals admitted. IC visited sick lines	Col. B
"	14.12.17		2 sick animals admitted	Col. B
"	15.12.17		3 sick animals admitted. 17 HK animals evacuated.	

Army Form C. 2118.

WAR DIARY
or
INTELLIGENCE SUMMARY.
(Erase heading not required.)

John Pinkney Sect
Whow Brigade

Instructions regarding War Diaries and Intelligence Summaries are contained in F. S. Regs., Part II. and the Staff Manual respectively. Title pages will be prepared in manuscript.

Place	Date	Hour	Summary of Events and Information	Remarks and references to Appendices
Ennemain	15.12.17		1 sick animal admitted	ChB
"	16.12.17		9 sick animals admitted. O.C. visited sick lines C.I.H.	ChB
"	17.12.17		O.C. visited "A" Battery sick el roco.	ChB
"	18.12.17		# 14 sick animals evacuated	ChB
"	19.12.17		Routine work as usual	ChB
"	20.12.17		Routine work as usual	ChB
"	21.12.17		3 sick animals admitted. O.C. visited sick lines B.H.Q.S	ChB
"	22.12.17		1 sick animal admitted	ChB
"	23.12.17		1 sick animal admitted	ChB
"	24.12.17		O.C. attended office of A.D.V.S.	ChB
"	25.12.17		Routine work as usual until 2pm.	ChB
"	26.12.17		1 sick animal admitted	ChB
"	27.12.17		1 sick animal admitted. O.C. proceeded to Paris on 6 days leave	ChB
"	28.12.17		"G" Battery. 14 Opthalmia cases admitted from for treatment. 18 Opthalmia cases admitted from 4th B.I.C. all	ChB
"	29.12.17		Vy sick animal evacuated	ChB
"	30.12.17		Routine as usual	ChB
"	31.12.17		Routine as usual	ChB

A Bruhn - Capt A.V.C.

CONFIDENTIAL

201.

WAR DIARY.

MOBILE VETERINARY SECT
MHOW BDE
for
JANUARY 1918

WAR DIARY
or
INTELLIGENCE SUMMARY

(Erase heading not required.)

Army Form C. 2118.

Mobile Veterinary Station
MHOW Cavalry Brigade

Place	Date	Hour	Summary of Events and Information	Remarks and references to Appendices
ENNEMAIN	1.1.18	—	Routine work as usual.	MVS
"	2.1.18	—	Visited B.I.H. Sick Horses	MVS
"	3.1.18	—	Admitted four Sick Horses	MVS
"	4.1.18	—	Evacuated to 8 Sick Horses to No 7 Veterinary Hospital from LA CHAPELLETTE.	MVS
"	5.1.18	—	Routine work as usual. Admitted 4 Sick Horses	MVS
"	6.1.18	—	Routine work as usual.	MVS
"	7.1.18	—	Visited G.H.Q Sick Horses.	MVS
"	8.1.18	—	Evacuated 14 Sick Horses to No 7 Veterinary Hospital from LA CHAPELLETTE.	MVS
"	9.1.18	—	Admitted 15 Sick Horses for treatment. Visited G.H.Q. Sick Horses.	MVS
"	10.1.18	—	Routine work as usual.	MVS
"	11.1.18	—	Routine work as usual	MVS
"	12.1.18	—	Routine work as usual.	MVS
"	13.1.18	—	Visited G.H.Q Horses.	MVS
"	14.1.18	—	Routine work as usual	MVS
"	15.1.18	—	Routine work as usual	MVS
"	16.1.18	—	Visited G.H. Sick Horses.	MVS
"	17.1.18	—	Routine work as usual.	MVS
"	18.1.18	—	Attended A.D.V.S. Office, B.H.Q	MVS
"	19.1.18	—	Visited G.H.Q. Sick Horses	MVS
"	20.1.18	—	Routine work as usual.	MVS
"	21.1.18	—	Routine work as usual.	MVS

J.W. Russell
Capt.

Army Form C. 2118.

Mobile Veterinary Section
MHOW Cavalry Brigade

WAR DIARY
or
INTELLIGENCE SUMMARY
(Erase heading not required.)

Instructions regarding War Diaries and Intelligence Summaries are contained in F. S. Regs., Part II. and the Staff Manual respectively. Title Pages will be prepared in manuscript.

Place	Date	Hour	Summary of Events and Information	Remarks and references to Appendices
ENNEMAIN	22.1.18	—	Evacuated 10 Sick Horses to No 7 Veterinary Hospital from La CHAPELLETTE.	App No 3
"	23.1.18	—	Visited B.I.H. Sick Horses.	App No 3
"	24.1.18	—	Routine work as usual. Attended A.D.V.S. Office.	App No 3
"	25.1.18	—	Visited B.H.Q. Sick Horses	App No 3
"	26.1.18	—	Routine work as usual	App No 3
"	27.1.18	—	Admitted 19 Sick Horses for treatment	App No 3
"	28.1.18	—	Visited C.I.H. Sick Horses.	App No 3
"	29.1.18	—	Evacuated 26 Sick animals to No 7 Veterinary Hospital	App No 3
"	30.1.18	—	Routine work as usual.	App No 3
"	31.1.18	—	Routine work as usual	App No 3

Capt AVC

CONFIDENTIAL.

WAR DIARY 4DIV

of

Mhow Mobile Veterinary Section

From. 1st February 1918. to 28th Bebruary 1918.

WAR DIARY
or
INTELLIGENCE SUMMARY.

(Erase heading not required.)

Army Form C. 2118.

Mobile Veterinary Section
MHOW Cavalry Brigade

Instructions regarding War Diaries and Intelligence Summaries are contained in F.S. Regs., Part II. and the Staff Manual respectively. Title pages will be prepared in manuscript.

Place	Date	Hour	Summary of Events and Information	Remarks and references to Appendices
ENNEMAIN	1.2.18		Routine work as usual. Evacuated 28 Sick Animals to No 7 Veterinary Hospital	OMB
"	2.2.18		Left ENNEMAIN on first day's march. Stopped at MARCELCAVE the night.	OMB
MARCELCAVE	3.2.18		Left for PONT de METZ. Stopped the night.	OMB
PONT de METZ	4.2.18		Left for COURCELLES. Received 4 Sick Horses.	OMB
COURCELLES	5.2.18		Visited Animals under my charge after arrival. Received 2 Sick Horses in Section.	OMB
"	6.2.18		Routine work as usual. Received 2 Sick Horses in Section	OMB
"	7.2.18		Routine work as usual. Attended QTVS's Office	OMB
"	8.2.18		Visited A.V.S. 2 Sick Horses	OMB
"	9.2.18		Routine work as usual	OMB
"	10.2.18		Visited B.H.Q. 2 Sick Horses.	OMB
"	11.2.18		Routine work as usual	OMB
"	12.2.18		2 Sick Horses. 2 Sick Horses	OMB
"	13.2.18		Routine work as usual.	OMB
"	15.2.18		Admitted 1 Sick Horse to Section. Evacuated 3 Sick Horses to No 7 M. Hospital	OMB
"	16.2.18		Casualties 6 Sick Horses to Section. Admitted 2 Sick Horses Section.	OMB
"	17.2.18		Visited H.Q. 4 Sick Horses.	OMB
"	18.2.18		Admitted 2 Sick Horses to Section.	OMB
"	19.2.18		Routine work as usual.	OMB

WAR DIARY or **INTELLIGENCE SUMMARY**

Army Form C. 2118.

Mobile Veterinary Section
MHOW Cavalry Brigade

Place	Date	Hour	Summary of Events and Information	Remarks and references to Appendices
COURCELLES	20	2.18	Routine work as usual	MVS
"	21	2.18	Visited 2nd Lancers Sick Animals	MVS
"	22	2.18	Routine work as usual	MVS
"	23	2.18	Routine work as usual	MVS
"	24	2.18	Visited R.H.A. Sick Horses	MVS
"	25	2.18	Visited 6 D.G. Sick Horses Routine work as usual	MVS
"	26	2.18	Routine work as usual	MVS
"	27	2.18	Evacuated 9 Sick Animals & 3 Cast mules	MVS
"	28	2.18	Routine work as usual	MVS

J.W. Newell Capt MVC

Mobile Veterinary Section 28.2.18 MHOW Brigade

www.ingramcontent.com/pod-product-compliance
Lightning Source LLC
Chambersburg PA
CBHW081434300426
44108CB00016BA/2368